PAPERS AND CORRESPONDENCE
OF
WILLIAM STANLEY JEVONS

Volume V

Also by R. D. Collison Black

CENTENARY HISTORY OF THE STATISTICAL SOCIETY
OF IRELAND

ECONOMIC THOUGHT AND THE IRISH QUESTION, 1817–1870

A CATALOGUE OF PAMPHLETS ON ECONOMIC SUBJECTS,
1750–1900

JEVONS'S THEORY OF POLITICAL ECONOMY (*editor*)

THE ECONOMIC WRITINGS OF
MOUNTIFORT LONGFIELD (*editor*)

READINGS IN THE DEVELOPMENT
OF ECONOMIC ANALYSIS, 1776–1848

PAPERS AND CORRESPONDENCE OF WILLIAM STANLEY
JEVONS, VOLUME I: BIOGRAPHY AND PERSONAL JOURNAL
(*editor with Rosamond Könekamp*)

VOLUME II: CORRESPONDENCE, 1850–1862 (*editor*)

VOLUME III: CORRESPONDENCE, 1863–1872 (*editor*)

VOLUME IV: CORRESPONDENCE, 1873–1878 (*editor*)

VOLUME VI: LECTURES ON POLITICAL ECONOMY,
1875–1876 (*editor*)

VOLUME VII: PAPERS ON POLITICAL ECONOMY (*editor*)

PAPERS AND CORRESPONDENCE
OF
WILLIAM STANLEY JEVONS

Volume V
CORRESPONDENCE 1879–1882

EDITED BY
R. D. COLLISON BLACK

M

in association with the Royal Economic Society

First published 1977 by
THE MACMILLAN PRESS LTD
London and Basingstoke
Associated companies in New York
Dublin Melbourne Johannesburg and Madras

ISBN 0 333 19978 2

Printed in Great Britain by
UNWIN BROTHERS LTD
Woking and London

CONTENTS

Letter

Letter

A complete index to the *Papers and Correspondence, Lectures,* and *Papers on Political Economy* will be contained in Volume VII.

PREFACE

With this volume, covering the brief period from January 1879 until Jevons's death, the series containing his professional and personal correspondence is completed. The fact that it contains a greater number of letters than Volume II, which covered thirteen years, and almost as many as Volume III, which covered nine, is indicative of Jevons's increased stature and wider circle of correspondents.

In the four years covered by this volume Jevons's contacts with such long-standing correspondents as Walras, Palgrave, Foxwell and John Mills continued. His other correspondence for the most part reflected his changing interests – sun spots and the trade cycle are discussed in letters from such men as A. M. de Foville and F. B. Edmonds, while the socio-economic problems which Jevons took up in papers such as 'Married Women in Factories'[1] generated a variety of letters from correspondents outside the usual circles of economists and statisticians. Within those circles perhaps the most notable new name to be added to the list of those with whom Jevons corresponded was F. Y. Edgeworth, but although the two men became close friends in these years few letters passed between them because both lived within a short distance of each other in Hampstead. Abroad, the number of Italian economists who corresponded with Jevons increased, with the addition of such names as Luigi Cossa and Amilcare Puviani.

In the preparation of this volume I have again received assistance from many quarters and wish to thank all those who so willingly gave me the benefit of their time and expert knowledge – especially Professor François Crouzet, of the University of Paris-Sorbonne who provided me with information from Paris libraries about Charles M. Limousin and Louis Raynaud; Miss H. E. Peek, Librarian, University Archives Cambridge, Dr Ian Jack, Librarian of Pembroke College Cambridge, and Dr F. Wild, General Secretary of the University of Cambridge Local Examinations Syndicate, all of whom provided information about the career of John Neville Keynes and his association with the last-named body.

I have many reasons to be grateful to Miss M. Canney for help with references in the Goldsmiths' Library of the University of London, but for this volume in particular she provided information on some of H. S. Foxwell's books and on the bookseller, Thomas Allen. My thanks are also

---

[1] *Contemporary Review*, 41 (1882) 37-53; reprinted in *Methods*, pp. 156–79.

due to Mr R. Walker, Librarian of Lincoln's Inn, for biographical information on Sir Francis Savage Reilly; to Mr Adrian Allan, Assistant Archivist of the University of Liverpool, and Miss N. Evette of the Liverpool Record Office for information concerning Edgeworth's application for the Chair of Political Economy at Queen's College, Liverpool; to the Director, India Office Library and Records, Foreign and Commonwealth Office for information about Milburn's *Oriental Commerce*, and about Robert Everest and J. H. Twigg; and to Dr D. A. Farnie of the University of Manchester for biographical information on Edward Herford. Similar information was kindly provided by Mrs G. Ryan, Post Office Records Department, London, for C. J. Willdey; by Miss E. D. Mercer, Head Archivist of Greater London Council, for James Beal; by Lt-Col. H. S. Francis, Curator, Museum of the Corps of Royal Engineers, Chatham, for C. H. P. Christie; by Mr W. Davies, City Librarian of Bradford, and Messrs John Emsley Ltd, Bradford, for George Townend; by Mr J. G. Watson, Secretary, Institution of Civil Engineers, London, for Richard Price Williams; by Mr J. C. Buckhurst, Borough Librarian of Penzance, for John Kinsman; by M. le Curé J. Perrin, Saint-Bernard, Zillisheim, France, for Eduard Moormeister; and by M. le Senateur-Maire de Boulogne-sur-Mer for Hugh McColl.

To my thanks to all these people must be added those which I owe to the Registrar-General, General Register Office, Belfast, who traced details of Harold Rylett's second marriage; to Mr S. Kearsey, Librarian of the Royal Statistical Society, who provided information about the Society's Assistant Secretary in 1882; to the Librarian, Science and Technology Research Center, New York Public Library, for details concerning the production of water gas in New York City; and to Mr D. Taylor, Calderdale Central Librarian, Halifax, Yorkshire, for information about the early telephone experiments mentioned in Letter 592.

For permission to make use of manuscript material of which they have custody or in which they hold the copyright my thanks are due to Mr B. I. Beal, Dr D. E. Butler, Mrs M. Barker, the Hon. Dame Frances Farrer, the Hon. Katherine, Lady Bridges, and the Hon. Anne Farrer; Mr Patrick S. Garnett; Mrs H. A. Mettam and Mr J. D. Mettam; Sir Geoffrey Keynes; Dr M. A. T. Rogers; the Master and Fellows of Trinity College, Cambridge; the Librarian and Library Committee of the University of Birmingham; the Trustees of the British Library of Political and Economic Science; the Provost and Fellows of King's College, Cambridge; Mr Piero Sraffa, Librarian of the Marshall Library, Cambridge; the President and Council of the Royal Society, the Cultural Services Committee of the Corporation of the City of Manchester; the Deputy Keeper, Public Record Office of Northern Ireland; the Goldsmiths' Librarian, University of London Library; the Council and Senate of the

University of Liverpool; the Editor of *The Economist;* the Directors of the Macmillan Press Ltd; *Times* Newspapers Ltd and *Guardian* Newspapers Ltd; and Baron W. J. d'Aulnis de Bourouill.

Queen's University   R. D. COLLISON BLACK
Belfast
12 November 1975

LIST OF ABBREVIATIONS
used throughout the volumes

Relating to Jevons material

LJ   *Letters and Journal of W. Stanley Jevons,* edited by his wife (1886).

LJN   Previously published in LJ; manuscript not now in Jevons Papers, or other known location.

LJP   Previously published in LJ, but only in part; fuller text now given from the orginal manuscript in the Jevons Papers or other indicated location.

WM   From a manuscript made available by Dr Wolfe Mays, University of Manchester.

Investigations   *Investigations in Currency and Finance,* by W. Stanley Jevons. Edited, with an Introduction, by H. S. Foxwell (1884). All page references to first edition.

Methods   *Methods of Social Reform and other papers,* by W. Stanley Jevons (1883).

T.P.E.   *The Theory of Political Economy* by W. Stanley Jevons (1st ed. 1871, 4th ed. 1911). All page references to fourth edition, unless otherwise stated.

Relating to other material

BM   British Museum, London (now British Library).

FW   Fonds Walras, Bibliothèque Cantonale de Lausanne.

HLRS   Herschel Letters, Royal Society, London

JRSS   *Journal of the London* (later *Royal*) *Statistical Society.*

KCP   Palgrave Papers in the Library of King's College, Cambridge.

LSE   London School of Economics, British Library of Political and Economic Science.

MA   Archives of Macmillan & Co. Ltd.

NYPL   New York Public Library.

RDF   From a manuscript made available by Mr R. D. Freeman.

TLJM   Isabel Mills, *From Tinder Box to the 'Larger Light'. Threads from the Life of John Mills, Banker* (Manchester, 1899).

Walras Correspondence   *Correspondence of Léon Walras and Related Papers* edited by William Jaffé (3 vols, Amsterdam, 1965).

Figures following any of these abbreviations denote page numbers.

LETTERS

[LJN, 393–4]

Hampstead, 2d January 1879

. . . It seems an age since I heard from you; indeed it was, I think, last year, and that is too far past to allow of my waiting longer before asking how you are. I see you now and then reported at the school board meetings, and I daresay the school work occupies you a good deal.[1] I suspect that they will gradually put more and more work upon you.

The main point, however, is, when will you come and pay the long-promised visit? Choose your own time, so that when you come we can have a good round of amusements. I am rather in want of diversion, having been sticking rather close to work from some months back. My health has been so remarkably better this autumn that I have taken to working double shifts, evening as well as morning.

How do you like my Parcel Post article?[2] It was rather hastily finished, and contains a few stupid blunders; but I think it is mainly unanswerable. I have plenty more articles to come, if Strahan does not tire of them.[3]

. . . But the burden of my letter is – come as soon as you can, and pay us a good visit, and in the meantime, write a line to say that the New Year promises well and happily for you, as it does for us. . . .

571. CH. – M. LIMOUSIN[1] TO W. S. JEVONS

Paris, Avenue d'Orléans 112
3 Janvier, 1879

Monsieur,

Permettez-moi de vous écrire en français. Je viens de lire votre volume sur la monnaie, et les nombreuses citations que vous faites d'économistes français me fait penser que vous comprenez cette langue mieux que je n'écris l'anglais.

---

[1] Broadfield had been elected to the Manchester School Board in 1878; he later became its Vice-Chairman and Chairman of the Finance Committee.

[2] See Vol.IV, Letter 566, n. 1.

[3] See below, Letter 626, n. 1, p. 74.

[1] Charles-Mathieu Limousin (d. 1909), French publicist; in addition to the positions listed by him in this letter, he was Vice-President of the Statistical Society of Paris, and an associate member of the International Institute of Sociology. Author of numerous publications on questions of current economic interest and (under the pseudonym of 'Le M ∴ Hiram') on Freemasonry.

Je suis membre de la Société d'économie politique de Paris,[2] rédacteur du *Journal des Economistes* et Secrétaire Général de la Société d'études économiques pour les réformes fiscales. C'est à ces divers titres que je prends la liberté de m'addresser à vous aujourd'hui.

Notre société a pour objet, ainsi que son nom l'indique, la recherche des moyens d'améliorer et même de réformer ou de transformer le système des impôts. Notre fondateur, M. A. Raynaud,[3] un grand industriel, a offert deux prix, l'un de 2,000 fr., l'autre de 500 aux auteurs des deux meilleurs mémoires sur cette question de la réforme des impôts. Ce concours ouvert et annoncé, il nous est venu 60 mémories. Sur ces mémoires, 59 ou se trainent dans les systèmes déjà proposés d'impôt sur le revenu, l'impôt sur le capital, de combinaison des deux, ou contiennent des projects absolument irréalisables.

Un seul, celui justement qui est inscrit sous le no. 60, est original et contient une solution.[4] Seulement, nous sommes absolument divisés dans le jury sur la mérite de cette invention. Les uns la trouvent excellente et disent que son seul défaut réside dans sa nouveauté et dans la révolution qu'elle fait dans les idées; les autres la trouvent absolument mauvaise, contraire aux lois de l'économie politique, etc.

M. Raynaud et moi, après avoir lu votre livre sur la monnaie, et constaté qu'il contient des apercus nouveaux et ingénieux, qu'en outre vous ne vous laissez pas dominer par des idées préconçus, nous avons pensé à vous demander votre avis.

Veuillez réfléchir à l'importance du sujet. Si le système qu'on nous propose était bon, il serait applicable dans tous les pays, et permettrait de supprimer toutes les taxes gênantes, tout en répartissant, équitablement les charges publiques entre les contribuables. Tout celà est accepté par tous; mais il y a un seul point de dissentiment qui est celui-ci; ce système pourrait-il fonctionner?

Ce système repose sur le papier monnaie et consiste dans une combinaison de ce que vous appelez: *méthode du dépôt simple, méthode de convertibilité déferée, méthode par le paiement des impôts,* en y ajoutant d'autres éléments que vous prévoyez dans le même chapitre de votre ouvrage.

---

[2] This society was founded in 1876 by the industrialist Raynaud (see below) with Limousin as secretary-general and Ernest Brelay, a merchant and member of the Paris municipal council, as president. Limousin and Raynaud at first undertook a campaign for the abolition of the *octrois* but their proposal to replace them by a tax on real property encountered considerable opposition. Raynaud then offered prizes for the two best essays on a new system of taxation, on the lines indicated by Limousin in this letter. After the contest had been held, the Society was wound up in May 1880.

[3] A. Raynaud, manufacturer of perfumes in Paris, sometime president of the *Union des Fabricants* and Mayor of Levallois-Perret, 1888.

[4] Mémoire no. 60, submitted under the pseudonym 'Go-Ahead', was afterwards published under the title *Revolution pacifique sur l'impôt sur les revenus. Système de Jacques Lorrain, premier lauréat du concours ouvert par la société d'études economiques fondée en 1878 par A. Raynaud . . . avec une Preface d'Augustin Galopin* (Paris, Guillaumin, 1888).

Voici brièvement en quoi consiste le système:

1° Emission par l'Etat de billets que l'auteur appelle *bons du Trésor*.

2° Constitution d'un encaisse de garantie, en or, de valeur égale au montant des billets (par un emprunt), soit, en prenant pour base le budget français actuel, une valeur de *trois milliards de francs*.

3° Emploi par l'Etat de ces bons du Trésor pour tous les paiements à faire par le dit Etat.

4° Soumission de ces bons du Trésor à un impôt de un pour mille et par jour, (soit dix centimes par cent francs), lequel impôt serait acquitté par l'apposition d'un timbre mobile dans des cases preparées pour celà et portant la date de chaque jour. Les dite bons ne circuleraient que revétus du timbre du jour.

5° Remboursement des bons du Trésor, au bout de trois ans, avec le prix des timbres qu'on aurait apposé dessus.

6° Réception de ces bons du Trésor, dans les caisses de l'Etat chargées de la vente des timbres, ce qui ferait que, quand le système serait en plein fonctionnement, l'Etat français, pris pour exemple, émettrait pour 280 millions de francs de bons du Trésor par mois, et vendrait pour 280 millions de francs de timbres ce qui amènerait la rentrée d'une somme égale au bons du Trésor, lesquels seraient alors détruits.

7° Pour activer la rentrée des bons du Trésor l'auteur propose deux moyens, l'un définitif, l'autre provisoire. Le premier consiste en une prime de 5% accordé sur la valeur des timbres apposés, soit au moment du remboursement, soit quand les bons seraient reçus en paiement. Ainsi un bon de cent fr. serait remboursé à 105 fr. 475 millièmes (il y a, en trois ans 1.095 jours; à 10 centimes par jour, cela ferait 109 fr. 50 qu'auraient payé les contribuables; et 5 pour cent de 109,50 font 5 f. 475). Il resterait encore à l'Etat pour ses frais divers ou pour bénéfices 4 f. 025.

Un bon presenté pour paiement aux caisses de l'Etat et portant 500 timbres serait pris pour 102 f. 50.

L'auteur du mémoire espère que la perspective de ce profit ferait rechercher les bons ayant beaucoup de timbres par toutes les personnes ayant paiements à faire à l'Etat. Par suite, cela amènerait la rentrée et la destruction de ces bons.

Le second moyen proposé consiste dans le maintien provisoire de certains impôts anciens, les moins impopulaires, pour l'acquittement desquels l'Etat accepterait des bons du Trésor, toujours avec une bonification de 5 pour cent sur les timbres apposés.

Par suite de l'emploi de ces deux moyens il n'y aurait pas à craindre la dépréciation pour cause de surabondance: la valeur en circulation n'étant jamais que de la valeur d'un budget, et le papier étant venu prendre dans la circulation la place du numéraire qui lui servirait de gage.

Il est vrai, que, ainsi que vous le faites remarquer, il faudrait payer l'intérêt de ce gage, soit, pour la France, 150 millions de francs par an; mais, d'autre part cette somme serait de beaucoup inférieure au montant de l'économie directe réalisée.

D'ailleurs, la génération future pourrait quand le système serait acclimaté, voir si le gage ne peut pas être supprimé en totalité ou en partie.

Toutes les objections que l'on fait à ce système se résument à ceci: Les marchands ne voudraient pas accepter ces bons du Trésor en paiement de leurs marchandises à cause de la dépréciation quotidienne, ou autrement dire des frais d'entretien qu'occasionnerait le maintien de leur valeur nominale par l'apposition des timbres.

A celà l'auteur répond: cette dépréciation n'occasionnerait qu'un change et si ce change était peu élevé, ce ne serait pas un inconvenient grave, ainsi que le prouve l'exemple des pays à papier-monnaie. D'autre part, les bons du Trésor n'ayant pas une valeur inférieure à cent francs ne circuleraient pas parmi les populations pauvres et ignorantes incapables de comprendre le mécanisme du change.

Quel serait ce change? Il serait de l'impôt qu'aurait à payer le déteneur pour le temps moyen pendant lequel il le garderait en main. Or, ce temps, dit l'auteur, serait au *maximum* de 13 ou 14 jours, ce qui provoquerait un change de 1.20 ou 1.40 pour cent; lequel ne se ferait sentir le plus souvent que dans le commerce de gros (Wholesale).

D'un autre côté, la prime accordée au bons du Trésor à leur rentrée dans les caisses de l'Etat, en provoquant la recherche de ces bons viendrait compenser le change et le diminuer, de même qu'il est très probable que la durée du séjour d'un bon entre les mains de la moyenne des détenteurs serait moindre de 13 ou 14 jours, ce qui diminuerait également le change.

A celà, les adversaires du système répondent que la dépréciation serait de la totalité de la valeur, ce qui me semble inadmissible puisque, à tout instant, les bons pourraient être présentés aux caisses de l'Etat et accepté pour leur valeur nominale majorée d'un certain *quantum*.

J'ai trouvé dans votre livre une indication qui m'a permis d'établir un raisonnement que je demande à vous communiquer.

Vous dites qu'à une époque le bétail a servi de monnaie. Or, à l'époque de transition quand les métaux ont commencé à circuler, il est probable que les marchands, en prenant les animaux comme instrument d'échange, faisaient entrer en compte les frais d'entretien pendant le temps moyen qu'ils devaient les garder. Or, la situation serait la même pour les bons du Trésor. Ce serait l'entretien pendant le temps moyen de garde qui determinerait le change. Si ce temps moyen était de 10 jours le change serait de 1 pour cent s'il était de 5 jours, le change serait d'un demi pour cent. Qui paierait cet impôt? Les commerçants? Non, car tout impot qui frappe l'ensemble des commerçants ou un groupe des commerçants vendant une même marchandise se reperçute sur le prix de la marchandise. Ce serait donc le public consommateur qui paierait proportionnellement à son revenu dépensé.

Vous me demanderez peut-être ce qui se passerait avec le système des *clearing-houses* que vous décrivez si bien. Il se passerait que les banquiers paieraient l'impôt en apposant les timbres, et qu'ils débiteraient leurs clients du montant, et que les dits clients le feraient entrer dans leurs frais généraux, c'est à dire dans le prix de leur marchandise.

Sans doute, un semblable système aurait l'inconvénient d'obliger les banquiers à faire coller des timbres tous les jours par leurs employés. Mais cet inconvénient peut-il être comparé à ceux des impôts indirects que nous avons en France, voire même à ceux de l'*income Tax* que vous possédez en Angleterre?

Le point spécial sur lequel nous desirerions avoir votre opinion – sans préjudice des autres bien entendu – est celui-ci: Quel serait le change auquel serait exposé les bons du Trésor du système que j'ai eu l'honneur de vous exposer? Subsidiairement, ce change s'il était faible, empêcherait-il la circulation des bons du Trésor?

Si vous le désirez, Monsieur, je vous ferai parvenir le mémoire lui-même; dans tous les cas, comme je pense qu'il sera prochainement imprimé, je vous l'addresserai.

En attendant, nous vous serions très obligé si vous vouliez bien nous donner votre avis sur les deux points ci-dessus.[5]

Je pense, Monsieur, que les questions du genre de celle que je vous ai exposée vous intéressent, je n'ai par suite qu'à m'excuser de n'avoir pas pu le faire plus brièvement.

Veuillez agréer, Monsieur et illustre confrère, l'assurance de mes sentiments de considération distinguée.

Ch. M. Limousin.

---

[5] There is no evidence that Jevons ever gave a written opinion on the Mémoire of Jacques Lorrain, but a report by Frédéric Passy was published along with the essay. Passy was critical of its proposals–'le système est compliqué, il n'est pas proportionnel et il n'est pas exempt de dangers' (op. cit., p. 113). Raynaud, however, gave an enthusiastic report on the scheme to the Council of the Society in 1880, and the first prize of 2,000 francs was accordingly awarded to Jacques Lorrain – *Société d'études économiques pour les reformes fiscales. Rapport à MM. les Membres du Conseil sur le Memoire no 60 . . . permettant de supprimer tous les impôts injustes, qui sont une entrave pour le commerce et l'industrie . . . par A. Raynaud* (Paris, A. Chaix, 1880).
See also 'L'Impôt sur la dépense par la monnaie. Analyse du "memoire" qui a obtenu le prix offert par M. A. Raynaud . . .', *Journal des Economistes,* mai 1880.

572.   W. S. JEVONS TO A. SCHUSTER[1]

2, The Chestnuts
7 January 79[2]

Dear Dr. Schuster,

I have just been reading the very interesting abstract of your paper on the sun, given in last week's *Nature*.[3] It is important to me in connexion with my Commercial Crises as I particularly want to decide whether the period is likely to be 10.45 as held by Broun[4] or 11.1 as by Wolf[5] – Stewart[6] & others Now your theory will allow us to select any period we like and it also opens great prospect of explaining the interruption at the beginning of the century. It seems to be superior to Stewart's planetary theory in the fact that the *modus operandi* is more apparent, it is what they call a *vera causa*.

Have you attended to Piazzi Smyth's temperature observations[7] which seem to show that a wave of high temp. intervenes[8] between two cold waves? while the heat waves at $10\frac{1}{3} - \frac{1}{2}$ year intervals seem only to be the higher crests of a series of heat waves.

I have been carefully reading up all I could find on the subject, and am strongly of opinion that the principal[9] solar period does not exceed 10.6 years & probably lies between $10\frac{1}{4}$ & $10\frac{1}{2}$. All that I have ascertained of late goes to confirm the theory of decennial com[1] crises, which I consider to be almost unquestionably true. Your theory tends to remove a lingering doubt about Jupiter and the planets which stood in the way.

I am writing an elaborate article for an American Review (The Princeton)[10] and if you have any printed copy of your paper a fuller

---

[1] [Sir] Arthur Schuster (1851 – 1934), Chief of the Eclipse Expedition to Siam, 1875; Professor of Physics in the Victoria University of Manchester, 1888 – 1907; secretary of the Royal Society, 1912 19; Foreign Secretary, 1920 – 4; secretary of the International Research Council, 1919 – 20; knighted, 1920.

[2] The original manuscript of this letter is now in the Schuster Papers, Royal Society, London.

[3] *Nature*, 2 January 1879, p. 211, contained a report of Schuster's paper 'Some results of the last total solar eclipse', a general survey of eclipse observations, which he had presented at a meeting of the Philosophical Society, Cambridge, held on 18 November 1878. The full text was published in the Society's *Proceedings*, 3 (1878) 209 – 16.

[4] John Allan Broun (1817 – 79), one of the first pioneers of scientific meteorology; Director of Sir J. M. Brisbane's magnetic observatory at Makestown, Dumfriesshire, 1842 – 9; and of the observatory at Trivandrum, 1852 – 65. See below, Letter 578, n. 2, p. 17.

[5] Johann Rudolf Wolf (1816 – 93). Swiss astronomer, discovered parallelism between sun – spots and magnetic variations in 1852.

[6] i.e. Balfour Stewart.

[7] See Vol. IV, Letter 561.

[8] In the original manuscript 'seems to' has been crossed out before this word.

[9] 'principal' has been inserted in the original manuscript.

[10] See Vol. IV, Letter 567, n. 2.

abstract which you could lend me for a day or two it would be of much service to me. Have you done anything more about the *vintages*?[11]

Yours truly

W. S. Jevons

573.· R. HAMILTON[1] TO W. S. JEVONS

3, Tenterden Street,
Hanover Square W.
13 Jan. 1879.[2]

Dear Professor Jevons,

I have only just found out that I have been at cross purposes with my friend Mr. Neison,[3] and I have to apologise for this tardy expression of my thanks for the pamphlet which you kindly sent for me. I should very gratefully receive the further papers to which you refer.

Will you do me the honour to accept a copy of my book on "Money and Value".[4] In the introduction I have referred to the question of the "Tabular Standard". It appears to me that the value of tables drawn out on the principle you propose is inestimable not merely for determining the fluctuations in the relative purchasing power of Gold, but also, yet more as a necessary step towards yet more important problems regarding the true value and economy of labour.

Yours faithfully,

Rowland Hamilton.

Professor Stanley Jevons

[11] See Vol. IV, Letter 491, n. 4; cf. also below, Letter 711, p. 167.

[1] Rowland Hamilton (d. 1897), F.S.S. 1879; a member of the council of the [Royal] Statistical Society, 1881–91, and 1892–6, before which he presented two papers.

[2] The original manuscript of this letter is in the British Library of Political and Economic Science, London School of Economics.

[3] Francis Gustavus Paulus Nieson (d. 1929), actuary; F.S.S. 1869; served on the council of the [Royal] Statistical Society for nearly thirty years from 1878; author of a number of papers, having a particular interest in statistics relating to occupational health hazards and mining accidents. Not to be confused with his father, F. G. P. Nieson, F. S. S., author of several papers, 1844–53, some of which were published collectively as *Contributions to Vital Statistics* . . . third edition (1857).

[4] Rowland Hamilton, *Money and Value; an inquiry into the means and ends of economic production. With an appendix on the depreciation of silver and Indian currency* (1878).

574.   W. S. JEVONS TO THE EDITOR OF *THE TIMES*[1]

SUN SPOTS AND COMMERCIAL CRISES.

Sir,

With reference to the article of January 14[2] on the above subject I should like to be allowed to explain that what I have hitherto published on the subject is of a preliminary and very incomplete character. Continued investigation of the subject produces almost perfect conviction that the principal – that is to say, the recurring – decennial crises of the 18th and 19th centuries are due to solar variations; but it is a matter of great difficulty to disentangle the requisite statistics in such a manner as to prove the exact *modus operandi*.

You point out what appear to be serious discrepancies between the epochs of *maximum* and *minimum* sun-spot frequency and the dates of crises as assigned by me, and you conclude that there are only four favourable cases out of 17. Indeed, you think that some of the cases are so unfavourable as to outweigh all the favourable ones, if not conclusively to negative the theory. This criticism proceeds, however, upon the assumption that the influence of the sun upon trade is of a direct and immediate character. Undoubtedly the connexion, if it exists at all, involves a long chain of causes and effects, so that the crisis will lag a good many years behind the wave of solar heat to which it is really due. The following is my present working hypothesis as to the production of decennial crises, a hypothesis quite open to modification by additional information. A wave of increased solar radiations favourably affects the meteorology of the tropical regions, so as to produce a succession of good crops in India, China, and other tropical or semi-tropical countries. After several years of prosperity the six or eight hundred millions of inhabitants of those countries buy our manufactures in unusual quantities; good trade in Lancashire and Yorkshire leads the manufacturers to push their existing means of production to the utmost and then to begin building new mills and factories. While a mania of active industry is thus set going in Western Europe, the solar radiation is slowly waning, so that just about the time when our manufacturers are prepared to turn out a greatly

---

[1] Published in the issue of 17 January 1879.

[2] This unsigned article, published in *The Times* on 14 January 1879 under the heading 'Sun-Spots and Commercial Panics', reviewed some of the evidence supporting the cyclical theory of sun-spots and the suggested connexion with meteorological phenomena. The author was not convinced that any link with famines and shipwrecks had been satisfactorily proved and ended by attempting to demolish Jevons's figures relating to commercial crises. He pointed out that the average interval between maximum and minimum sun-spot frequency was 5¼ years and that if the theory was to be proved every commercial crisis should occur within a year or so on either side of a minimum frequency: this only occurred in relation to four out of the seventeen crises cited by Jevons.

increased supply of goods famines in India and China suddenly cut off the demand. This is, I believe, the simple explanation of the over-production so much complained of at present. Our practical men, despising all theory and leaving the main factor in affairs (the sun) out of their calculations, just manage to make demand and supply not meet. Their arrangements are made about five years too late; just when they are in the depths of despondency they ought to be actively preparing for the coming favourable change in the Indian trade, and when they are all hopeful and excited the real opportunity has already slipped by.

Although the examination of a great series of statistical and physical facts leads to the conclusion that the trade with tropical countries is the principal disturbing cause, a European mania is almost always complicated by variations in home industry, due to speculative sympathy.

To return to the sun spots. As the crisis is separated by a good many years from the wave of solar heat to which it was originally due, precise coincidence of crises with *maxima* or *minima* is not to be expected. When it is asserted that the commercial period is 10.466 years, and the solar period 10.45, it does not mean that there is any like precision in the events, but only that 17 solar waves have been followed by 17 commercial waves. Moreover, it is quite open to question whether the sun spots are an accurate sign of solar variations, and whether, again, Wolf's numbers, from which you probably argue, are always to be relied upon. Wolf has been proved by Mr. Brown* to have made a mistake of eight months in the average solar period (11·1 years, instead of 10·45 years), and we are not bound to accept all his *dicta* as infallible. As to the very doubtful crisis of 1804–5, I could show, did space admit, that the discrepancy is probably due to the remarkable failure of solar activity and of auroras about the beginning of this century, with which is probably connected the famine prices of corn and the succession of bad seasons, commented on by the late Mr. Tooke in his history of prices. [3]

Finally, you adduce the American panic of 1873, which occurred when spots were very numerous, as evidence overweighing that of the crises of 1866 and 1878. But the American crisis of 1873 was not one of the decennial series at all; it was an exceptional event, due to the breakdown of inflated paper currency prices. The fact is that the decennial crisis duly occurred in the United States about the year 1876, as conclusively proved by the following statistics of bankruptcy in the States, published by Messrs. John Kemp and Co. (*Nature*, Dec. 5, 1878, p. 98):— "1870, 3,551; 1871, 2,915; 1872, 4,069; 1873, 5,183; 1874, 5,830; 1875, 7,740; 1876, 9,092; 1877, 8,822." [4] These numbers and multitudes of other facts teach an impressive lesson concerning the regular decennial march of

[3] Cf. Vol. IV, Letter 564, n. 1.
[4] *Nature*, 15 December 1878, pp. 97–8.

commercial disaster, and it is sad to think how many go to ruin and to death because they will not attend to the teachings of true experience. Let our so-called practical men give up the idea that theory is all nonsense. Give us facts, they say, not theory; but the facts on which a theory of this kind rests fill a library, and their collection and study, so far as I am concerned, has been the work of a quarter of a century.[5] Apologizing for the length to which the nature of the subject extends my letter,

I am, your obedient servant,
W. Stanley Jevons.

University College, W. C.

575.   R. HAMILTON TO W. S. JEVONS

3 Tenterden Street,
Hanover Square,
17 January.[1879]

Dear Professor Jevons,

I have to thank you very much for your note of the 14th[1] and your pamphlets which reached me last night. My work has been done very much alone and I am very glad to hear that it is of any use when it gets into the world.

I remember hearing of Sir James Stewart,[2] but have not read his works and could not find them referred to in the catalogue of the British Museum. I shall get them however for I do find some of the earliest writers the clearest. I do not wonder at the late revolt against the dogmatism of some Political Economists, but we seem likely to get a full supply of rubbish on the other side of the question.

The enclosed is an extract of a note I sent to Nature early last month,[3] but they did not find place for it. My experience of "panics" has been very much on the practical side and you may care to see how entirely a view from that side agrees with your own as I read it in the "Times" the other day.[4]

I remain
Yours faithfully
Rowland Hamilton.

Professor Stanley Jevons.

[5] Jevons was presumably referring to his meteorological researches begun in Australia in 1855. See Vol. II, Letter 52, p. 113; Letter 66, p. 161; Letter 92, n. 2, p. 239, and Letter 107, p. 297.

[1] The Editor has not succeeded in tracing Hamilton's papers.

[2] So rendered by Hamilton, but the reference is clearly to Sir James Steuart (1712 80), author of *An Inquiry into the Principles of Political Economy* . . . (1767).

[3] The 'enclosed extract' is not now among the Jevons Papers.

[4] Since Jevons's letter to *The Times* did not appear until 17 January 1879 (see above, p. 10) this is probably a reference to the account of his views given in *The Times* of 14 January 1879.

576. A. M. DE FOVILLE[1] TO W. S. JEVONS

Ministère des Finances,
Cabinet du Ministre,
Bureau de Statistique,
Paris, 17 j[anvi]er 79

Monsieur et cher maitre

Je vous suis très reconnaissant de l'aimable empressement que vous avez bien voulu mettre à m'envoyer, en double exemplaire, votre très curieux article sur les Crises Commerciales. Permettez-moi de joindre à mes remerciements quelques renseignements peutêtre nouveaux pour vous.

Dans l'*Annuaire du Bureau des Longitudes de 1878* ont paru plusieurs notices de M. Faye,[2] successeur de M. Leverrier à L'Observatoire de Paris, sur les Taches du soleil et sur leur influence magnétique ou thermique. Si vous n'avez pas cet ouvrage à votre disposition, j'aurai grand plaisir à vous l'adresser.

Un économiste français assez distingué, le Dr. Juglar, a publié, il y a déjà plus de 20 ans, une *Etude sur les Crises Commerciales* qui a été couronnée par l'Académie des Sciences Morales et Politiques.[3] Je n'ai pas lu ce livre jusqu'ici; mais j'ai vu les diagrammes qu'il contenait continués par M. Juglar jusqu'en 1876; et si vous désiriez prendre connaissance des travaux de cet écrivain, je lui demanderais de vous les communiquer. Sur les diagrammes, je remarque que les années 1803–1804 correspondent, comme les époques de crises ultérieures, à un minimum des Reserves metalliques et à un maximum des Escomptes pour la Banque d'Angleterre. Pour la Banque de France il y a maximum d'escompete en 1804–09 et un minimum d'encaisse en 1806. Si je rencontre d'autres éléments d'information sur cette époque, au point de vue qui vous occupe, je les recueillerai avec soin à votre intention. Les cours du 5% ont été très peu accidentés à cette époque, malgré la paix d'Amiens (27 mars 1802) et la reprise des hostilités dès mai 1803. Mais ce calme plat des fonds publics le retrouve en 1827, 1837, 1847, 1857 . . . époques de crises commerciales bien caracterisées.

Je vous signale encore à titre de document, l'article "Crises Commerciales" du Dictionnaire d'Economie Politique de Guillaumin,[4]

---

[1] Alfred de Foville (1842–1913), French statistician and economist; Directeur de l'Administration des Monnaies de France; director of *Bulletin de Statistique* published by the French Ministry of Finance; became Professor of Industrial Economy at the Ecole des Arts et Métiers in 1885 and later Professor of Political Economy at the Ecole Libre des Sciences Politiques; Membre de l'Institut.

[2] 'Sur la Metéorologie Cosmique', par M. Faye, *Annuaire pour l'an 1878*, publié par le Bureau de Longitudes (n.d.) 608–88.

[3] See Vol. IV, Letter 564, n. 2.

[4] Coquelin et Guillaumin, *Dictionnaire de l'économie Politique*, 2 vols (1854) 1, 526–34.

article qui est de Coquelin, un économiste mort depuis peu;[5] Coquelin, dans cet article, ne signale que très vaguement le caractère périodique des crises commerciales, et il croit – lequi me semble une complète illusion – qu'il suffirait de substituer la liberté absolue des Banques au système des Banques privilègées pour prévenir dèsormais toute crise nouvelle.

Ce qui jusqu'à présent m'inspire encore un certain scepticisme à l'égard de votre théorie, malgré les arguments saisissant que vous avez si habilement groupés, c'est qu'à en juger par le diagramme de l'Annuaire du Bureau des Longitudes, les maxima des sun's spots, bien que donnant une periodicité *moyenne* de 10 ans et quelque chose, ne sont pas très egalement échelonnés. Ces maxima correspondraient d'après ce diagramme aux dates ci-dessous; ou à peu près:

1750	1848
1761	1860
1770	
1779	L'intervalle varierait ainsi de
1788	9 à 17 ans, et la périodicité serait
1805	moins précise que pour les crises
1816	commerciales, ce qui me detournerait
1828	un peu de croire avec vous que le plus
1837	regulier de ces deux mouvements puisse

être le contre coup de l'autre. Si vous aviez de bonnes raisons de croire que ces irrégularités de la courbe des sun's spots sont le resultat d'erreurs d'observation, je vous saurais gré de me le dire.

Pardonnez moi ce long bavardage et croyez moi votre très dévoué et sympathique lecteur.

A. M. de Foville

577.   E. MOORMEISTER[1] TO W. S. JEVONS

Altkirch (Elsass), 24. Jan.
79

Hochgeehrtester Herr Professor!
Unterstützt durch die gütige Empfehlung der verehrlichen Verlagshandlung von Macmillan & Co. nehme ich mir die Freiheit Sie, hochgeeh-

---

[5] Charles Coquelin (1805–52), at one time actively engaged in the French textile industry; wrote numerous articles on economic policy for *Revue des Deux Mondes* and *Journal des Economistes*.

[1] Eduard Moormeister (1845–94), obtained his doctorate at Münster in 1869, and taught at Oberehnheim from 1871 until 1874 when he was appointed Director of the Realprogymnasium at Altkirch in Alsace; director of the Realgymnasium at Schlestadt, 1881–92, and of the Gymnasium at Hagenau, 1892–4. Author of *Die ersten Elemente der Wirtschaftslehre* (1879) and *Uber volkswirtschaftliche Belehrungen im Unterrichte des höheren Schulen* (1889).

rter Herr, um freundliche Auskunft in einer mir höchst wichtigen Sache zu bitten.

Damit beschäftigt, die Nothwendigkeit der Einführung der Grundlehren der politischen Oekonomie in einer kleinen Schrift darzuthun liegt mir sehr viel daran auf die in diesem Punkte in Ihrem Vaterlande gemachten Erfahrungen und erzielten Erfolge hinzuweisen. Es wird Ihnen nicht unbekannt sein, dass in Deutschland in der betreffenden Sache bis jetzt noch gar nichts geschehen ist und in wirthschaftlichen Sachen bis oben hinauf eine erstaunliche Unwissenheit herrscht, weil in der Schule nicht für die Aufnahme solcher Kenntnisse praedisponirt wird. Schon W. Roscher hat auf das Beispiel Englands hingewiesen und nach ihm Böhmert,[2] Contzen[3] u. a. m. Allein greifbare Ergebnisse und praktische Vorschläge fehlen bis jetzt gänzlich. – Auf die Gefahr, Ihnen, verehrtester Herr, unbescheiden vorzukommen habe ich es desshalb gewagt, mich an Sie mit der ergebensten Bitte zu wenden, mein Vorhaben durch Ihre reiche Erfahrung gütigst unterstützen zu wollen. Besonders wäre es mir wünschenswerth zu erfahren, ob in den englischen Staatsschulen – ich habe die Elementar- oder allgemeinen Volksschulen im Auge – die Anfangsgründe der politischen Oekonomie gelehrt werden, in welcher Klasse (rücksichtlich des Alters) und etwa in dem Umfange, wie Sie ihn in Ihrem Primer vorgezeichnet haben. Sodann wäre es für die Frage von Belang zu wissen, ob für den Lehrer die Kenntnisse dieser Anfangsgründe obligatorisch sind und darüber examinirt wird. – Ueber die Erfolge liesse sich nur insofern sprechen, als darauf hinzuweisen wäre, ob die einfachen Gesetze der pol. Oek. von dem jugendlichen Geiste leicht aufgefaßt werden. In Bezug auf diesen Punkt ist hier in Deutschland wenig Glauben verbreitet und wenn man von der Nothwendigkeit spricht, solche Kenntnisse in den Jugendunterricht einzuführen, der ist gleich mit der Phrase bei der Hand, man könne Schulkinder nicht das lehren, worüber selbst die Professoren an den Universitäten nicht einig wären. – Ferner möchte ich gern einiges daruber erfahren, wie es mit der pol. Oek. an den höheren Schulen (Gymnasien – Colleges – Technische Anstalten) steht. Ist in denselben ein besonderer Kursus für pol. Oek. eingerichtet oder werden die Hauptlehren nur gelegentlich vorgetragen; folgt der Unterricht bestimmten Leitfäden, wie z.B. dem Buche von Mrs. Fawcett: Political Economy for Beginners![4]

[2] Karl Viktor Boehmert (1829–1918), editor of *Bremer Handelsblattes* and secretary of the Bremen chamber of trade, 1857–66; Professor of Political Economy and Statistics at the University of Zürich, 1866–75; became Professor of Political Economy at the Technische Hochschule in Dresden and Director of the Statistical Bureau of Saxony in 1875. His writings included *Die Gewinnbeteiligung: Untersuchungen über Arbeitslohn und Unternehmergewinn* (Leipzig, 1879).

[3] Karl Wilhelm Heinrich Contzen (1835–88), author of *Die Nationalokonomie, ein politisches Bedurpriss unserer Zeit* (1872); *Geschichte der volkswirtschaflilichen Literatur* (1872).

Um Ihnen anzudeuten, wie es hier mit dem Verständnis der Wichtig-keit der pol. Oek. aussieht, nur dieses: In den Gewerbeschulen (6–9 jähriger Cursus) wird in den oberen Classen Comptoir=oder Handel-swissenschaft getrieben; das dies Studium aber wenig fruchtbar ist, ohne eine Einsicht in das Wirthschaftsleben überhaupt zu haben, daran hat noch niemand gedacht.

Es bleibt hier noch sehr Vieles zu thun, und Sie würden Sich gewiss den Dank Vieler verdienen, wenn Sie durch meine Vermittlung nur einige greifbare Thatsachen über die Möglichkeit die Anfänge der pol. Oek. auch in den Volksschulen, noch mehr aber in den höheren Schulen zu lehren, einem weitern Kreise wollten zukommen lassen.

Nehmen Sie schon im voraus, hochgeehrtester Herr, meinen vollen Dank für Ihre gütige Mühewaltung hin. Indem ich noch um Entschul-digung bitte, dass ich mich meiner Muttersprache bedient habe, bemerke ich, dass ich das Englische besser verstehe, als schreibe. Mit der Versicherung meiner ausgezeichneten Hochachtung

Ihr

ganz ergebener Diener

Dr. Moormeister

Director am Realprogymnasium zu

Altkirch (Elsass)

578.   W. S. JEVONS TO A. M. DE FOVILLE

[LJN, 394–5]

Hampstead, 1st February 1879

. . . I am much indebted to you for your very kind letter on the subject of Commercial Crises, which I have been thinking over for a week or more. As regards the book of M. Juglar, I have had a copy for some time, though I have not read the whole of it with the care which it deserves. His information about the crisis of 1804–5 is valuable, in addition to others I have since gained, but it does not satisfy me, inasmuch as the crisis of 1809–10 was in any case a much greater one, and is the *only great* exception to the decennial periodicity.

I have a good deal of information about the sun-spots and other physical fluctuations, but am yet far from fully acquainted with the facts of this complex subject. I shall have an opportunity of consulting the *Annuaire du Bureau des Longitudes de 1878*, in London, and expect to get from it the latest information.

---

4 Millicent Garrett Fawcett, *Political Economy for Beginners* (1870): see Vol. III, Letter 271, n. 2.

I cannot easily explain the greater regularity of the commercial series as compared with the physical series of events. The proper working out of so complex a subject must be a matter of time, and what I have printed is only the first germ of what I hope to publish in the course of some years. Other engagements will prevent me from following the matter up as rapidly and fully as I should like, but when I write anything more on the subject (in an American review or elsewhere) I shall have the pleasure of sending you a copy. In the meantime *I will take the liberty of assuring you, with great confidence, that the theory is a true one, and will ultimately be proved to be so.*[1] But this must be a matter of time and labour.

P.S. – The apparent irregularity of the sun-spot curve at the beginning of the century – 1779, 1788, 1805, 1816 – has been carefully discussed in England, and Mr. J. A. Broun has shown (*Transcations of the Royal Society of Edinburgh*, 1876, vol. xxvii., p. 563)[2] that Wolf was probably wrong. For Wolf's minimum in 1776 he substitutes a maximum, and he thinks that there was a small maximum in 1797 overlooked by Wolf. Broun is a very able meteorologist, and he throws great doubt on the accuracy of some of Wolf's numbers. He conclusively proves, too, that the average period is not the 11.1 years of Wolf, but 10.45. Eventually it may be found that the physical fluctuations are more regular than is supposed, but the facts are numerous and complicated. . . .

[1] De Foville evidently remained sceptical. He wrote shortly afterwards in an article, 'Les Tâches du Soleil et les Crises Commerciales', *L'Economiste Français*, 15 February 1879, pp. 191-3, '...M. Stanley Jevons est un des économistes les plus distingués de la Grande-Bretagne. Esprit à la fois très original et très-encyclopédique, il considère que l'étude des questions économiques n'exclut ni les inspirations subites du poëte, ni les procédés de calcul du mathématicien, et il n'est pas rare que, sous sa plume alerte, un vers de Virgile ou de Shakespeare se trouve encadré entre une équation algebrique et une figure de géometrie. On comprend qu'avec une semblable nature d'esprit, M. Jevons ait été plus facilement séduit qu'un autre par l'espoir de surprendre une intime connexité entre certains faits sociaux et certains phénomènes astronomiques. . . .'
    De Foville was therefore incorrect when he recalled in an obituary of Juglar (*Economic Journal*, 15 (1905) 294) that 'it was through my having gently railled the author of this fantastic theory (i.e. Jevons) in the *Economiste Français* (15 February 1879), that I was drawn into amicable relation with this always ingenious and frequently profound thinker . . . ,' as clearly their correspondence had begun before the publication of his article. He went on to assert 'shortly before his tragic death he wrote to me once more on the subject, in the firm conviction of the truth of his sun-spot theory.' However this letter, with its strong assertion of the truth of the theory, is the last from Jevons to de Foville which can now be traced and it seems possible, after a lapse of so many years, that it may have been the letter which de Foville had in mind.
[2] 'On the Decennial Period in the Range and disturbance of the decennial oscillations of the magnetic needle and in the sun-spot area', loc. cit.

579.   W. BROWN[1] TO W. S. JEVONS

13 Grove Place,
Brompton,
February 12,   79.

Professor W. Stanley Jevons, M.A., LL.D., F.R.S.,
Hampstead.

Dear Sir,

I have received your note and I am glad my letter will have been of some service to you however slight.

I wrote on the subject of having the Primers translated into various Indian Vernaculars because I thought you might be able with Brother "litterati" to bring sufficient influence to bear upon the authorities at the India Office to get this object effected under Governmental auspices.

I fear the task could not be efficiently undertaken by Englishmen alone. Natives thoroughly conversant with the grammatical structure of their own tongue and possessing facility of expression would be the most suitable persons to do the work of translation while Englishmen could afterwards supervise and see that the sense of the original was aptly rendered without pedantry which is as much a snare to the Hindu scholar as to our German cousins.

No doubt native children attending Government schools will be able to get excellent instruction directly through the medium of English books but there will ever be millions whose parents either cannot or will not send them to such institutions and who must needs be content with such instruction as they can derive from inane fables spawned perhaps when Buddha taught and happy if they attain to the fantastic poetry of the "Ramayanam."

This is the soil wherein the Primers might strike their roots and infuse a love of knowledge which when once kindled can never be quenched.

I have always since becoming personally acquainted with India at least, thought that our system of forcing on it our own tongue down the throats of the native population a very faulty one.

No doubt in the beginning of our connection with the country the contrary mode of proceeding would have been almost impossible but now that we have excellent dictionaries and grammars of nearly all the chief vernaculars no such excuse remains.

It seems therefore the first duty of an Englishman living in India to make himself master of the language and the people he is among instead

---

[1] This seems the most likely interpretation of a signature which is almost illegible. No other clues as to the author's identity are traceable; according to the *Post Office London Directory* for 1879 No 13 Grove Place, S.W., was a lodging-house kept by a Mrs Harriet Lewis.

of leaving the country as the majority do after a protracted residence with no literary knowledge of the native tongue except perhaps a score of dictatorial phrases expressive of daily needs ever emitted in like manner as the imperfect utterances of a parrot.

Were on the other hand European literature offered to the reading native public in a palatable form I feel convinced a firmer bond would link this country and India together than is knit expecting myriads of famished mortals destined to live and die in the gross mental darkness where unto they were born.

We may too learn much even from Hindu literature barbarous though it seems to us. I myself possess a very imperfect acquaintance with Tamil one of the chief languages of the South acquired during intervals snatched from other occupations during a short sojourn in the country. But the little I was able to learn taught me what an expressive and rhythmically beautiful language it is. Permit me to quote a short couplet from one of their poets which might not be an unfitting motto where with to head a work upon Political Economy and must seem pregnant with meaning to those who reflect upon some of the recent occurrences that have dyed with a blacker hue the cloak now resting upon our mercantile world.
"Vanikagn seivarkken varrikam pēnip
"Piravirur tham poōr sēyyin."
i.e. Let merchants trade with caution treating their neighbours goods as though they were their own.

I hope many more primers may be written and that they may meet with the success they deserve. To you personally it must be an imperishable source of gratification to know that your life and work have been of benefit to your fellow men.

I beg to remain
Yours very faithfully,
W. Brown.

580. R. HAMILTON TO W. S. JEVONS

3 Tenterden Street, W.
14 Feb. [1879]

Dear Professor Jevons,

I was called out of town the last few days or I should have more promptly answered your note of the 10th.

I found only a french translation of Sir James Steuart's Vol:[1] in the

---

[1] Sir James Steuart, *Recherche des principes de l'économie politique, ou essai sur la science de la police intérieure des nations libres*. Traduite par. E. de Senovert, 5 vols (1792).

British Museum and the essay on Money [2] bound with other pamphlets. I have only had time to glance at the former, but have read a considerable part of the latter with much pleasure. There is a wonderful grasp and power of insight in it, though he is dealing with far narrower conditions of trade and more artificial surroundings than we have now to consider. I feel much indebted to you for mentioning his work to me.

So much of my time has been spent abroad and I have had so little opportunity of collecting books that I can hardly give an opinion of any value as to the reprint of old works, but my impression is that it would be most interesting and of considerable value. It will help us to realise the present evils against which they fought and over which they eventually triumphed and as I think should bring home to us in our day the duty of meeting the evils with which we have to deal, in their spirit, rather than by an over-refinement of the letter handed down by them. It may be too that the reactionary spirit may be strong enough to call for a new statement of the old argument for free trade. It is perhaps not quite beyond the limit of possibility that Imperialist instincts might find it wisdom to divide class against class by granting protection to some favored interests who would thus become dependent upon those who would support their pretensions.

I remain
Yours faithfully,
Rowland Hamilton.

Professor Stanley Jevons.

581.   L. WALRAS TO W. S. JEVONS

Ouchy sous Lausanne
17 fevrier 1879 [1]

Cher Monsieur,

Je vous serais bien obligé si vous pouviez m'envoyer d'ici à quelques jours des programmes des cours des Universités anglaises, particulierè-

---

[2] Idem, *Principles of Banks and Banking of Money, as Coin and Paper, with the Consequences of any Excessive Issue on the National Currency, Course of Exchange, Price of Provisions, Commodities and Fixed Incomes* (1810).

This was in fact a reprint of the monetary sections of Steuart's *Principles*. There is a copy 'bound with other pamphlets' in the British Museum, press mark 1028. e (11) (6).

[1] The version of this letter published here is an exact copy of the original manuscript received by Jevons and now in the Jevons Papers. Jaffé, *Walras Correspondence*, 1, 596–7, publishes the version based on the draft in Fonds Walras FW 1, 278/13. Minor differences between the two versions are listed below:

	Walras Correspondence	*Jevons Papers*
para 2	numéro de décembre	no de Xbre
para 3	une traduction	ma traduction
para 3	dans toute notre liste	de toute notre liste.

ment des cours de droit. Je m'occupe en ce moment d'une étude sur *l'enseignement des sciences morales et politiques* dans les divers pays de l'Europe;[2] et je voudrais savoir ce qui se fait à cet égard en Angleterre. Il va sans dire que tous les renseignements que vous voudriez bien joindre à cet envoi me seraient infiniment précieux et agréables.

Vous avez dú trouver votre *Bibliographie* d'économie politique mathématique dans le no de Xbre dernier du *Journal des Economistes*.[3] M. Garnier a jugé à propos, je ne sais pourquoi, d'y ajouter votre signature que je n'y avais pas mise. J'espère que ce détail ne vous aura pas contrarié. Je me suis fait donner une quarantaine d'exemplaires tirés à part de ce document. Je vous en envoie un par la poste, et en tiens d'autres à votre disposition s'ils pouvaient vous être utiles.

J'ai réussi tout dernièrement à me procurer pour six semaines un exemplaire de l'ouvrage de Gossen que vous m'avez signalé, et j'ai trouvé ce livre si remarquable que j'ai voulu en garder la traduction que j'ai faite avec l'aide d'un de mes collègues[4] et qui va être terminée sous peu de temps. Un jour que j'aurai plus de loisir qu'aujourd'hui, je m'entretiendrai plus longuement avec vous des théories de cet auteur. Pour le moment, je vous dirai seulement qu j'ai le plus vif désir de publier ma traduction en français dès que les circonstances me le permettront; ét que je saisirai aussi avec empressement la première occasion qui s'offrira de signaier l'ouvrage dans le *Journal des Economistes;*[5] car c'est assurément le plus important de toute notre liste.

Recevez, Cher Monsieur, l'assurance de mes sentiments bien dévoués.

Léon Walras

582.   W. S. JEVONS TO L. WALRAS

21 Feb. 1879

My dear Sir

I am very much obliged to you for getting the Bibliographical list printed in the Journal des Economistes and for the important additions which you have made thereto. I now hear that there was an Italian Economist who took the mathematical view early in the last century, called Ceva.[1] His work is said to have been described in the Giornale

---

[2] Léon Walras, 'De la culture et de l'enseignement des sciences morales et politiques', *Bibliothèque Universelle et Revue Suisse*, 3 (1879) 6–32 and 223–51.

[3] See Vol. IV, Letter 532, n. 2.

[4] The translation was made by Charles Secrétan but not published: the manuscript is now in the possession of M. Georges Lutfalla of Paris. Cf. Jaffé, *Walras Correspondence*, 1, 597.

[5] In fact, Walras's article on Gossen did not appear until 1885; see Vol. IV, Letter 536, n. 2.

[1] Giovanni Ceva (1647–1734), engineer of Mantua whose *De re nummaria quod fieri potuit geometrice acta* (1711) became the earliest entry in Jevons's 'List of Mathematico-Economic Books' as finally published in *T.P.E.*

dell'Economista recently,[2] but I do not know the particulars.

I have decided to print the second edition of my "Theory of P.E." without waiting for the full bibliography, but I will put the list in the appendix and also give a full preface with references. My idea now is to produce a considerable volume with full references, descriptions and quotations from works on the math. method, also including translations of Cournot's and your works, and with the best abstract I can get of Gossen.[3] My impression is that the mathematical method is really making great progress though little is said about it. I expect my new edition to be published in 2 or 3 months and will then send you a copy. You will find some improvements and extensions, particularly concerning negative value and also concerning the dimensions of economic quantities.

In regard to courses of instruction in moral and political sciences, I have already posted you some papers giving information. There is however no single publication which would in any degree give a correct idea of the whole.

You are aware I suppose that the Revue Philosophique of Th. Ribot (Germer Bailliére) has given lists of the courses of philosophy (Tome III pp. 210–17) in various parts of Europe.[4]

In England the greater part of the philosophical teaching is done at Oxford and Cambridge, but comparatively little attention is paid to the Professor's lectures. A good deal of reading is done with private tutors, and the rest by College lecturers. At Cambridge, as well I believe as at Oxford, they now have inter-Collegiate lecturers, that is lecturers who receive students from any college indifferently, by a kind of exchange. The chief authority in Ethics and Mental and Logical Philosophy is Mr. Henry Sidgwick, author of the 'Methods of Ethics.' In political economy Professor Fawcett, as you know is professor but much of the lecturing is done by Mr. H. S. Foxwell.

Until the last few years the legal education of England was mostly done in the offices of the lawyers (attorneys and barristers) where young men went as apprentices to 'read,' partially acting however as clerks and assistants. There were courses both at Oxford, the Scotch Colleges, in University College London where Austin[5] gave his celebrated lectures on

[2] F. Nicolini, 'Un Antico economista matematica', Giornale degli Economisti, 3 (Anno v) (1878) 11–23.

[3] This idea was never carried into effect; the preceding sentence describes all the additions which were ultimately made to the second edition of T.P.E.

[4] 'Les universités de France et d'Allemagne. Programme des cours de philosophie professés pendant le semestre d'hiver (1876–1877)', Revue Philosophique de France et de l'étranger, 3 (1877) 210–17.

[5] John Austin (1790–1859), was appointed to the Chair of Jurisprudence in University College London at its foundation in 1826.

jurisprudence. Now the Inns of Court in London have appointed professors whom you will find in the enclosed list. But Sir James Fitz James Stephen[6] having been just appointed judge and being engaged on the new Criminal Code of England has resigned the Common Law Professorship.

In University College London Professor A. W. Hunter[7] has just been appointed to the chair of jurisprudence, instead of Roman Law the chair of which is at present vacant.

To obtain the detailed prospectuses of the Philosophical Courses in England, Ireland and Scotland would be a matter of considerable time and trouble. I know no single work which gives them. The separate regulations of each would have to be obtained and in the case especially of Oxford and Cambridge nothing but personal inquiry on the spot could give a precise idea of the method of instruction. I am

Yours very faithfully
W. S. Jevons.

583. W. S. JEVONS TO H. SIDGWICK

2 The Chestnuts,
West Heath,
Hampstead N.W.
28 Feb. 1879

Dear Mr. Sidgwick,

I am greatly obliged to you for your kindness in sending me printed copies of Professor Marshall's Theory of Trade.[1] The examination answers of some of his pupils had given me an inkling of their nature and I am now glad to see them at least privately printed. I suppose they will be eventually published.

There can be no doubt that his problems are exceedingly ingenious & very important for throwing light on difficult points of political economy. It will not be possible to enter into the matter now. I notice however that you speak of the method of diagrams as being *opposed* to that of symbols, whereas I should not attribute this meaning to Marshall's remarks in the

[6] Sir James Fitzjames Stephen (1829–94) had been appointed Professor of Common Law at the Inns of Court in 1875.

[7] William Alexander Hunter (1844–98), Professor of Roman Law, University College London, 1869–78, of Jurisprudence, 1878–82; M.P. for North Aberdeen, 1885–96.

[1] A. Marshall, *The Pure Theory of Foreign Trade* and *The Pure Theory of (Domestic) Values*. These two papers were printed for private circulation in 1879, and first published as No. 1 in the London School of Economics Series of Reprints of Scarce Tracts in Economic and Political Science in 1930. Cf. Pigou, *Memorials of Alfred Marshall*, pp. 23–4.

first half of p.5.[2] I should prefer to say that if not ultimately the same methods they are parallel methods, the difference being one of convenience of apprehension.

I have for some time past been inquiring into the history of the mathematical treatment of Economics, and the truth gradually dawns upon me that the mathematical method is as old as the science of Economics itself. The details are curious & in the long course of time I may perhaps hope to publish them. But it is quite plain that no recent writers have any claim to novelty, or priority of method, apart from originality. The *Recherches sur les Principes Mathématiques de la Théorie des Richesses* par Augustin Cournot, (Paris, 1838) which Mr Todhunter pointed out to me some years ago, is in my opinion a very beautiful piece of mathematical analysis applied to the laws of supply & demand, & he employs both the differential calculus and diagrams.

I forget whether I sent you the enclosed list to which however many additions have recently been made. In the new edition of my Theory I will take the liberty of adverting to Prof. Marshall's inquiries.[3]

I am pleased to have your ideas about my attack on Mill, but while quite agreeing that most philosophical writers break the law of non-contradiction, I should hold that in Herbert Spencer's case, the breaches are in matters of detail & that after striking off all errors there remains a new & true philosophy. In Mill, contradiction is of the essence of his method, I am sorry to hold. Some day I hope to complete my criticisms & pursue my assertions but I am not equal to finishing all I undertake.

I am

Yours very faithfully

W. S. Jevons.

[2] 'The pure theory of economic science requires the aid of an apparatus which can grasp and handle the general quantitative relations on the assumption of which the theory is based. The most powerful engines for such a purpose are supplied by the various branches of mathematical calculus. But diagrams are of great service, whenever they are applicable, in interpreting to the eye the processes by which the methods of mathematical analysis obtain their results. It happens that with a few unimportant exceptions all the results which have been obtained by the application of mathematical methods to pure economic theory can be obtained independently by the method of diagrams'. – Marshall, *Pure Theory of Foreign Trade*, p. 5.

[3] *T.P.E.*, Preface to the second edition, p. xl: 'I ought to add, however, that at Cambridge (England) the mathematical treatment of Economics is becoming gradually recognised owing to the former influence of Mr. Alfred Marshall, now the principal of University College, Bristol, whose ingenious mathematico-economic problems expounded *more geometrico*, have just been privately printed at Cambridge.'

584.   G. H. POWNALL[1] TO W. S. JEVONS

Manchester & Salford Bank,
St. Annes Street.
[March 1879]

Dear Dr. Jevons,

It is with great pleasure that I now enclose a copy of the paper which I read on the 5th inst[2] at the Statistical and which has just reached me. I dont send it because I am so in love with the paper that I fancy everyone else will be, but because I feel sure that it will pleasure you to see me trying to do any work. I am thinking of trying to make something out of my old friends the London Clearing House Returns, and when I have disentangled my notion of what I want to do, if you will allow me, I should like to ask you if you think it worth doing. I dont know that I ever shall do any strikingly good work but I have not got past the age when the wish to do so is always present. But it does not take long before one finds out that dropping grains of sand into the whirlpool of the public mind is an occupation which may go on unnoticed for ever and by and by I shall be amused at the wish to be noticed. Mr. Dickins's Presidency is over this year and we hope that he will be succeeded by Mr. Helm who is in every way more suitable. Trade in Manchester continues very greatly depressed and I think with many people there is a disposition to throw the whole blame upon free trade – my own theory in explanation is that the arguments which persuaded the last generation of the soundness of the doctrine are well nigh forgotten and that when protectionisst fallacies are advanced most people have nothing to reply with – but I suppose that is inevitable with every doctrine which reaches the dogmatic stage.

You will be afraid that I am going to inflict another paper upon you if I go on much longer.

Mr. Beardsalls testimonial reached near £40 and was expended in a drawing room clock with side ornaments.

Now wishing you a very pleasant spring when the long winter goes.

I remain, Dear Dr. Jevons,
Yours most sincerely,
Geo. H. Pownall.

[1] George Henry Pownall (1850–1916), banker, one of Jevons's students at Owens College; began his career with the Union Bank of Manchester, becoming manager of the Deansgate Branch; joined the Manchester and Salford Bank in 1877, becoming manager of the St Ann Street Branch in 1900; Joint Manager of the London Office of the Manchester and District Bankers' Institute, 1895; elected to the Council of the Institute of Bankers, 1901; Vice-President, 1910; President, 1916. Nominated by Jevons for membership of the Manchester Statistical Society, before which he read five papers concerned with banking and local government; President of the Society, 1896–8. Pownall became one of the four Honorary Secretaries of the Jevons Memorial Committee. See below, Letter 676, p. 129; also T. S. Ashton, *Economic and Social Investigations in Manchester, 1855–1933*, p. 175.

[2] This letter is undated but must belong to March 1879 in view of the reference to 'the

585.   W. S. JEVONS TO H. SPENCER

2, The Chestnuts,
West Heath,
Hampstead, N. W.
12 March 1879[1]

Dear Mr Spencer

Last night I received from the Secretary the formal notice of my election to the Athenaeum Club. I suppose this is a kind of literary apotheosis, and I am somewhat surprised at my early election.[2]

It adds much pleasure however to the event to remember that it was through your kind intervention that I was admitted and it does not need many words to say how highly I esteem the honour, and the kindness which you have thus done me.

I am
Yours faithfully
W. S. Jevons.

586.   W. S. JEVONS TO J. MILLS
[LJN, 395-6]

2 The Chestnuts, West Heath,
Hampstead, N.W., 12th March 1879.

. . . It is very kind of you to ask me to go to Manchester for the silver debate,[1] and to stay with you at the same time. I should like much to see you again at Northwold, and will hope for some opportunity of doing so. But the silver question would interfere with my class, which is held on Wednesdays; and as there is only just time before the end of the term to finish my promised course, it would create some inconvenience. After two

---

paper . . . read on 5th inst.'. On 5 March 1879 Pownall read a paper entitled 'Some Considerations affecting the relations of Capital and Labour' before the Manchester Statistical Society: in the autumn of 1879 Elijah Helm succeeded Thomas Dickins as President of that Society.

[1] The original manuscript of this letter is now among the Spencer Papers, London University Library.

[2] Jevons was apparently elected to the Athenaeum under a rule of 1864 which allowed the committee to elect each year a limited number of persons 'who have attained to distinguished eminence', without a ballot of members. Herbert Spencer had been a member of the committee since 1874. There was a sixteen-year waiting list for ordinary membership at this period. See Ralph Nevill, *London Clubs, Their History and Treasures* (1911) pp. 278-9. Cf. below, Letter 593, p. 36.

[1] Probably a reference to the meeting of the Manchester Statistical Society on 13 March 1879 when E. Langley presented a paper on 'The Silver Question'. See *Transactions of the Manchester Statistical Society for the Session 1877-78*, pp. 75-88. Langley's paper is not bound with those for the Session 1878-9, although Ashton, op. cit., p. 172, lists it there.

weeks more of lectures I shall be free for the summer. As regards silver, I do not think there is much if any good in discussing it. The matter must be left to take its course. *Nothing can be done*, and it is beating the winds to talk as if we could set everything right as we like. Above all, the Indian currency problem is one which admits of no solution except that of *laisser faire et laisser passer*. In fact, any attempt to tinker it up would inevitably fail, and if a gold currency could be introduced there, which I do not believe, it would only intensify the comparative superfluity of silver and scarcity of gold, which is, or rather has been, at the bottom of some of our troubles here. . . .

587.   C. L. MADSEN[1] TO W. S. JEVONS

Copenhagen, the 14th of March 1879.
41. Gamle Kongevei.

Professor W. Stanley Jevons,
University College,
London.

My dear Sir,
A few days ago I had the great pleasure to send you a copy of "New Researches on the Law of International Traffic", containing "Denmarks, Sveriges og Norges Samkvem med Udlandet" ["The Intercourse of Denmark, Sweden and Norway with foreign countries, 1871–1877"];[2] and you will see, that I thus have endeavoured to follow your advice to extend as much as possible the statistical materials upon which the law is founded. I have now added the statistics for 3 years more to each of the three countries, so that I now dispose of 186 groups of differently composed international traffic against 77 groups which formed the basis for the first series of Observations. Besides this I have also added the international post traffic, the freight and the regular international means of communications (telegraphs, railways, steamers) to the main tables, so that you in the three annexed tables will find in 27 columns for each year the reply to the frequent question: which are the moments together forming the sum of international commercial interests or intercourse between Denmark (Sweden, Norway) and England, Germany, Russia etc. etc. The tables are constructed so as to allow space for completion up to 1880 or for a period of 10 years.

---

[1] See Vol.IV, Letter 524, and introductory notes thereto.
[2] Copenhagen 1879. This work was included by Jevons in his 'List of Mathematico-Economic Books', *T.P.E.,* fourth edition, p. 339.

As to the Law I have found it to hold good for the years added just as for the first period (see page 17–19 and remarks), but in this treaty[3] the new observations and applications of the Law concern mainly the remarkable stability in the geographical distribution of commercial interests (page 7–12), in regard to which I would call your attention to the table given page 10 and conclusions thereof. Next follows the international post and telegraphic traffic and the regular communications and you will observe the nearly constant relation of the post to the Telegraph traffic (page 13), showing that the Law is applicable also to the former, and thus explaining the fact, that the great reform in the foreign post-tariff which dates from 1st July 1875 has not to any perceivable extent exercised any influence on the post traffic itself (see also page 18 and 19 and remarks). The Chapters from page 17 are devoted to a discussion on the Law, in the course of which I demonstrate the Equation (3) – page 22 –, showing how the definition of progress given by Herbert Spencer (page 24) may be mathematically applied to the development of international intercourse and with results [the more interesting as they are *absolute* figures][4] (co-efficients page 23) which are in the strictest accordance with the geographical situation of the countries concerned, means of regular communications etc. etc   The discussion of the Law leads to the introduction of a new commercial term, composed of passenger-traffic and tonnage of steamers and trains, provided particularly for this traffic, the post, etc. In the concluding words I compare the development of the *international* and the *inland* traffic (represented in the factor p in the traffic-equation), and after a few remarks on the difference of the leading principles, I explain why many reforms, which exercise the most distinct power to develop the inland traffic, according to experience and the equations necessarily must fail [to][5] do so in the international intercourse.

When the Law or rather the strict consequences of the Law thus again and in new directions shows itself able to throw fresh light over and to give a clear insight into the international movement, and when it up to the present moment through numerous applications have been proved, that the factors, of which this movement is composed, in all respects work harmoniously together, I think I am right in feeling myself more and more convinced that the Law is as exact and perfectible as the statistics itself. I shall therefore continue to work for the same, at the same time being well aware, that I am only a pioneer and that one day, when much more materials have been collected, we shall be able to dissolve even the commercial terms in factors composed of the geographical elements, the nature and economical conditions of the countries, attributable to and

---

[3] Madsen clearly wrote 'treaty' here although he evidently meant 'treatise'.
[4] These passages have been inserted by Madsen in the margins of the original letter.
[5] Omitted in the original manuscript.

concentrated in their commercial centres of gravity. But I shall feel quite content if I can get through my share of the work, which will still include the determination of as many commercial centres of gravity as possible and of the commercial distance between the countries, by means of which the yearly amount of progress (p) can be accurately defined.

But I am afraid I take up too much of your precious time and I shall therefore take leave for the present; I shall only add that I have commenced to study your excellent work, "the Principles of Science" (1877) and that I long to see your new edition of "Theory of Political Economy", mentioned in your letter of 25th of February last year – with many compliments and in the hope this will find you quite well, I remain, dear Sir.

Yours very faithful
C. L. Madsen

588.   E. MOORMEISTER TO W. S. JEVONS

Altkirch, (Elsass)
18 March 1879.[1]

Very honoured Sir,

I may be allowed to express you in your own language the most sincere thanks I feel for your highly benevolent letter.

You can believed that I am very surprised to see that the Pol. Econ. is instructed in a considerable number of Primary Schools, while this science is unknown at all in the middle schools of Germany. If I am not mistaken, W. Newmarch published in his Transactions of social science or in the Perspectives several notions upon the propagation of Pol. Econ. in schools.[2] I would be very glad to receive more exact information on this matter.

Especially it is important for me to know, if Pol. Econ. is an obligatory object of learning for all schools depending from the government, in other words, Is there in your country a school-law, prescribing the instruction of Pol. Econ. for all schools? An other question would be, if in the commercial schools this object did not be instructed. I am very obliged to you if you have the kindness to give me the direction of Mr. Templar[3] and

---

[1] The text of this letter has been reproduced as a literal copy of the manuscript.

[2] Newmarch, in his address as President of the Economy and Trade Department of the National Association for the Promotion of Social Science meeting at Leeds on 10 October 1871, reported that a Committee on Labour and Capital set up by the Association had had an interview with the President of the Educational Committee of the Privy Council 'to urge the desirableness of teaching elementary economics in schools under public inspection'. See *JRSS*, 34 (1871) 481.

[3] Possibly Benjamin Templar, author of *Reading Lessons in Social Economy for the use of schools* (1858), *Graduated School Arithmetic* (1872) and other school textbooks.

other masters of school who have a large experience in the instruction of Pol. Econ.

Perhaps you will find some articles concerning the instruction of this science, which could be adapted to my purpose, that is, to give a review of the propagation of Pol. Econ. in the institution of youth by other peoples.

Multa quae occurrent scribendi vitia te excusatarum spero meque eximiae tuae in me benevolentiae gratiam quam maximum habere, ut persuasum habeas, vehementur cupio. [4]

I remain Sir
Yours faithfully,
E. Moormeister.

589.   C. H. P. CHRISTIE[1] TO W. S. JEVONS

My dear Sir,

I must trust to the subject of my letter, to excuse me, a perfect stranger to you, for addressing you:—that subject is the 'Theory of Political Economy'.

In the preface to your work on that subject you say, "it is very likely that I have fallen into errors of more or less importance, which I shall be glad to have pointed out", and my object in now writing to you is to ask you to allow me to send you the M.S. of a paper in which I have attempted inter alia an examination of your theory, and in which – and I say it with the utmost diffidence – I have pointed out what, in my humble opinion, is a cardinal error in that theory.

I have seen many criticisms of your theory, but none which in my opinion, has gone to the root of the matter; – for instance the criticism of the late Professor Cairnes. [2] But it seems to me that I have put my finger on a real flaw; – at any rate if I am wrong I should be extremely glad to have my error pointed out to me.

As to the mathematical character of the science I fully agree with you, and in the paper to which I refer, and which I ask you to let me send for your perusal, I have endeavoured to arrive at accurate quantitative notions of Demand and Supply with a view to showing the relation of Price to these; and this conclusion to which I have been reluctantly driven, is that 'price'—what Cairnes called 'the proper price of the

---

[4] Moormeister seems to have decided to use Latin as an 'international language' here; the passage is certainly not identifiable as a quotation from any Latin author.

[1] Probably Charles Howard Peregrine Christie (d. 1906), a regular officer of the Corps of Royal Engineers; promoted Captain, 31 December 1878; retired as a Colonel.

[2] *Fortnightly Review*, 11 (1872) 72 - 7.

market'[3] – is connected with Demand and Supply, rightly indicated, by some law which might possibly be qualitatively stated by some general mathematical formula; but that it seems hopeless to expect that for any given commodity we shall ever be able to determine the numerical values of the constants involved in the expression, – that is to state quantitatively the law of the price of any given commodity.

If you will let me send the paper for your perusal, will you kindly let me know to what address I should send it.

I enclose my card,[4] and

I am, Sir,
Your obedient servant,
Charles H. Christie.

2, Coleherne Road,
South Kensington.

20th March, 1879.

590.   G. BOCCARDO[1] TO W. S. JEVONS

Genoa March 28th 1879

Dear Sir,

Allow me to tender you my heartfelt thanks for the coveted favour you have been pleased to bestow on me, by proposing me as a member of the London Statistical Society.[2]

To belong to so distinguished a body and to be brought forward under

---

[3] '. . . in all states of supply and demand there is always a certain price beyond which, if the markets rise, consumption is unnecessarily checked, and the stocks in the country pass off more slowly than is needful. In time the error is discovered, and a competition sets in among holders of the commodity, which issues in a fall of price, tending to stimulate consumption as much as it had previously been unduly checked. On the other hand, supposing the market price to be set too low, stocks become exhausted too soon, and the undue fall will need to be compensated by a corresponding advance at a later period. Such oscillations are at variance with the interests of the consumer; and the price, therefore, which renders them unnecessary, which is just sufficient and no more than sufficient to carry the existing supply over, with such a surplus as circumstances may render advisable to meet the new supplies forthcoming, may, I think, be conveniently designated as "the proper price" of the market.' – Cairnes, *Some Leading Principles of Political Economy Newly Expounded* (1874) p.108.

[4] No longer with the original manuscript.

[1] Gerolamo Boccardo (1829–1904), Professor at the University of Genoa; succeeded Francesco Ferrara as editor of the *Biblioteca dell'Economista*.

[2] Boccardo had been elected an Honorary Member of the Statistical Society on 18 March 1879, under the Society's rules allowing the admission of distinguished foreigners proposed by members of the Council. See *Annals of the Royal Statistical Society, 1834–1934* (1934) pp. 280–3.
Membership was obviously much sought after by European economists and Boccardo's election aroused the envy of at least one of his compatriots: cf. below, Letter 610, p. 59.

the auspices of so illustrious a Collegue, would be flattering to the self-esteem of one who can lay claims to weightier titles than I myself can boast of.

I have the pleasure of herewith forwarding to you, Sir, a copy of a late publication of mine entitled=Sulla Legge di periodicita delle crisi: Perturbazione economiche e Macchi Solari[3] in which I have endeavoured to enlighten the men of science of my own country on the highly important inquiries made by you on this very interesting question.

Please, accept, once more, my warmest acknowledgements, and believe me

   Dear Sir

         Yours truly
Prof. W. Stanley Jevons   G. Boccardo
 M.A., F.R.S.
   London

591.   C. H. P. CHRISTIE TO W. S. JEVONS

            2 Coleherne Road,
            South Kensington,
          28th March. [1879]

My Dear Sir,

I must thank you for your consideration of the paper that I sent you, and also for allowing me an opportunity of perusing the M.S. which reached me yesterday evening.[1]

On the latter I should like to offer a few remarks. I am probably wrong, but I am not convinced that you have really shown that 'time', or 'extension of commodity etc. in time', can be eliminated from economic formulae. Indeed, it seems to me, that you may have allowed yourself to be misled by an oversight, very similar to that which, as you have yourself pointed out, has been made in the case of 'interest'.

Consider the expression $v = \frac{1}{t}$ as ordinarily written. What does it mean? The usual interpretation, I take it, is velocity = *length* divided by *time*. But is this right? It seems to me that the operation thus assumed, is an impossible operation. You cannot multiply or divide one concrete quantity by another concrete quantity. You can no more multiply or

[3] Gerolamo Boccardo, *La legge di periodicità delle crisi: perturbazioni economiche e macchie solari* (Genoa, 1879).
[1] From the context of the Preface to the second edition of *T.P.E.* it is evident that this was the manuscript, or possibly a first proof, of the section of 'Theory of Dimensions of Economic Quantities' in chapter III of that book.

divide *length* by *time*, than you can *oranges* by *lemons;* and *length* divided by *time* no more yields *velocity*, than do *oranges* divided by *lemons* yield *grapes*.

Your expression, indeed, is not precisely '*length* divided by *time*'; — you say '*units of length*' divided by '*units of time*'; but if you would just try what can be made of '*units of oranges*' divided by '*units of lemons*', I think you would allow that your expression is hardly admissible.

I take it that the operation really denoted by $\frac{1}{t}$ is the division of a rate by an abstract number, producing another rate; — that is the division of a concrete quantity by an abstract number, producing a second concrete quantity of the same denomination as the first; — the rate for 't' units of time divided by 't'. v, l, and $\frac{1}{t}$ seem to·be in reality three quantities of the same denomination, — they all three represent *rates*, i.e. distances travelled in a certain time, — 'l' is the distance travelled in 't' units of time, — and 'v' or '$\frac{l}{t}$' is the distance travelled in 'one' unit of time; or, to vary the phase slightly, 'l' is the rate per unit 't', and 'v' or '$\frac{l}{t}$' is the rate per unit 1.

The notation ordinarily used is, I think, partly responsible for concealing the nature of the operations denoted. The nature of the operation would, I think, be more clearly brought out, if, instead of writing $v = \frac{l}{t}$ we wrote

$$v = l_{(1)} = \frac{l_{(1)}}{1} = \frac{l_{(t)}}{t} = \frac{l_{(n)}}{n}$$

thereby keeping prominently in view the fact that '$l_{(n)}$' involves 'time', just as the rate of interest involves 'time'.

And as in the operation denoted by $\frac{l}{t}$, you do not divide *length* by *time*, but divide, a *rate* by a *number*, producing a second rate, so, if you multiply $\frac{l}{t}$ or v, by t, you multiply *a rate by* a *number*, and the result is not a length but a rate.

Applying precisely the same reasoning to commodity or supply, I come to the conclusion that M and $\frac{M}{T}$ or $M.T^{-1}$, are two quantities of the same denomination, — both 'rates of supply', — rates calculated for two different units of time (T and unity) but nevertheless *rates* of supply, both of them, and *both involving time*, just as rate of interest and rate of motion involve time.

Therefore it seems to me that, except *in particular cases* perhaps *as an approximation* you cannot eliminate 'time': − that you *must* represent 'total utility' as a solid. It *may* be that it is only an infinitely thin lamina of this solid $\left(\dfrac{dM}{dt}\right)$ that you have to consider at one time, but it seems to me that it *is* a lamina, and *not* a 'surface'; and, moreover, that the equation to the curved surface limiting the entire solid which represents 'total utility' must be known before $\dfrac{dM}{dt}$ can be known. Must it not?[2]

2.   Touching the use of the symbol M, − the symbol of mass, to denote quantity of commodity, you have of course considered the fact that there are many things exchanged of which 'mass' cannot be predicated, − certainly the entire class of 'services', and, may I not say also, time and space, − for are not time and space sometimes bought and sold. Do you not think that Q, as symbolising quantity in the abstract, without implying any particular kind of quantity − mass, extension, weight or what not might in some respects be preferable?[3]

3.   With regard to the ambiguity of the word 'value', it seems to me that there is a fourth meaning in which the word is often used; − that when people talk of a commodity having increased or decreased in value; they do in general mean that it is more or less difficult to obtain, − that the 'difficulty of attainment' has increased or decreased. I think people commonly confound 'value' and 'difficulty of attainment', − 'value' and (according to my views) the 'ground of value'.[4]

I return your M.S. with many thanks and

I remain
Yours faithfully
Charles H. Christie

W. Stanley Jevons Esq.

P.S. Pray consult your own convenience about returning my M.S. I am in no hurry for it.

---

[2] Jevons gave his answer to this question in the text of *T.P.E.* (fourth edition, p. 67): 'This would be erroneous, because the third dimension T enters negatively into the quantity represented by the horizontal axis. Thus time eliminates itself, and we arrive at a quantity of two dimensions correctly represented by a curvilinear area, one dimension of which corresponds to each of the factors in MU.'

[3] Jevons accepted this point − in the Preface to the second edition he paraphrased Christie's argument with the comment: 'In this objection I quite concur, and I must therefore request the reader either to interpret M with a wider meaning than is given to it in p. 64, or else mentally to substitute another symbol' (fourth edition, p. xii).

[4] Christie seems to have in mind here what would now be called a positive shift of the supply curve, which in Jevons's theory would be subsumed under the head of 'degree of productiveness of labour in producing X or Y'. This point is not treated in chapter III of *T.P.E.*, but in chapter V (fourth edition pp. 191−3).

592.   W. F. BARRETT[1] TO W.S. JEVONS

Milner Field,
Bingley, Yorkshire.
Mar. 28 [1879]

My dear Prof. Jevons,

Very many thanks. I will return the extract from the Times. Your letter I read in part in your art in Nature.[2] I am glad you are so in earnest. Balfour Stewart's 24 day cycle wonderfully confirms the correctness of your reasoning. But surely the true secret of the apparent capriciousness of "the weather" is to be found (when local causes are eliminated) in the superposition of many waves of different periods and in different phases. The origin of these waves is doubtless the sun and through it the other members of our solar system. For they possibly set on the sun and the sun on us. Hence our weather is like a complex musical sound and the "timbre" of the weather at any moment would thus result from the number and the intensity of the period of the "partial" weather "tones" operating in conjunction with the fundamental tone of ray the 10–11 yearly sun spot cycle. Fourier's Law[3] ought thus to apply to the analysis of the "combination" weather "tone" which we daily experience. And so one might be led to hope an harmonic engine might be devised to analyse the weather into its constituent "partial tones" – as no doubt each elementary wave is of a simple pendular type. Of course the combinations resulting from the superposition of these waves in various phases is infinitely great and hence the vast variety of our weather changes according to this view. I should like to see Lockyer's & Hunter's art. if you have the reprint.[4] My address on Wednesday – Friday is New Athenaeum Club, Suffolk Street, Pall Mall, S.W., after that Dublin.

I have just been taking part in the most wonderful telephonic experiment I have yet had. I have listened to a sermon in Halifax 18 miles from here and the whole service not a word lost and the singing was

---

[1] [Sir] William Fletcher Barrett (1844–1925), Science Master, International College, 1867–9; Lecturer in Physics, Royal School of Naval Architecture, 1869–73; Professor of Physics in the Royal College of Science, Dublin, 1873–1910; chief founder and President of the Society for Psychical Research; knighted, 1912.

[2] Presumably references to Jevons's letter published in *The Times*, 17 January 1879 (see above, Letter 574, p. 10) and his short article 'Sun-Spots and the Plague', *Nature*, 13 February 1879, p. 338, in which he published a table showing that outbreaks of plague in Europe between the sixteenth and eighteenth centuries coincided with solar years, if based on the $10\frac{1}{2}$-year period.

[3] The trigonometric series used in mathematics to fit sets of data and represent functions, devised by the French mathematician Jean-Baptiste Joseph, Baron Fourier (1768–1830), applicable to the mathematical analysis of musical sound.

[4] J. N. Lockyer and W. W. Hunter, 'Sun-Spots and Famines', *Nineteenth Century*, 2 (1877) 583–602.

accompanied in perfect time by friends in different places 2, 10 and 18 miles from the chapel, all in one circuit.[5]

Yours,

W. F. Barrett.

593.   W. S. JEVONS TO T. E. JEVONS
[LJN, 396–7]

Athenaeum Club, 31st March 1879.

. . . Since last I wrote to you I have become, as you see, quite a swell, having been elected to this club under the rule allowing a limited number to be elected specially by the committee.[1] It is a most luxurious place, with all kinds of swells about. I daresay I shall like it more and more as I become accustomed to it.

I have been very busy of late with many things, but have rather run myself down, and need a few days' holiday. Just lately I have fortunately found the required keystone to my commercial crisis theory, in the prices of corn in India, which in a large part of the last century show a wonderful periodicity. I have got tired of my proposed *Princeton*[2] article, but I must try what I can do soon.

We are all well at home, the children very lively, and Winefrid becoming very winning and pretty. Yesterday I began a little lesson to 'boy' on the making of bread, and told him it was made of flour. 'Do you mean cauliflower, papa?' was what the little fellow asked, after some reflection.

P.S. – I am the more pleased at my election to the club, inasmuch as it was Herbert Spencer who moved and managed it; and as he is a constant frequenter of the club, it will give me an opportunity of becoming well acquainted with him. . . .

[5] Apparently a reference to one of a number of experiments being conducted at the time by Louis John Crossley (1842–91), a prominent Halifax businessman who pioneered telephone development in the north of England. In the process of developing the 'Crossley Transmitter' which he later patented, he carried out several experiments centred on Square Congregational Chapel, Halifax, where a transmitter had been installed in the pulpit. The first transmission to receive wide publicity took place shortly after this letter was written, on 13 April 1879, when a sermon preached in Halifax was heard in Manchester.

[1] See above, Letter 585, n. 2, p. 26.
[2] See Vol. IV, Letter 567, n. 2.

594. A. PUVIANI[1] TO W. S. JEVONS

Prof. Stanley Jevons
Most Hon. Sir,

Having had the fortune of reading your Political Economy, in a french translation by Mr. Henry Gravez,[2] and persuaded to perform not only a useful but an indispensable work for my fellow Citizens, especially to the working classes by offering them its plain translation, I firmly resolved to go to work at it, humbly asking your full consent.[3] I hope also that the welfare of the cause could excuse the translator before the public for any faults perhaps committed by him. Since that your generous impulse has undertook to do good to the working classes' condition (which thing nobody else could have done better than yourself, who occupy so a distinct place in the Departments of Economical science) it would be, it seems to me, a great loss in its integrity and efficacity, remaining confined only in a restrict and special local point while now a days on the contrary the conditions of all States contribute to confer an international and universal character. Allow me to add that your book represent rather most special characters of opportunity for the Italians. As our intellectual and phisical power has been till now absorbed in two great undertakings, we could not even free our public opinion from old and pernicious prejudices, a poor inheritance of sistems since long condemned by the civil conveniences and science. The composition of the political unity – the establishment of the relations between Church and State in a permanent and conform way to the wants of the times: these are the high and perilous works happily accomplished with great perseverance, with shrewdness and courage, with a noble sacrifice of life and property. Thus, we could give life to that sturdy and generous thought, which the civil dissentions of the middle ages lightened in the high mind of the subtle Florentin Secretary.[4] Likewise we have fulfilled the program of Count Cavour's, synthesis of the Italian wants and tendencies: neither the wrath of Vienna nor that of the Vatican has been able to stop its way: for the power wavers whenever it is not faithful to his mission.

[1] Amilcare Puviani (1854–1907), graduated from the University of Bologna in 1876, and for a few years taught Public Finance and Administration there; from 1890 to 1907 he taught Economics and Public Finance at Perugia University. His published works included *Del sistema economico borghese in rapporto alla civiltà* (1883) and *La Teoria dell'illusione finanziaria* (1903). The text of this letter has been reproduced as a literal copy of the manuscript.

[2] See Vol. IV, Letter 553, n. 2.

[3] As the letter of 3 April 1879 from Luigi Cossa shows (see below, Letter 595, p. 42), Hoepli had already commissioned him to undertake a translation of Jevons's *Primer of Political Economy* into Italian.

[4] Niccolò Machiavelli (1469–1527), author of *The Prince*, who in 1488 was appointed secretary of 'The Ten', a board charged with the management of the foreign affairs of the city-state of Florence.

The forming, then, of the political and religious interests, hindered us to turn seriously our attention to economical interests, rather sacrificed to the exigencies of them. It is, at length, time to occupy ourselves of the economical part, if we do not wish to see in danger the conquests laboriously achieved, for, by the prosperity of the economical interests may derive strength and respect to the State, elevation of the humble classes in the interior, general welfare and security. – If we were allowed to draw auspices from the present, we could but pronosticate well of the future, for, though the times were not propitious, nevertheless we can member some clever and hot supporters of the good economical doctrines, both in old and new generation, although, helas! we are very far from seeing descend the sound leading truths in the conscience of suffering crowds. Therefore, the endeavours done till now have been able to give Economical Politics an honourable and official place in Universities and Technical Establishments, but they have not yet been able to make it known as far as where want is more pressing, and we have not yet tried to give them that elementary and practical character, which is indispensable in order that it may bring all those fruits, that it is capable, which the illustrious J.B. Say referred to, when he wrote: "Les sommités des sciences sont de peu d'usage dans la vie ordinaire. Elles ne servent qu'à confirmer et coordonner les principes élémentaires, les seuls dont on ait besoin dans les applications que les arts font des sciences aux besoins de l'espèce humaine" (Cours compl. – Des établissements d'instruction). [5]

Some erudite monographies and valuable treatises have also appeared, but their nature and object were not fit to be read in the few moments of leisure, that remain to the working classes, which do not like bulky books. They are in want of plain written books, in the meantime clear and concise, in which, difficulties that are presented to their understanding, may be gently cleared up, that they may be within the reach of their scarce pecuniar means; they want books full of useful and elementary truths advantageously suitable to daily wants of life, and that may be shield against subversive doctrines and dangerous exagerations of factions and ambitious men. It is true that elementary works procure but little glory and less profit, and that only the most learned men can do it, for who has not a deep intelligence of all parts of a given science cannot expose and set in good order the principles of it in a more rigorously logical manner so that one may draw useful directions from them, and settle an elementary principle, which might not then be deprived of its efficacy by a deeper examination of the subject.

To the detriment of our condition of things, and to the scarcity of italian productions suitable the imparting of the principles of economical

---

[5] Jean-Baptiste Say, *Cours Complet d'Economie Politique Pratique*, 6 vols (1828–9) v, 296.

science in an elementary way to all classes, we may add then, that we have made no endeavour to supply our lack by the spreading out the elementary treatises of enlightened and well deserving Strangers, for in these first years of political liberty, our few champions of the economical doctrines they had in view, either to resolve the controversial points of the science or to discuss in the high spheres of politic against the ties and difficulties, which were left to us by the perverse times of discordies and by the despotism.

The want then urges, and it urges the more, in as much (that though we must give praise to the temperance of our lowest classes, which never were pushed to those furious anarchicals phrenzies, which have saddened other countries) we were though for recent deeds, forced to be persuaded, that also in Italy boils a deep and rancorous discontent of the present, and there is propagating such a subversive mania, which is formidably organizing throughout the whole Continent, and which it is impossible to appease neither with severe and restraining Laws, nor with inhuman sentences and with an imponent parade of forces.

It is also necessary to persuade ourselves how indispensable is, be to the security be to the prosperity of nations, the diffusion of the good economical doctrines; which besides dissipating the ferment of the pernicious opinions that menacing the overthrow of the whole social edifice, will be able progressively rarefy the causes of the dissatisfied, and render the Citizens active and concord in the common welfare. From which derive the duty of every illuminated and prudent Citizen, to apply himself to economical study and endevour to usefuly spread it: and as to a government, that holds in its hands the monopoly of instruction, it will concern to provide, that in the schools, where the Children of the people run in crowds, be imparted "wholesome and firm ideas on the economy of the society and on the laws, to which its development and life are infallibly subordinated"; with it "the sophists and mountebanks perhaps now a days would not have so a favourable position among the contemporary generations and so easily would be not found complices to overthrow these laws with violence, and substitute to the naturale society, which we have always under our eyes, an unknown fictitious society, upon the end and order of which they all disagree".

To these words, the most celebrated Dunoyer,[6] that plausibly greeted the appearance in France of the precious elementary work of Garnier,[7] added "If we had taken the trouble of teaching the generations the function practised in the social economy by the security of persons and properties, by the liberty of work and transactions, and to what point the

---

[6] Charles Dunoyer (1786–1862), author of *Traité théorique et pratique d'économie politique* (1858) and *De la liberté du travail* (1845) among the other works.

[7] *Eléments de l'économie politique* (1845). On Garnier see Vol. III, Letter 337, n.1.

observation of these natural laws is necessary to all, and particularly to the less advanced classes; at what point, for instance, the respect of property, so desirable by them who possess a fortune acquired, is particularly indispensable in the interest of those, who have all to acquire: if, I say, these primordial truths were given them, fruit of the best and most instincts of humanity, source of all the prosperity, that she possess, we would not have to day . . . the humiliation to see put in doubt in our Country the most elementary bases of Society, and to be obliged in particular to defend the principle of property against an unchaining of attacks, the most strange and unheard, the one from the others''.

In order that, the great principle of nationality and also that more comfortable and providential of humanity, assisted by the progress of exact and moral sciences, may accomplish, their full development, and succeed to fraternize the peoples, by engaging the single action in a vast, common and pacific laboratory of industry, it is a duty of the actual age to persuade, everywhere, the peoples of the fraud of many doctrines, of the emptiness of many shadows, that the despotism, or the license or the wanted examen and to short views of the economical science have sowed on the path that they ought to tread on. The harmony of views will drive out the distrusts and rancours, which today separate the different classes of Citizens with a great loss to the prosperity, credit and to the common vigor.

I trust, most honored Professor, that, as you have not disdained to mix yourself among the working classes, with the noble object of contributing to their instruction and welfare, you will not find it inopportune, that I may avail myself of your learn words, in order to promote more efficacely the work, to which you have so generously dedicated yourself. And if to the darkness of my name and to the humility of my forces, little conveying to me the translation in the Italian language your thought, in all its integrity, neatness and precision, my effort will not be totally reproachable, when it will be of use, as I hope, to excite others worthier than me, to the proof.

With which it would appear to me to see the Italians to push forward in that way, which only can lead them to the highness, which seems to them reserved among Civilized Nations. It is useful to hope that Rossi's[8] Country, that had seen in the last Century on the walls of Naples, the Genovesi[9] occupy the first Economical Cathedra, and that in the two

[8] Pellegrino Rossi (1787–1848), Professor of Criminal Law at Bologna, 1812–16 and at Genoa, 1816–33; Professor of Political Economy at the Collège de France, 1833, and of Criminal Law at the University of Paris, 1834. French envoy to Rome, 1845; entered the service of Italy in 1848 and formed a ministry under Pope Pius IX; assassinated 15 November 1848.

[9] Antonio Genovesi (1712–69), Professor of Ethics and Moral Philosophy, and later of Commerce and Political Economy, in the University of Naples; author of *Lezioni di economia civile* (1765).

precedent Centuries, had given such a copious harvest of good monographies, of diligent studies, will concede to this part of the knowable, all the interest that now shows Adam's Smith country: and that Italy in her fecund bosom will find emolors and admirers of the learned and well deserving Archibishop Whately and of that illustrious legion, of which you make a part. Which has contribute to enlighten the public English opinion, following Cobden's paths, the obscure Muslin Manufacturer, who with five or six of his friends, raised (as the celebrated Ferrara said) an association whose power is unexampled in the history of the pacific Reforms: preparing thus with Manchester's Examples and with his own triumphs that celebrated "Association for the freedom of Exchanges" in France, which formed the greatest glory of the beloved and complained Bastiat.

Finally, I write herewith to my excuses for having abused till now of your patience and kindness, the prayer to favour me with your biographical particulars holding I for sure, that the Italians will be glad to be acquainted as near as possible with him, who already enjoy a so much deserved fame be in science be in philanthropy.

Your devoted and humble Servant
Dr Amilcare Puviani
Via Saragozza N° 11   Bologna (Italia)

April 2.^{d} 1879.

595.   L. COSSA[1] TO W. S. JEVONS

Illustre et très honoré Collègue,

Pavia, (Italie) 3 Avril 1879.[2]

Ayant appris par Mr. Ferraris le jugement très flatteur pour moi que vous avez bien voulu donner de ma *Guida alla Studia dell' economia politica*, je me prends la liberté de vous faire hommage d'un exemplaire, que je vous prie d'accepter avec bienveillance.

J'espère qu'il puisse se présenter l'occasion de faire connaître mon travail au public anglais par quelque article de journal. Une citation seule de votre part me serait très utile. Si quelque jeune économiste de votre pays voulait par aventure le traduire, il serait bien facile de s'arranger pour le *copyright*.[3]

---

[1] Luigi Cossa (1831–96), Professor of Political Economy in the University of Pavia, 1858–96. The *Guida* referred to in this letter was first published in 1876; his *Saggi d'Economia Politica* in 1878. Cf. below, Letter 603, p. 53.

[2] The original letter is thus set out, with the address and date below the opening phrase.

[3] Cf. below, Letters 603 and 651, pp. 53 and 101.

J'espère pouvoir vous envoyer enfin un exemplaire du numéro du Journal des Economistes (italien) où se trouve le mémoire que j'ai fait rédiger par mon savant écolier Mr. Nicolini sur l'ancien économiste mathématicien Ceva. [4]

Il vous sera peut-être agréable de savoir que dans le courant de l'année l'éditeur milanais Hoepli publiéra une *traduction italienne* de votre *Primer of Political Economy* qui paraître *sous ma direction*. [5]

Je vous serais bien obligé s'il vous était possible de me procurer un éxemplaire de la réimpression des *ancient tracts on money* et *on commerce*, editée jadis par les soins de feu Mr. J. R. McCulloch. [6]

En faisant nommer Mr. Boccardo, *membre honoraire* de la *Statistical Society of London*, vous avez donnée une preuve très distinguée de votre prédilection pour les savants italiens. Il est désirable que l'occasion se présente à vous de donner le même témoignage d'éstime à d'autres auteurs des études économiques de notre pays.

Vous trouverez ci-jointe une note de *trois anciens économistes mathématiques*. Il vous sera peut-être agréable d'y voir mentionné un auteur anglais (le général Lloyd) qui vous était échappé dans votre *bibliography*. [7]

Je me prends la liberté de vous faire remarquer que vous avez oublié beaucoup d'*auteurs allemands*, comme *Helferrich*,[8] *Laspeyres, Knapp, Brentano*,[9] *Schumacher*,[10] *Falk*[11] qui ont fait le critique du *Salaire naturel* de

[4] See above, Letter 582, nn. 1 and 2, p. 21.

[5] There is no record of this translation in the Bibliography of Jevons's writings, *T.P.E.*, appendix IV. Here, and throughout this letter, passages in italics were underlined by Cossa in the original manuscript.

[6] *A Select Collection of Early English Tracts on Commerce, from the Originals of Mun, Roberts, North and others* . . . and *A Select Collection of Scarce and Valuable Tracts on Money, from the Originals of Vaughan, Cotton* . . . *and others*, both edited by J. R. McCulloch (1856). McCulloch also edited a second collection of *Scarce and Valuable Tracts on Commerce* (1859).

[7] Henry Humphrey Evans Lloyd (1720–83), major-general in the Austrian army. The work referred to was *An Essay on the Theory of Money*, published anonymously in 1771. Jevons included it in his bibliography, acknowledging his indebtedness to Cossa in the Preface to the second edition of *T.P.E.*, p. xlii.

[8] Johann Alfons Renatus von Helferich (1817–92), Professor of Political Economy at Freiburg, 1844–9; Tübingen, 1849–60; Göttingen, 1860–9; Munich, 1869–90.

[9] Lujo Brentano (1844–1931), a founder member of the Verein für Sozialpolitik; Professor of Political Economy at Berlin, 1871–2; Breslau, 1872–82; Strassburg, 1882–8; Leipzing, 1889–91 and Munich, 1891–1931. His early works included *Über J. H. von Thünens Naturgemässen Lohn und Zinsfuss* (Göttingen, 1867).

[10] H. Schumacher, of Zarchlin, Mecklenburg: editor of Johann Heinrich von Thünen's *Ein Forscherleben* (Rostock, 1868) and *Der isolerte Staat* (Berlin, 1875); author of *Ueber J. H. von Thünen's Gesetz vom natugemässen Arbeitslohn* . . . (Rostock, 1869), *J. H. von Thünen und Rodbertus. Kapital-isationsprincip oder Rentenprincip* (Rostock, 1870) and *Grunderbrecht im Lichte der Rentenprincips* (Rostock, 1871).

[11] Georg von Falck, author of *Die Thünen'sche Lehre vom Bildungsgesetz des Zinsfusses und vom naturgemässen Arbeitslohn* (Leipzig, 1875), *Kritische Rückblicke auf die Entwickelung der Lehre von der Steuerüberwalzung seit Adam Smith* (Dorpat, 1882) and *Russische Wirtschafts und Finanzfragen* (Reval, 1889). Only von Falck, Brentano and Schumacher, of the names listed by Cossa, later found a place in Jevons's Bibliography.

Thünen – Vous pouvez trouver leurs indications dans les *bibliographies allemandes*. Si cela ne vous était pas possible, je suis disposé à vous en donner l'*indication exacte* et détaillée.

Agréez, Mr. le Professeur, l'expression de ma considération très distinguée

Prof · Luigi Cossa
at the University of Pavia.
Italy.

596. W. S. JEVONS TO HARRIET JEVONS
[LJN, 397]

The Three Swans,
Salisbury, 8th April 1879

. . . I have just received your letter, and am glad to find that all is right at home. I have decided to stay here the rest of my visit, only making excursions in the neighbourhood.

This afternoon I shall probably go to Romsey, as the church there is said to be very well worth seeing.

I like Salisbury very much; and it fortunately happens that they are having special musical services in the evening – 8 to 9 p.m. – at the cathedral, which occupy the time very pleasingly. They have a fine new organ, with a good organist, and very careful singers, and with the cathedral lighted up by gas, the effect is very beautiful. Two nights they are going to have portions of Bach's *Passion* music.

. . . I have done a great stroke in book-buying, having bought a remarkable collection of nearly five hundred economical and political pamphlets at about a halfpenny each.[1] Some of them are evidently valuable and rare. One of them contains copperplate diagrams of prices for some centuries. One or two are by Robert Owen. I also got a carefully-written list of them all, as good as a catalogue.

The cathedral has been elaborately restored, and looks much better than when we saw it. . . .

[1] Jevons's large collection of economic pamphlets is now in the British Library of Economic and Political Science.

597. W. S. JEVONS TO R. H. INGLIS PALGRAVE

Address Hampstead.
16 April 79.

My dear Palgrave,

I find that Newton's reports on the currency, concerning which you inquired of me, are reprinted in the 'Select Collection of Tracts on Money' printed for the Political Econ. Club by MacCulloch, which however is very scarce, as only 125 copies were printed. There are three reports, all brief, of which the third alone (1717) needs notice. After reading it carefully I think it is *untrue* that Sir Issac Newton recommended a double standard.

He was required by the Lords of the Treasury to give his opinion "What method may be best for preventing the melting down of the silver coin", and he gave the opinion that if the guinea were reduced in nominal value from 21s. 6d. to 21s – "*it would diminish the temptation to export or melt down the silver coin, and by the effects, would shew hereafter better than can appear at present, what further reduction would be the most convenient for the public*".[1]

He was asked what would diminish the exportation of silver compared with gold and he gave a correct answer, all his reports showing a perfect comprehension of the subject, but there is no advocacy of bi-metallism.

I fear the labour and worry that might be involved in the Adam Smith Society, and do not feel inclined to venture on it at present.[2]

Yours faithfully,
W. S. Jevons.

598. W. S. JEVONS TO THE EDITOR OF *THE TIMES*[1]

SUN-SPOTS AND COMMERCIAL CRISES.

Sir,

Some months since you did me the favour to insert a letter on the subject of commercial crises, in which I endeavoured to answer objections against the notion that the activity of commerce in England

---

[1] 'Representations of Sir Isaac Newton on the Subject of Money, 1712–1717' in *A Select Collection of Scarce and Valuable Tracts on Money*, with a Preface by J. R. McCulloch (1856) p. 277 (italics supplied by Jevons).

[2] For fuller details of this proposed society for reprinting economic works, see below, Letter 631A, p. 81.

[1] Published in the issue of 19 April 1879. This letter, together with that published in *The Times* on 17 January 1879 (see above, Letter 574, p. 10) formed the basis for Jevons's paper 'Commercial Crises and Sun-Spots', *Nature*, 24 April 1879, pp. 588–90; reprinted in *Investigations*, pp. 235–43.

ultimately depends upon the solar activity. Public men ask again and again what is the cause of the recent, and it may perhaps still be said the present depressed state of trade. Yet the only answer which refers this state of things to a definite cause is treated with ridicule. I am repeatedly told that they who venture to connect commercial crises with the spots on the sun are supposed to be jesting.

So far as I am concerned in the matter, I beg leave to affirm that I never was more in earnest, and that after some further careful enquiry I am perfectly convinced that these decennial crises do depend upon meteorological variations of like period, which again depend, in all probability, upon cosmical variations of which we have evidence in the frequency of sun-spots, auroras, and magnetic perturbations. I believe that I have, in fact, found the missing link required to complete the first outline of the evidence. About ten years ago it was carefully explained by Mr. J. C. Ollerenshaw, in a communication to the Manchester Statistical Society ("Transactions," 1869–70, p. 109), that the secret of good trade in Lancashire is the low price of rice and other grain in India.[2] Here again some may jest at the folly of those who theorize about such incongruous things as the cotton-gins of Manchester and the paddy-fields of Hindostan. But to those who look a little below the surface the connexion is obvious. Cheapness of food leaves the poor Hindoo ryot a small margin of earnings, which he can spend on new clothes; and a small margin multiplied by the vast population of British India, not to mention China, produces a marked change in the demand for Lancashire goods. Now, it has been lately argued by Mr. Hunter,[3] the Government statist of India, that the famines of India do recur at intervals of about ten or eleven years. The idea of the periodicity of Indian famines is far from being a new one; it is discussed in various previous publications, as, for instance, "The Companion to the British Almanack for 1857," p. 76.[4] The principal scarcities in the North-Western and Upper Provinces of Bengal are here assigned to the years 1782–3, 1792–3, 1812–20, 1826, 1832–3. Here we notice precise periodicity up to 1812–3, which, after being broken for a time, seems to recur in 1832–3.

Partly through the kind assistance of Mr. Garnett, of the British Museum,[5] I have now succeeded in finding the *data* so much wanted to

[2] See Vol. III, Letter 347.

[3] Sir William Wilson Hunter (1840–1900) entered the Indian Civil Service in 1862 and became Director-General of the Statistical Department of India in 1871. Jevons's 'Commercial Crises and Sun-Spots, Part II', contains the statement "Efforts have, I believe, been made by Dr. Hunter, Mr. J. H. Twigg and probably others, to obtain facts of this kind, which would confirm or controvert prevailing theories" – *Investigations*, p. 237. See above, Letter 592, n. 4, p. 35.

[4] *The British Almanac* . . . and *The Companion to the Almanac* . . . were published annually by the Society for the Diffusion of Useful Knowledge from 1827 to 1887.

[5] See below, Letter 667, n. 1, p. 120.

confirm these views – namely, a long series of prices of grain in Bengal (Delhi).

These *data* are found in a publication so accessible as the "Journal" of the London Statistical Society for 1843, vol. 6, pp. 246–8, where is printed a very brief but important paper by the Rev. Robert Everest,[6]

PRICE OF WHEAT AT DELHI.

Year	Price	Note	Year	Price	Note
1763	50	M. C.	1800	22	
1764	35		1801	23	
1765	27		1802	25	
1766	24		1803	65	M.
1767	23		1804	48	C.
1768	21		1805	33	
1769	24		1806	31	
1770	23		1807	23	
1771	33		1808	36	
1772	38	C.	1809	40	
1773	100	M. C.	1810	25	C.
1774	53		1811	23	
1775	40		1812	44	
1776	25		1813	43	
1777	17		1814	39	
1778	25		1815	2 7	
1779	33		1816	28	
1780	45		1817	41	
1781	55		1818	39	
1782	91		1819	42	
1783	167	M. C.	1820	46	
1784	40		1821	38	
1785	25		1822	35	
1786	23		1823	33	
1787	22		1824	39	
1788	23		1825	39	C.
1789	24		1826	48	M. C.
1790	26		1827	30	
1791	33		1828	22	
1792	81	M.	1829	21	
1793	54	C.	1830	21	
1794	32		1831	26	
1795	14		1832	22	
1796	14		1833	33	
1797	15		1834	40	M.
1798	8		1835	25	
1799	17		1838	—	C.

[6] Rev. Robert Everest (1798–1874), geologist; chaplain to the East India Company, 1829–48;

chaplain to the East India Company, "On the famines that have devastated India and on the probability of their being periodical." Here we have a list of prices of wheat at Delhi for 73 years, ending with 1835, stated in terms of the numbers of seers of wheat – a seer is equal to about 2lb. avoirdupois – to be purchased with one rupee. As this mode of quotation is confusing, I have calculated the prices in rupees per 1,000 seers of wheat, and have thus obtained the foregoing remarkable table.

The letter M indicates the *maxima* attained by the price, and we see that up to 1803, at least, the *maxima* occur with great regularity at intervals of ten years. Referring to Mr. Macleod's "Dictionary of Political Economy," pp. 627–8,[8] we learn that commercial crises occurred in the years 1763, 1772–3, 1783, and 1793, in almost perfect coincidence with scarcity at Delhi. M. Clément Juglar, in his "History of Commercial Crises," also assigns one to the year 1804.[9] After this date the variation of prices becomes for a time much less marked and regular, and there also occurs a serious crisis about the year 1810, which appears to be exceptional; but in 1825 and 1836 the decennial periodicity again manifests itself, both in the prices of wheat at Delhi and in the state of English trade. The years of crisis are marked with the letter C.

Taking this table in connexion with a mass of considerations of which I have given a mere outline at the last meeting of the British Association (see "Journal" of the Statistical and Social Inquiry Society of Ireland, August, 1878, pp. 334–342; *Nature*, November 14, 1878, vol. xix., pp. 33–37), I hold it to be established with a high degree of probability that the recurrence of manias and crises among the principal trading nations depends upon commerce with the East. This conclusion is confirmed by the fact that these fluctuations are but slightly felt by the non-trading nations, and that what these nations do feel is easily accounted for as an indirect effect.

It has been objected by the *Economist* that this explanation cannot be applied to the earlier crises in the years 1711, 1721, and 1732, because trade with India was then of insignificant dimensions. But the reading of many old books and tracts of the 17th and 18th centuries has convinced me that trade with India was always looked upon as of the highest importance. A large part of the political literature of the time was devoted

---

assisted his brother Sir George Everest (1790–1866) in the Survey of India, 1833–4. Author of a number of papers on geological and meteorological topics, also *A Journey through Norway, Lapland and part of Sweden* . . . (1829) and *A Journey through the United States and part of Canada* (1855).

[7] There appears to be a gap in the table here, presumably a printer's error. The entry should read '23'.

[8] Henry Dunning Macleod, *A Dictionary of Political Economy* (1863).

[9] Clement Juglar, *Des Crises Commerciales et de leur Retour Periodique en France, en Angleterre et aux Etats-Unis* (1862); second edition (1889) pp. 404–5.

to the subject, and under the Mercantile Theory the financial system of the country was framed mainly with an eye to Indian trade. The published returns of exports and imports probably give us little idea of the real amount of trade, as smuggling was very common in those days, and much of the Indian trade went on secretly in private ships or indirectly through Holland.

Dr. George Birdwood[10] has lately been studying the records of the India Office, and he gives as the result of his extensive reading "that the history of modern Europe, and emphatically of England, has been the quest of the aromatic gum resins, and balsams and condiments, and spices of India and the Indian Archipelago." ("Journal" of the Society of Arts, 7th February, 1879, vol. xxvii., p. 192). This closely corresponds with the view which I have been gradually led to adopt of the cause of decennial crises.

Let it be remembered, too, that because the impulse comes from India it does not follow that the extent of the commercial mania or crisis here is bounded by the variation of the Indian trade. The impulse from abroad is like the match which fires the inflammable spirits of the speculative classes. The history of many bubbles shows that there is no proportion between the stimulating cause and the height of folly to which the inflation of credit and prices may be carried. A mania is, in short, a kind of explosion of commercial folly followed by the natural collapse. The difficulty is to explain why this collapse so often comes at intervals of ten or eleven years, and I feel sure the explanation will be found in the cessation of demand from India and China occasioned by the failure of harvests there, ultimately due to changes of solar activity. Certainly the events of the last few years, as too well known to many sufferers, entirely coincide with this view, which is, nevertheless, made the subject of inconsiderate ridicule.

> I am, yours obediently,
> W. Stanley Jevons.

2, The Chestnuts, West-heath, Hampstead.

---

[10] See the following Letter 599, n. 1, p. 49.

599.   G. C. M. BIRDWOOD[1] TO W. S. JEVONS

India Office,
April 19/79.

Dear Sir,

I see you do me the honour of quoting from my lecture[2] in "The Society of Arts Journal".

I take the liberty to send you by this post a late proof of it in the official form in which it will presently be published.

I do this because my paper in the Journal is full of misprints, which I am too blind to detect in such small type myself. In fact the Society was hard up for a paper. When they appealed to me I rather weakly consented to read the official report I was then writing from the first revision of my rough notes.

I have always maintained that pepper is responsible for a good deal of human history. The pepper of the Indian Archipelago and the herrings of the North Sea have kept coming and going between Northern Europe and Australasia. And there is beside the trade worked by pepper and the spices between Australasia and Kamchatka all along the back side of Asia.

I do not suppose you have come across my little 'Handbook' on the Indian Council at Paris.[3] I therefore do myself the pleasure to send you a presentation copy. In it I point out the remarkable facilities the southern coast line of the Euro-Asian continent presents for the growth of trade and how it was that the great to and fro trade which sprung up between the Indian Archipelago and the North Sea came to be engrossed by the Phoenicians. These are quite original points but I could not develope* them as I would have wished in a popular Handbook, which moreover I had as it happened to do in twelve days.

I am very glad you have taken India up. I have lived there all my life, and a speech like that by Mr. Bright published yesterday cuts me to the quick. I know well what India means for us, and when I find a man like Bright making light of its possession, almost indeed suggesting our giving it up, I tremble for England's own position in the world. It is not only the trade of India its possession secures us, but of all the East – the whole "Levant" in the mediaeval sense of term – from Const^ople to Pekin. When

[1] Sir George Christopher Molesworth Birdwood (1823–1917), Professor of Anatomy and Physiology, and of Materia Medica and Botany, Grant Medical College, Bombay; Registrar of the University of Bombay and Curator of the Government Museum there. Served in Bombay until 1868, and in the India Office from 1871 to 1902.

[2] See above, Letter 598, p. 48. The paper was entitled 'The Quest and early European Settlement of India'.

[3] G. C. M. Birdwood, *Handbook to the British Indian Section* (1878), published for the Paris Exhibition of 1878.

the Dutch got the upper hand of us in the Indian Archipelago, they drove us away from trading there and had they or the French got hold of India they wd. have kept us out of all our Eastern Trade. Egypt wd. long ago have been shut against us. [4]

I beg to remain with many apologies

Yrs faithfully,

Geo. Birdwood

P.S. You must kindly regard my proof as confidential until the paper is published.

600.   J. H. TWIGG [1] TO W. S. JEVONS

East India United Service Club,
St. James Square.
20 April 1879.

Dear Sir,

I am much interested in the evidence of Indian rain-fall periodicity supplied by your letter to the "Times" of Saturday last. [2] I did not expect such striking results for I thought that at Delhi the levelling influence of trade disturbed in its turn by the movement of troops and retainers would have obliterated any natural periodicity in prices. I have accordingly been trying but without effect to get from India some record of prices in localities unaffected by great external commerce particularly the Central Provinces nor could Sir W. Muir [3] of the Indian Council or Dr. W. Hunter give a clue to such statistics. I sent them a copy of some numerical notes on the periodicity question which you would perhaps like to read though they are somewhat confused, I am afraid, and curious rather than useful. I may perhaps explain the method by saying that I assumed the rain-falls of the first year of each cycle to be a series of quantities

---

[4] In a long speech to an election meeting in Birmingham on 16 April 1879, reported in *The Times*, 17 April 1879, p. 11 (Birdwood evidently misremembered the date), John Bright criticised the government's foreign policy, which he stated was based on fear of the supposed Russian threat to the Indian Empire. He declared that in terms of trade India was worth less to Britain than either France, Germany or the United States, yet cost twice as much to administer as the value of the trade produced. If British attitudes towards India could be rationalised, and relations with Russia thereby improved, the potential economic advantages were considerable. He did not suggest giving up India.

[1] John Hill Twigg (1841–1917) was educated at the Royal School, Dungannon, and Trinity College Dublin; entered the Indian Civil Service in 1863 and served in the North-West Provinces, 1864–90. This letter was written during a period of leave for health reasons from May 1877 to October 1879.

[2] See above, Letter 598, p. 44.

[3] Sir William Muir (1819–1905), member of the Council of India in London, 1876–85; Principal of Edinburgh University, 1885–1905.

distributed round their own average according to the law of error. I made the same assumption with regard to the rainfalls of the second year of each cycle and so on. It was thus possible to calculate the probability that the rainfall of any year of a cycle would differ from its average by any assigned amount such for instance as the amount in defect, say, 15 or 20 inches, which would imply famine. It was also possible on the same theory to calculate the probability that the sum of the rainfalls for one half of a cycle would exceed the average of all the years observed or for the other half fall short of the same—the principle being this, that, having eleven known quantities, namely the average rainfalls for the eleven years of several cycles and the "modulus" of error (i.e. of variation) for each of those eleven quantities we can tell the probability that the sum of any $5\frac{1}{2}$ of them that is any hemicyclic total will depart from the average by an assigned amount namely the quantity necessary to bring it above or below the general average of all observed years. The calculation depends on the fact that the variation-modulus of the sum of several quantities is the square root of the sum of the squares of their several moduli. This mode of calculation gives a result agreeing with that devised from the simple rule that as periodicity at Madras has been manifested in 10 out of 12 recorded hemicycles the chances are 11 to 3 that it will occur in the next hemicycle. I urged Mr. J. Elliott[4] the govt. meteorologist for Bengal more than a year ago to look out for old price lists of good grain but I presume he has found none. When I return to India however I shall search myself and send you any information I can get. I was sorry to see so much written by Mr. Procter in depreciation of evidence like this. He said there was similar evidence of periodicity in the boat race victories of Cambridge or Oxford[5] forgetting that though there may be such evidence it is overborne by contrary proof ab extra which does not exist in the case of rainfall.

Your obed. servant

J. H. Twigg

Bengal Civil Service.

To W. Stanley Jevons, Esq.,

F.R.S.

---

[4] [Sir] John Eliot (1839–1908), F.R.S., Fellow of St John's College, Cambridge, 1869–76; Professor of Mathematics, Roorkee Engineering College, 1869–72, and at the Muir Central College, Allahabad, 1872–4; Professor of Physics at the Presidency College, Calcutta; Meteorological Reporter to the Government of Bengal, 1874–86; Meteorological Reporter to the Government of India and Director-General of Indian Observatories, 1886–1903; author of *Hand-book of Cyclonic Storms in the Bay of Bengal. For the use of sailors* (Calcutta, 1890) and a number of meteorological reports of cyclones in the Bay of Bengal and the Arabian Sea.

[5] An unsigned article entitled 'University Boat Races and Sun-Spot Cycles' published the previous month in *JRSS*, 42 (1879) 328–9, was probably the work of the astronomer Richard Anthony Proctor(1837–88). Proctor, Secretary of the Royal Astronomical Society, 1872–3, and

P.S. Would you kindly let me know if think this method of calculating the value of evidence is fairly applicable to the rain-fall statistics? I was led to it chiefly by your very valuable work on Scientific Method but most questions of probability are so difficult that one can never be sure of not having overlooked something. There is a very interesting question for instance which has suggested itself to me but I do not feel sure as to its solution. Government in India are attempting without any prospect of success to determine the average length of life by statistics of the whole population and I have been trying to determine what degree of error would attach to statistics derived from a few specific individuals. Something similar was done by Laplace[6] in France – I would send you some papers stating the problem if you take an interest in the matter.

601.   R. ADAMSON TO W. S. JEVONS

2, Osborne Terrace, Edin[h].
20th April 1879.

Your card has just reached me. The notice of or rather reference to Gossen's work was in Kautz, *Geschichte der National-Okonomie*.[1] If you wish, I shall send you pages etc. when I get home.

R.A.

602.   W. S. JEVONS TO A. MACMILLAN
[MA]

2, The Chestnuts,
West Heath,
Hampstead N.W.
22 April '79

My dear Macmillan,
I now forward the MS of the preface of Theory of Pol. Econ. together with contents and everything to complete the copy for the book.
I have this morning received the proofs of the appendices so that if you will kindly ask the printers to finish up the text and prefaces as quickly as they can we shall not be much longer over it.

---

founder of *Knowledge* in 1881, was author of numerous articles on astronomical and related subjects and enjoyed poking fun at ideas to which he was opposed. Cf. Meadows, op. cit., pp. 97–103.
[6] Pierre Simon de Laplace (1749–1827), *Essai d'arithmétique morale* (1777).
[1] Cf. Vol. IV, Letter 536, n. 1.

I have not yet been able to turn up Cliffords Logical paper,[1] but I am sure I have a copy and can probably send it tomorrow.

I will also post Cossa's guide[2] tomorrow after looking into it a little more.

I am

Yours faithfully,

W. S. Jevons

P.S. I have no copy of the preface and so hope the Post will not lose it.

603. W. S. JEVONS TO A. MACMILLAN
[MA]

2 The Chestnuts,
West Heath,
Hampstead, N.W.
24 April '79

My dear Macmillan,

I have now found a copy of Clifford's curious paper[1] which I enclose; it is entirely at your service for reprinting.

I am posting Cossa's Guide to the Study of Pol. Econ. to your house. Miss Macmillan[2] will be able to give you a clear idea of its contents. It seems to me well fitted to open up to English students a great deal which is beyond their reach at present.

An Italian Professor of Pavia and a publisher at Naples asks permission to translate my Pol. Econ. Primer but at the same time Cossa says it is being translated for Hoepli of Milan under his own supervision.[3] As I suppose you have some sort of arrangement with Hoepli, it is no doubt all right, and I had better answer the other people in the negative. It is desirable however to mention the matter to you first. I enclose the notes referring to the matter.

The proofs of the 'Theory of P.E.' are now mostly in hand and the preface alone remains.

I am,

Yours very faithfully,

W. Stanley Jevons

[1] W. K. Clifford's paper 'Of Boundaries in General' was published in *Macmillan's Magazine*, 11 (1879) 359–68.

[2] *Guida alla Studia dell'Economia Politica.* See above, Letter 595, p. 41.

[1] See above, Letter 602, n. 1.

[2] Alexander Macmillan's daughter, Margaret: she prepared the translation of Cossa's *Guida.* See below, Letter 651, n. 1, p. 101.

[3] See above, Letters 594 and 595, pp. 37 & 41; also below, Letter 613, p. 62. It is not clear whether the Neapolitan publisher was in contact with Puviani; no letter from such a publisher is now among the Jevons Papers.

604.   G. C. M. BIRDWOOD TO W. S. JEVONS

April 25/79

Dear Sir,

I will see if what you want is to be found in the records: but to put everything on a strictly official footing – which is what is liked by the authorities here, & which will indeed ensure your being served thoroughly – would you write a private note, addressed to the Under Secty of State, asking for a copy of my official report. I find there are several applications for it, & it has been promised when ready to all who have applied. Also ask if you may have access to the Office Library. This request also is sure to be complied with & then you will find in Milburn [1] – valuable tables of prices: – & you will be allowed to keep any of our books at home for three months. Meanwhile I will quietly have the records looked through, so that I may know to which to direct your attention. There is a capital room in the library to work in, & of course the old records would not be lent out of office, although probably an exception w^d be made in your case.

I beg to remain,
Yours faithfully
Geo. Birdwood.

605.   W. S. JEVONS TO H. RYLETT
[LJN, 379]

Hampstead, 25th April 1879

. . . My interest in Ireland [1] is rapidly increasing, and when I had a run of a week through some parts, I resolved to come again. I think that when you have had time to become thoroughly acquainted with your part of the country I should much like to spend a few days with you, and see the state of things with my own eyes. My impression is increasing to the effect that landlordism is a terrible burden on the country, and that the just laws of England are rather a myth. In the middle of the summer I shall have to go to Norway for the benefit of my health, and perhaps it is too soon to suggest any definite time yet. The climate of Ireland in the middle of the summer would, I fear, be too relaxing for me, and I need bracing up a good deal. . . .

[1] William Milburn, *Oriental Commerce; containing a geographical description of the principal places in the East Indies, China and Japan, with their produce, manufactures and trade* . . . 2 vols (1813). Tables of prices current included in this edition were deleted from the second edition, published in 1825. The India Office Library held copies of both editions in 1879.

[1] Rylett at this time had just moved to Moneyrea, near Belfast.

606.   R. ADAMSON TO W. S. JEVONS

60 Parsonage Road.
27th April 1879.

Dear Jevons,

I hope the one or two corrections I made in your most comprehensive list will be of service. The additions, of course, I merely inserted in order that you might consider whether it was worth while entering them. The ? at Cournot's second work[1] refers to the fact that no mathematical treatment of any economical problem is given there. I doubt if Rau should be inserted. The passage referred to is a mere comment on the fact that certain economists (Buquoy etc.)[2] had applied Math. Rau himself does not.[3]

I am very glad to know that your new edition is so far advanced and am only sorry that it should have been out of my power to offer you any assistance, even in regard to Gossen's book. If you are printing anything like a full account of that work, you might let me see the proof of the passage.

I shall have rather a busy month with lectures, for I have several extra ones to give, but I feel much refreshed by the holiday I have taken. I think I shall run up to London for a day or two in the beginning of June and may manage to see you then.

With kind regards,

Yours very truly,
Robert Adamson.

607.   J. D'AULNIS TO W. S. JEVONS

Utrecht 31 April 1879[1]

Dear Sir!

I have the honour of sending back to your honourable address the book of T. Noble on the Queen's taxes[2] which you had the kindness to put at my disposition.

The proposed taxation on the "Capital en portefeuille" is at this moment the subject of scriptory discussion between the parliament

[1] A. Cournot, *Principes de la Théorie des Richesses* (1863).

[2] Georg von Buquoy, *Die Theorie der Nationalwirtschaft* (Leipzig, 1815).

[3] K. H. Rau, *Grundsatze der Volkswirtschaftslehre* (Leipzig, 1868). In spite of Adamson's comments, both Rau and Cournot's 1863 volume were included in Jevon's bibliography.

[1] The original manuscript of the letter is quite unambiguously dated in this form; it was presumably a mistake on d'Aulnis's part for 30 April 1879.

[2] John Noble (1837–98), *The Queen's Taxes: an inquiry into the amount, incidence and economic result of the taxation of the U.K.* (1870).

(second Chamber) and the Minister of Finances. The theoretical part of the question was scrutinised in innumerable articles of the periodical litterature and in brochures; now it seems me exhausted as for the Netherlands. The parliamentary papers, of which I received indication in your honourable letters of 28 Sept 1878, were also consulted; but, however they contain a fulness of information upon the operation of a general Income tax, they were scanty at the particular point of a taxation on the incomes drawn from public papers (effets, fonds publics, in the Dutch "effecten"). The book of *Gossen* "Entwickelung der Gesetze des Menschlichen Verkehrs" Braunschweig 1854, is appointed [3] by me for the Academian "bibliotheque", but not yet received. When I will have received that book, I will be very curious to observe in how far M. Gossen was our predecessor. – It was, notwithstanding the very pain which I took for reading the second part of Mr. Walras' book, till yet impossible for me to understand the mathematical theories of our colleague at Lausanne on the wages, the profits and the interest. How ingenious these theories may be, they seem me to complicated and in every case more complicated than was needed for the simple exposition of the problem and its solution. Indeed I regret that this amiable man, – friends of me who did meet with him at Lausanne, abound in praising his cordiality and loveliness – has preferred to adopt a so abstract and complicated form to new theories, which at the bottom of the matter must be simple, while they treat of phenomena, which occur daily and can be exposed, nay, must be exposed in their most simple relations.

Dear Sir, I pray you to agree the expression of my thankfulness for your treatises, which I did receive, – and to believe me

truly yours

J. d'Aulnis

608. E. D. ARCHIBALD [1] TO W. S. JEVONS

3 St. George's Villas,
Beckenham,
May 5. 1879.

My Dear Sir,

In view of the probable rise in importance of the question just now engaging the attention of men of science as well as an increasing section of the general public, viz. the Relation between sunspots and terrestrial meteorology, and hence Economy; I have thought that it would conduce very much to the present solution of the problem, as well as to render its

---

[3] Substituted for 'commanded', deleted by d'Aulnis in the original manuscript.
[1] E. Douglas Archibald, Professor of Mathematics in Patna College.

subsequent elucidation of more immediate practical utility, if the sporadic efforts at present made to solve it in its various aspects could be amalgamated into one united, systematic, and harmonious whole.

To be brief, it appears to me that what we want in the matter is cooperation and that this would be best ensured by eminent leaders in the Enquiry, such as yourself, Prof. Balfour Stewart, Mr. J. Norman Lockyer, Mr Alexander Buchan, [2] Dr. W. W. Hunter, and others, forming a society for the collection and discussion of evidence bearing on the general question, the adoption of common methods of comparison to be employed, the publication of results etc.

At present, though we are all working towards a common end we are guided by no common principles and we even use different lengths for the sunspot cycle. By such a plan as I propose, we should gain the strength which is necessarily associated with combination as well as the further knowledge that would come of being acquainted with every aspect of the question, and so materially hasten its progress and developments. For my own part, I can only reecho your words in Nature "I was never more in earnest", [3] the result of three years investigation having convinced me that through all the perplexing mist of irregularity there is an undoubted relation between sunspot and meteorological variation. The problem however can never be solved without a careful study of 'differentia' as well as 'similia' and it is to the former that I have more particularly turned my attention because I found it at the outset an almost entirely untrodden field. Your recent interesting communications on "sunspots and commercial crises" as well as your former investigations on the price of corn etc. have emboldened me to take the liberty of asking your attention to my proposition, which though unworthily advocated I beg of you to consider.

I remain Dear Sir
Yours faithfully,
E. Douglas Archibald.

[2] Alexander Buchan (1829–1907), Scottish meteorologist; Secretary of the Scottish Meteorological Society, 1860, which inaugurated the observatory at the summit of Ben Nevis, 1883.
[3] W. S. Jevons to the Editor of *The Times*, 19 April 1879 (see above, Letter 598, p. 45); reprinted, slightly modified, in *Nature*, 24 April 1879.

609.   T. HANKEY[1] TO W. S. JEVONS

59, Portland Place, W.

5 May 1879.

Dear Sir,

I venture to write to ask a question of you on a subject which I believe is more familiar to you than to almost any one else in London – and that is relating to the present annual consumption of gold – I have before me a book of yours – published in 1863 called "a Serious Fall in the Value of Gold, etc." I do not know whether the diagrams therein have been in any subsequent publication continued but they were very curious as making out as I believe you then contended the rise in prices from 1852 when the new gold discoveries occurred consequent on these events. I translated a little work of Léon Faucher on the gold discoveries[2] in which I then took a good deal of interest having been governor of the Bank at that period 1851 to 1853. I am not sure whether you are of opinion that the late fall in prices is in any way to be attributed to a late rise in gold – or rather to a falling off of the former large supply – but it would be very curious to have a continuation of the diagram which was made in the little book I have referred to – the consumption of gold for coinage during the last 2 years must have been enormous. The United States will not require to coin gold to any considerable extent – nor shall we I fancy. Russia is not likely to resume specie payments at present and I have no reason to suppose that Spain or Italy or Austria or any other country will come forward in 1879 or 1880 as abnormal buyers of gold – if so there is apparently no reason why gold should not steadily increase – and the consumption be under the production even if the latter is only about 17 or 18 million £. The additional consumption from wear and tear and the increase of gold in Germany and the U. States cannot be very great on its new coinage for a year or two; if I am right in my notion. I see by a letter I have lately received from Sir E. Thornton[3] our Minister at Washington that last years gold coinage in the U.S. amounted to 52 million dollars whilst the whole of their production of gold was only 41. What amount the Germans have coined since the commencement of their gold coinage I do not know but I fancy that the whole gold coinage in 1877 and 1878 must have been at least double the amount of the production of gold in the world. But now I should fancy there must be for this next year probably a great lull in gold coinage and a considerable increase in consequence of uncoined gold. I

[1] Thomson Hankey (1805–93), M.P. for Peterborough, 1853–68 and 1874–80; Director of the Bank of England and Governor, 1851–3.

[2] Léon Faucher (1803–54), *Remarks on the Production of the precious metals and on the demonetization of Gold in several countries in Europe.* Translated by Thomson Hankey, Junior (1852).

[3] Sir Edward Thornton (1817–1906), British Attaché, Mexico, 1845; Minister Plenipotentiary to the U.S.A., 1867; Ambassador at St Petersburg, 1881; Constantinople, 1884.

should think that France must have either in coin or in bar gold much more than will suffice for their wants for coinage for the next and this year; ditto Germany, probably, and that the late fall in prices has had little connection with the increased demand for gold. I incline to think that gold will begin now to accumulate again and if it is possible that some little effect has been produced by the abnormal demand it will now very soon resume the position it has held for now many past years – as considerably in excess of the demand and consequently it is likely again to increase prices of all commodities. I am ashamed at having troubled you at such length – but I hope you will excuse it. I should not have done so had I known any other equally high authority, to apply to.

Sir E. Thornton wrote me that though there is a great lull in the production of silver a great many persons think that large masses may be again discovered in the same abnormal manner in which it has already been found from time to time in Nevada etc. if so we shall have I fear a long continuance of this annoying question about silver currency in India.

> I am Dear Sir
> Yours faithfully,
> Thomson Hankey.

W. S. Jevons Esq.

What I really most want is the total amount of gold coinage in 1877 and 1879. I have it for America here it is easily obtained. I fancy none has been coined in Russia or Turkey – it must therefore be only Austria, Italy, Spain and Switzerland, Holland and Belgium and Norway.

610.   L. COSSA TO W. S. JEVONS

Monsieur et très honoré Collègue,

Pavie, 5 Mai 1879.[1]

Milles remerciments pour votre lettre. Je vous prie d'employer *toute votre autorité* pour persuader votre éditeur M.Macmillan à la publication d'une édition anglaise de ma *Guida* – Pour faciliter la chose j'*ai obtenu* de mon éditeur (M. *Ulrico Hoepli*, Libraire, Milano, Galleria De Cristoforis N°. 59, 60), le même qui publie la trad. ital. de votre *Primer,* qu'il se contente [pour le copyright] de l'honoraire très modeste de *huit*/8/livres sterling.

[1] As in his earlier letter of 3 April 1879 (above, Letter 595, p. 41) Cossa placed the address and date below the opening phrase. Here again, all words in italics were underlined by Cossa in the original manuscript.

– Il me tarde donc de savoir que l'affaire soit combinée. Une mention de mon ouvrage dans la préface de votre Theory (dont j'attends avec impatience l'exemplaire que vous me promettez!) rendra la chose encore plus facile.

Je pense aussi que pour rendre *mon nom* encore plus connu en Angleterre et pour augmenter le nombre de ceux qui le chercheront il serait très utile que je pourrais mettre sur le frontispiece le Titre de *Fellow* of *the Statistical Society* of *London*, si Vous croyez bien par votre entremise de me le procurer, comme vous avez fait pour M. *Boccardo*.[2]

J'ai reçu l'exemplaire de votre *Primer* avec les corrections, qui sont déjà pratiquées dans la traduction italienne – Dans deux semaines, au plus tard, l'impression va commencer et elle pourra s'achever très vite.

N'ayez pas de doute sur l'affaire Lloyd (1771.) Un *extrait* de son ouvrage (en italien) se trouve en *appendice* à certaines éditions de l'*économie politique* de *Verri*,[3] et enfin dans la *Collection* des *Economistes italiens* de *Custodi*.[4] – Le général Lloyd est entré en correspondance epistolaire avec Verri, et cette correspondance constate qu'il est l'auteur du livre sur la monnaie.

Je vous prie de me faire savoir tout de suite la décision qu'aura prise M. *Macmillan* quant à la traduction de ma *Guida* – Quant à l'honoraire il pourra le faire venir directement à M Hoepli; dans la mésure déjà indiquée, bien entendu après la publication.

A la hâte j'ai l'honneur de me dire, *faithfully and respectfully.*

votre dévoué
Prof. Luigi Cossa

611.   R. ADAMSON TO W. S. JEVONS

60 Parsonage Road,
6th May, 1879.

Dear Jevons,

Your preface I like very much and I think the account of Gossen's book is as good as could be given without entering a minute analysis of it. I have only had to note one or two slight misprints.

There is one name I think ought to be given rather more prominence in your preface, i.e. von Thunen. Of course he has nothing on utility, value etc. but his mathematical investigations on capital, interest and wages

---

[2] Cf. above, Letter 590, p. 31.

[3] [Count] Pietro Verri (1728–97), officer in the Austrian government of Milan; author of *Elementi del Commercio* (1760) and *Meditazioni sull'Economia Politica* (1771). It was to this latter work that an abstract of Lloyd's *Essay* was appended.

[4] Pietro Custodi, *Scrittori classici Italiani di economia politica*, 50 vols (1803–16). Verri's *Meditazioni* was included in this collection.

seem to be remarkable, and a good deal has been done on the subject in Germany.

I would be rash to give any opinion on what you tell me regarding your present views on wages and rent. It seems to me probable that stress laid on uniformity of conditions would lead to what may be called the Ricardian view, while stress laid on inequality would give something like what you hint at. In both cases the results are probably limits and do not express the real thing. I shall be anxious to see what you have got to.

Might I suggest with reference to the 'mincemeat' man[1] that your language regarding him is a little bitter. It is, so far as I can see, needless to select *his* definition of value, as if it were special to him and surely 'unutterably tedious' is a little strong, particularly when it must be acknowledged that to the majority of readers any amount of cloth and linen is less fatiguing than the simplest symbolic treatment.

'Victoria' is a *pis aller*.[2] In all you otherwise say I agree. The thing has come to a bad end, mainly I suspect through our want of courage.

Yours very truly,
Robert Adamson

612.   R. ADAMSON TO W. S. JEVONS

60 Parsonage Road,
8th May, 1879.

Dear Jevons,

I send herewith the remainder of your proof. With the exception of one or two slight misprints, there seem only the following to be noted:

(1)   In the previous portion you speak of the work on logic "attributed to Kant". The only work on logic which is ever called Kant's is undoubtedly his: it is not a treatise prepared in form by Kant himself, but is printed from the MS notes used by him in his lectures. 'Attributed' is a wrong term.

(2)   Gossen calls himself on the title page of his book "Royal Prussian Government Assessor – out of employment." I am a little puzzled with

---

[1] i.e. J. S. Mill. In his chapter on the Theory of Exchange, Jevons wrote: 'Let us turn to Mill's definition of Exchange Value, and we see at once the misleading power of the term' – *T.P.E.*, p.77.

The passage in the Preface to the second edition relating to Mill's method of treating the theory of international values (p. xxiv) refers to those 'difficult and tedious chapters' – presumably Jevons modified the phrase in response to Adamson's criticism.

[2] This refers to a decision to rename Owens College, on its receipt of a charter as a University, 'The Victoria University of Manchester'. This name was a compromise, the authorities of the Yorkshire College having objected to the conferring on the new University 'the name of a town or of any person whose claims to such distinction are merely local'. Cf. Thompson, *Owens College*, pp. 530–6.

the last terms and shall ask Ward[1] more definitely about them. So soon as I know I shall send you the exact translation for your preface.[2]

(3)   I think you should notice that Mill is quite alive to the fact that *inequalities* artificial or natural, give rise to *rent* (See Bk.III cap. 5. §4 last parg. but one).[3]

As to your theory itself I should require longer time than I have given it to feel qualified even to have an opinion. I hope you will put very definitely what you understand by cost of production, for on one view of that ambiguous quantity, the apparently radical difference between your theory and Ricardo's would be only apparent. Assuredly we want an economic terminology.

Yours very truly,
Robert Adamson.

613.   A. PUVIANI TO W. S. JEVONS

Bologna 11 May 1879,[1]
Via Saragozza N 11.

Most Honourable Sir,

I warmly beg of you to excuse my delay in answering your most gentle and precious letters; but before complying to such an agreable duty, I did want to recurr to pr. Louis Cossa in order to know if he would really undertake the translation, of which matter I have already spoken to you in my previous letters, or if instead he would have no difficulty to commit the honourable charge to others, submitting to him the approval of it. And as I perceive by a letter written to me just now by pr. Cossa that he has already finished the translation in matter, and that shortly it will come to the light, for me it rests nothing but to welcome with fervid pleasure the appearance among us of a book, that for remarkable preciousness of the text will unite (I am sure) others of translation; and to rejoice in stating how your book could never more worthily be presented to the Italian public.

To this regard, I thought it my duty to let you know how I have permitted myself to put at the pr. Cossa's disposition those biographical particulars which you so kindly deigned yourself to forward me. I would

---

[1] [Sir] Adolphus William Ward; cf. Vol.IV, Letter 462. It was no doubt because of Ward's unrivalled knowledge of European history and politics that Adamson referred to him.

[2] The translation which appeared finally in the Preface was 'Royal Prussian Government Assessor, retired' – *T.P.E.*, p. xxxviii.

[3] 'I ought to say that Mill, as pointed out to me by Professor Adamson, has a remarkable section at the end of chapter v of Book III of the *Principles*, in which he explains that all inequalities, artificial or natural, give rise to extra gains of the nature of Rent.' – ibid., p. li.

[1] The text of this letter has been reproduced as a literal copy of the manuscript.

be very sorry indeed if such a proceeding would have displeased you: but the reason it was that I judged that it would have been for me an act of great egoism to deprive my fellow Citizens of all that could greatly interest and affectionate them to your person, for the only fact that the good chance to cooperate to the translation of your fine pages it is for me forbidden.

Meanwhile I beg you, illustrious professor, to accept the most distinct and affectionate regards of whom, that professes himself besides a sincere admirator and a studious of your works, and also grateful and proud witness of your goodness and perfect courtesy.

In fine I would beg you to present my high thanks and my respects to your much esteemed lady.

Your devoted servant
Dr Amilcare Puviani.

614. W. S. JEVONS TO A. MARSHALL [1]

Hampstead
12 May, 79

Dear Mr. Marshall,

I have for some time back felt very guilty about retaining a book of yours (Rau) [2] which you kindly sent me some years since. I have been always on the point of finishing with it and always delaying. However now my new edition of the "Theory of Pol. Economy" is almost out of the printers hand and I have no further excuse for keeping your book. I have posted it to-day registered and hope you will get it safely. I have to thank you much for your kindness.

I hope you will be interested in my new preface. Mr. Sidgwick having sent me a copy of your printed papers [3] I have been able to refer to them tho not as much as I should have liked the work having been mostly done before I received the copy. Your problems are rather stiff and I have hardly succeeded in mastering them.

Hoping that Mrs. Marshall is pleased with her lecturing work and satisfied with her class, which however is seldom the case with a teacher.

I am,
Yours faithfully,
W. S. Jevons.

---

[1] The original manuscript of this letter is now in the Marshall Library, Cambridge.

[2] Rau, *Grundsätze der Volkswirtschaftslehre* (Leipzig, 1868).

[3] *The Pure Theory of Foreign Trade* and *The Pure Theory of Domestic Values*, which were privately printed at Cambridge in 1879. Jevons listed the papers in his Bibliography for the second edition of *T.P.E.* See above, Letter 583, p. 23.

615.   W. S. JEVONS TO A. MACMILLAN
       [MA]

2, The Chestnuts,
West Heath,
Hampstead, N.W.
22 May '79

My dear Macmillan,

I have now sent off the last proofs of the new edition of the "Theory of Pol. Economy" and I suppose you can get it out in a couple of weeks. It is already very near the holydays.*

I shall be much obliged if you will direct the printers to strike off fifty extra copies of the Prefaces and appendices. These contain certain statements and explanations which I wish to distribute. Any extra expense thus caused can be charged to me.

As this new edition is rather important as representing the acceptance by many of the theory it would be well to send a certain number of copies to the Press, and to treat it to a great extent as a new book.

The long new preface, appendixes and certain other parts contain much new matter.

Has Miss Macmillan read Professor Cossa's Guide yet?[1]

Believe me,
Yours faithfully,
W. S. Jevons

P.S. The printers will I suppose require your order about the extra copies pretty soon.

616.   W. S. JEVONS TO A. MACMILLAN
       [MA]

2 The Chestnuts,
West Heath,
Hampstead, N.W.
1 June 1879

Dear Mr. Macmillan,

I now return list of press copies of 'Theory', with the suggestion that two copies for the chief French periodicals should be substituted for two provincial papers.

---

[1] Cf. below, Letter 651, p. 101.

A good deal might be done abroad but it is very troublesome to know to whom precisely to send them.

The list seems an ample one.

Hoping to see the volume out soon and with thanks for your reply about separate copies of preface and appendixes.

I am,

Yours faithfully,

W. S. Jevons

617.   W. S. JEVONS TO T. E. JEVONS
      [LJN, 400]

Chestnuts, Hampstead Heath,
18th June 1879.

. . . I have been much pleased to get your recent letters, especially as they give one a cheerful idea of your family and business. I think trade must revive now by degrees, and probably more in the United States than here, where there has been a considerable shock to credit. The extract about *seccas* in Brazil[1] may prove to be of great importance, and I will try to follow it up as soon as possible, but I am engaged in so many things that, like the six omnibuses abreast through Temple Bar, they block each other's way.

On 9th July I sail to Norway with Arthur Jevons,[2] and hope to have a healthy, pleasant tour of five weeks. Until then I shall be almost taken up with examinations, as, in addition to the University of London, I am to examine this summer for the Indian Civil Service in logic and political economy, for which I shall get £40.

I am thinking of bringing out my essay on the *Amusements of the People* as a popular Mudie book, and have just written to Macmillan proposing it.[3] The subject is being a good deal taken up in England (though, perhaps, not in consequence of my article) and I hit the right moment to write upon it. Although we were neither of us very well, I always think our Dano-Swedish tour was a most instructive and interesting one.

---

[1] The extract has not been traced. Jevons was evidently referring to climatic records of the semi-arid sugar and cattle-producing area of north-eastern Brazil, which suffered twenty-nine serious droughts in two hundred years. A disastrous drought from 1877 to 1880 cost 200,000 lives and resulted in total loss among the region's cattle. See R. F. Whitbeck and F. E. Williams, *Economic Geography of South America* (New York, 1940) p. 376; Celso Furtado, *The Economic Growth of Brazil. A Survey from Colonial to Modern Times,* translated by R. W. de Aguiar and E. C. Drysdale (Berkeley, 1968) pp. 145–6. There is no evidence that Jevons carried out his intention of following up the question.

[2] A cousin. See Vol. II, Letter 155, n. 4, p. 438.

[3] Nothing appears to have come of this proposal. Cf. Vol. II, Letter 140, n. 5, p. 401.

. . . Our children progress rapidly. The 'boy' is very wide-awake. 'Oh, silly papa,' he remarked the other day, when I ran his kite into the middle of a fir-tree, and dragged it out with the loss of half the tail. He shows considerable musical taste, and conducts a band consisting of his own self, by the hour together, singing very melodiously to his own tunes.

Winefrid is a shy little thing, but is for all the world like some of Reynolds' pictures. She is just beginning to talk. . . .

618. A. MARSHALL TO W. S. JEVONS

30 June 1879[1]
1 Glen Oran Villas,
Apsley Road,
Clifton.

Dear Professor Jevons,

I take up the pen with some shame to acknowledge your letter of May the 12th, and the safe arrival of "Rau". When your letter came I was in an unusual press of work which as I was not very well, I could hardly get through; and when the pressure was over I forgot your letter till just now.

I am looking forward with the greatest interest to the new edition of your book. During the last two years I have been too much occupied with practical work to do any considerable amount of study or writing. I hope better days are in store and I think soon I may begin on a book of curves of which the papers sent you by Mr. Sidgwick will form the basis. The pure theory of international values I don't much care about. I don't think it can be made easy without curves, and I think I shall leave it very much as it stands; but in the rest of the book I propose to give only a subsidiary place to curves, and to develop the application of the theory somewhat. In this way I hope to contribute my mite towards that work of "real"-ising the results of abstract quantitative reasoning in Economics of which I recognize in you the chief author. The *Economics of Industry,* the 2s. 6d. book which my wife and I are writing, is nearly finished. You may be sure that one of the first copies that are bound will find its way to Hampstead.

Yours faithfully,
A. Marshall.

[1] Printed in *Memorials of Alfred Marshall,* p. 371.

619.   E. J. BROADFIELD TO W. S. JEVONS

Roseleigh
Prestwich
Manchester.
JULY 9/79.

My dear Jevons,

I hope you will receive a copy of the *Examiner*[1] today in which is a short notice of your second edition. You are I venture to think too generous to your anticipators and perhaps go a little too far in trying to show that there is not much novelty in your theory. People multiplied before the multiplication tables were drawn up and reasoned before figures were invented – but there was novelty of the most important practical character in these things. It is just possible that careless readers in glancing at your preface may be disposed to say Oh – there is nothing here but what everybody knew and therefore it cant be much good. I suppose 'scheme out' must be a good phrase because you use it on page xxxviii but I don't like 'as Cournot and myself have done' – on xxxix – why not 'Cournot and I' you would never say 'as myself has done'. I am writing this knowing the uncertainty of your being at home. If you are still in London let me hear from you. I shall be here the greater part of July. The University charter is under our consideration just now and I suppose it will interfere with the length of some of the holidays of our friends. With kind regards to Mrs. Jevons, Believe me,

Yours very truly,
E. J. Broadfield.

620.   T. E. CLIFFE LESLIE TO W. S. JEVONS

July 27, 1879.

Dear Jevons,

I send the Academy of July 26[1] with a review of your book. I made reference to it elsewhere in the same paper – see Notes and News p. 66. Ingram[2] who is an excellent mathematician and got his fellowship in

---

[1] *The Manchester Examiner and Times*, 9 July 1879, p. 3, contained a review of the second edition of *T.P.E.*, which dealt at some length with Jevons's account of early mathematical economists in the new Preface and commented–'With the instincts of a true philosopher, he cares more for the truth than for his own claims to priority. . . .' The review was unsigned, but presumably by Broadfield.

[1] *The Academy*, 26 July 1879, pp. 59–60. Not surprisingly, Leslie approved of those parts of the book in which Jevons advocated inductive studies, but disapproved of his use of mathematical techniques. 'Were the application of mathematical processes and symbols to all economic reasoning . . . possible, it does not follow that it would be expedient. . . . *The Times* might be printed in shorthand, and much ink and paper thereby saved, but would it conduce to the enlightenment of the public to make that economy?' See Vol. VII, p. 160.

[2] See below, Letter 672, n. 1, p. 124.

T.C.D. (for his mathematics, for classics did not then count for a Fellowship) quite agrees to my view that we must be content to be logical in economics. I only wish the greater part of the hitherto accepted theory were so much as logical. It is on the contrary largely a make up of *petitio principii,* reasoning in a circle, and *ignoratio elenchi.* Cairnes to my mind had a singularly illogical way of working out his results.

I am at the Final Examination of I.C.S. Candidates selected in 1877. Perhaps I shall make London my headquarters during the vacation; going for a few days each week to some watering place or country house. I have plenty of invitations to the latter, but am not in certain regular health enough for visiting unless under peculiar circumstances. And if I go to a rich relative I particularly face the difficulty and privation of being forbidden to ride; an exercise of which I was very fond in earlier days. One feels too rather awkward when asked to go out riding with the ladies. It looks comical to say one's doctor forbids it.

I hope to hear you have had a pleasant and invigorating trip. Laveleye comes to England at the end of August for the marriage of his son, but I don't know whether I shall meet him.

Ever truly yours,
T. E. Cliffe Leslie

621.   W. S. JEVONS TO A. MACMILLAN
       [MA]

2 The Chestnuts,
West Heath,
Hampstead, N.W.
23rd August 1879

My dear Macmillan,

I enclose a letter from Italy. I should much like my 'Elementary lessons' to be used in Italian Schools as it might lead to its further extension and shall be satisfied with an almost nominal show of profit. But it would be well that the book should come out from some first rate publishers like Hoepli, and, as Sig. Sergi[1] belongs to Milan, he could, I dare say, arrange with Hoepli. However, I had better leave the matter in your hands.

I shall not be able to get the projected "Essay on the Amusements of the People" ready for this next Christmas.

I do not give up the idea, but need more time to do it deliberately.

---

[1] Presumably the author of the enclosed letter from Italy, which is no longer with the original manuscript. I have been unable to trace any detailed information about Sergi.[Editor].

At present I am getting on with "Exercises in Logic", a book which I proposed to you many years ago, and which is much wanted. But of this anon.

When Miss Maçmillan has completed her translation of Cossa's book, I shall be happy to do anything which may seem likely to conduce to its successful publication.

I am,

Yours faithfully,

W. S. Jevons.

622.   W. S. JEVONS TO R. O. WILLIAMS
    [LJN, 406]

Hampstead, 29th August 1879

. . . I beg leave to thank you for your kindness in informing me of the adoption of my *Political Economy Primer* in Oakland.

I believe I shall receive a certain royalty on the copies or editions sold by Messrs. Appleton and Company, though the profit on the American sale is usually not half that on copies sold in England.

Among those who consider the subject dispassionately, there can be but one opinion about the justice and expediency of international copyright, and I quite expect that the American nation will presently feel this. It is only the interests of a limited number which lead them to persuade the people to the contrary.[1]

I do not pretend that the income from my books is a matter of indifference to me, as it makes a convenient and increasing addition to a very limited income. But I must also say that were there no profit – as there practically is not – upon certain translations, it is always pleasing to hear that the books are in use and are liked. I believe that school-books are one of the most important departments of literature, and I hope to be able to produce several others in logic or political economy.

I am at present engaged rather arduously upon a *Logical Exercises*,[2] designed for college use, and intended to exercise students in accurate thinking. . . .

[1] The underlying principle of American copyright law emphasised the importance of providing an incentive to creative effort, rather than protecting an author's rights. Works became freely available after a limited period, which nineteenth-century legislation extended to forty-two years. This copyright protection, however, applied only to the works of American citizens or residents. International efforts to establish certain minimum reciprocal rights of copyright protection for authors culminated in the Berne Convention of 1886: member countries adopted as a standard period of copyright protection the author's lifetime plus fifty years. The United States declined to become a signatory to the Convention and has remained outside subsequent international agreements.

[2] *Studies in Deductive Logic, a Manual for Students*, published in October 1880: cf. LJ, p. 418.

623.   SIR A. MUSGRAVE TO W. S. JEVONS

Stockbridge
Massachussetts, U. S.
5th Sept., 1879.

My Dear Sir,

I scarcely deserved from you so agreeable a reply to my last letter as I received a short time before I left Jamaica last month on a half a years furlough. Without being exactly ill I felt that two years pretty close work in a Tropical climate was beginning to tell unpleasantly, and I thought it wise to take the proverbial stitch in time by applying for leave of absence. My intention is to winter in Italy, and as every one nearly is out of London in the early Autumn I fear it is not likely that you will be in Town when I pass through next month. On my return in the Spring I shall hope to be able to find you, and to renew the pleasant personal acquaintance begun two years ago.

My official occupation is so constant while in Jamaica that I have not the leisure I could wish for to deal with abstract questions; but enough is brought within my knowledge to convince me that the present condition of Jamaica is encouraging and the prospect for the future far from the hopeless outlook which it is believed very generally to be. But the place must cease to be regarded principally as a Sugar colony. Unfortunately hitherto it has been thought of almost only in that character; whereas in fact although the production of sugar and its accompaniment rum, has not much if at all declined during the last forty years, this industry does not afford employment to *five per cent* of the total population of both sexes and all ages. But other cultivation – of coffee, of pimento, of fruit, of ginger – and other occupations as of sapwood cutting – are increasing. The Savings Bank deposits have annually and steadily increased during the last two years. The black population are far from being the idle and thieving set which they are commonly said to be. They are in fact the taxpayers who furnish the largest part of the more than half a million of Revenue for public and parochial purposes; and among them are to be found as prosperous and contented a body of peasant proprietors as any probably in any country. I could write an essay upon this subject and possibly I shall some day. Meantime when I get some printed copies which I shortly expect I will send you one of my last annual report upon the condition of the community which is in fact an Essay as well as a resume of statistics.

The field of work is extensive and very interesting in the variety it affords. Railway extension and construction of a line of Telegraph of about 200 miles engage our attention just now. Among other things, in connection with a mail coach on a short line of road from the present

Railway terminus, we have established what I think may be the germ of a more complete and extensive parcel post. I quite recognize the importance and convenience of this if it can be accomplished.

In a place where the Govt. has to undertake so much that elsewhere is dealt with by private enterprise the Administrator has no bed of roses – inter alia the Government is responsible for the work by which Kingston is supplied with Gas, and we have recently been pretty well abused because the Kingstonians are expected to pay for what they enjoy. You can understand that the cost of Gas is a matter which comes home to my business and my bosom. Have you heard of the recent process by which Gas is obtained from the decomposition of water! The oxygen is disposed of, and the hydrogen carburetted by passage of some sort through coal and Naphtha; the product being a gas of 22 candle illuminating power, at a cost 40 per cent less than that of gas produced by the best ordinary process under the most favourable circumstances. The New York Gas Co. is using it successfully and supplying gas at one dollar (4/2d.) per thousand feet. [1]

The periodicity of droughts and epidemics is an interesting subject of enquiry. Some speculation upon it I have heard made in Jamaica where the ten years interval is said to have been observed both as to dry weather and Yellow Fever.

General Mann R.E., [2] our Director of Public Works, who is fond of science has promised to gather what information he can for me and when I get back I will see what I can extract for you.

Believe me, my dear Sir,
Very faithfully yours,
A. Musgrave

W. Stanley Jevons, Esq.,

[1] A method of producing water gas was devised and patented in 1869 by Henry Wurtz (1828–1910), who spent most of his career as a consulting chemist in New York City and from 1868 to 1871 edited the *American Gas Light Journal*. The manufacturing process consisted of super-heating steam to about sixteen hundred degrees F, mixing it with the vapour of naptha or other hydrocarbon oil at an equally high temperature, and passing the mixture through incandescent coal. This fixed the gas, converted the hydrogen into light carburetted hydrogen and enriched it with carbon monoxide. Water gas was first introduced into New York in 1877 by the Municipal Gas Light Company, one of several companies serving the City at this period.

[2] James Robert Mann (1823–1915), entered the Royal Engineers as a Lieutenant, 1840; retired as a Major-General, 1873; Director of Public Works, Jamaica, 1866–86.

624.   W. S. JEVONS TO R. H. INGLIS PALGRAVE

Cliff House
Galley Hill
Bulverhythe
Near Hasting
24 Sept. 1879

My dear Palgrave,

I enclose a document concerning the trade of Holland and England
which has been forwarded to me by my Dutch Correspondent Dr. W
Vissering. His father also an excellent economist is now I understand
Finance Minister of that Kingdom and from all that I believe the article i
a most reliable and authoritative one. If you can I should like to see i
published in the *Economist*,[1] but as no name is appended and I have no
express authority (although no prohibition) it *must be given anonymously*

The paper seems to me important both as to the distinct assertion of a
free trade policy which it makes, and also as regards the doubt it throw
upon the value of our trade statistics.

If you cannot publish it *in extenso* you might give the contents and
comment upon them. To do both would be best. If you see any objection
to making use of the paper I shall be much obliged by your returning it to
the above address, as the contents of the paper ought certainly to be made
known one way or another.

I shall be here for about ten days more in a very quiet seaside retrea
favourable to head work.

Yours very faithfully,
W. Stanley Jevons.

In case of publication perhaps you will kindly send me a copy or two o
the Economist to above address.

---

[1] Palgrave did publish the article, which appeared in *The Economist* for 1 November 1879, pp.
1258-9, over the signature 'A Constant Reader'.

625.   W. S. JEVONS TO R. H. INGLIS PALGRAVE
       [KCP]

(Hastings)
29 Sept. 79.

My dear Palgrave,
    Thanks for your letter about Vissering's article. His address is
                    Dr. W. Vissering
                 de Ruyterstraat 2c,
                    The Hague, Holland.
It will be well to send him a proof. I do not know nor care much about
Dutch Finance but the Visserings seem so far as I can judge from
correspondence to be men of very sound economical views, and it will be
no harm for you to be in correspondence with them. Fancy an
Englishman writing in Dutch so that a Dutchman would not know that it
was by a foreigner. So far as I know the article was written by father or son
or both and yet I could not detect any faulty expression of the least
importance.
    I have written you what occurs to me about Free Trade in America,
but tho no doubt it is requisite to meet special objections the true
argument in favour of Free Trade is a general *a priori* one that trade must
be profitable to individuals because otherwise they would not carry it on.
If it were governments which exported and imported in theory, as it were,
arguments against trade might be as valid as they are against the Afghan
campaign. *But free trade being carried on by individuals for their own benefit, is not
a theory. It is a kind of constant experiment, and verifies itself.* It is the proof of its
own benefit.
    I cannot get the idea of a reprinting society out of my head tho I
hesitate to involve myself in it without clearly seeing the way.[1] We now
have in connection with our College Mr. Edward Arber,[2] who has done
so much in reprinting old English literature. He is an oldish man
apparently rather in want of occupation and acting as Professor
Morley's[3] assistant. I will try to get into acquaintance with him sufficient
to judge whether he would do for the working secretary.
    How would it do if you and I were joint Honorary secretaries, all the
detail work, communication with publishers, accounts etc, being done by
Arber or other good paid secretary. Sir J. Lubbock might be asked to be
President. Newmarch Treasurer. When I last saw him Newmarch asked
me spontaneously what we were doing about it.

---

[1] Cf. above, Letter 597, p. 44.
[2] Edward Arber (1829–1912), Fellow of King's College, London; Professor of English Language
and Literature in the University of Birmingham until 1894. Issued many reprints of rare books.
[3] Henry Morley (1822–94), Professor of English Language and Literature at University College
London, 1865–89; editor of the *Examiner,* 1859–64.

In a week or two I will try to call on you for a few minutes in the Strand. In the mean time you can turn the matter over.

The editing would have to be volunteer work with the clerical assistance of the paid secretary in proof reading etc.

I have recently had urgent requests from Italy to procure old English economical works to which I had to reply that it was impossible to procure them except by chance and at high prices. I believe many foreign and American economists and libraries would become subscribers. But we must not be troubled with want of funds — £700 a year is a minimum.

| Ordinary subs | £1. | 1. | 0 |
| Large paper copies | £3. | 3. | 0 |

Yours very faithfully,
W. S. Jevons.

626.   W. S. JEVONS TO A. STRAHAN[1]

Address

5 Oct. 1879[2]
Bulverhythe,

Hampstead

near Hastings

My dear Sir:

I shall be happy to send you an article as soon as I can, but I have been hard at work on an exhausting logical work of late and do not feel equal to writing anything immediately.

I was intending in the course of the next month or two to finish an inquiry in which I have been engaged off and on for some time back on "The local distribution of Intemperance in England" partly founded on the Lords Reports on Intemperance and partly on information obtained direct from Chief Constables. It might go as one of the series of Social Reform articles if you wish it, but it might be a question whether it is not better to drop the general title.[3]

As regards the Mill articles I have written some further portions but doubt whether they are fitted for a further critical article, which ought to be both strong and 'round'. I am afraid of weakening the former articles. But when I get home tomorrow or the next day I will look over what I have written and see if anything can be made of it.

---

[1] Alexander Strahan (1833–1918), Scottish publisher; founder of the *Contemporary Review* in 1865 and its editor from 1870 to 1881.

[2] The original manuscript of this letter is now in the Ford Collection, New York Public Library.

[3] This ultimately developed into an article different not only in title, but to some extent in content – 'Experimental Legislation and the Drink Traffic', *Contemporary Review*, 37 (1880), 177–92, reprinted in *Methods*, pp. 253–76.

A few days ago a friend asked me to submit to you an article bearing on the Church of England. I have not yet seen it but may perhaps take the liberty of communicating with you about it in the course of a week or so. It is by the Rev. Mr. La Touche,[4] vicar of Stokesay near Ludlow.

I am

Yours very faithfully,
W. S. Jevons

627. W. S. JEVONS TO H. SIDGWICK (postcard)

Chestnuts West Heath Hampstead
NW

13 Oct 79.

Can you without trouble give me the exact reference to the letter in which Bentham uses the term 'Utilitarian' as mentioned by you in Fortnightly Review May 1877, Vol XXI p.648?[1]

W. S. Jevons.

627A. W. S. JEVONS TO H. S. FOXWELL
[RDF](postcard)

2, The Chestnuts,
West Heath,
Hampstead, N.W.
2 Nov. 79.

Best thanks for the parcel of books which I duly received. I have been over the exam^n papers & found some capital questions therein. I shall return the papers shortly.

---

[4] James Digges La Touche, educated at Trinity College Dublin; ordained, 1851; Curate of Ardstraw, Co. Tyrone, 1851–5; Vicar of the Church of St John the Baptist, Stokesay, in the Diocese of Hereford, from 1855. No article meeting this description by La Touche appears to have been published in the *Contemporary Review*.

[1] Jevons sought this information for use in his own article 'John Stuart Mill's Philosophy Tested – IV. Utilitarianism' which appeared in the *Contemporary Review*, 36 (1879) 521–38. In this Jevons wrote: 'It is pointed out . . . by Mr. Sidgwick in his article on Benthamism, that Bentham himself suggested the name "Utilitarian", in a letter to Dumont, as far back as 1802.'

628.   J. D'AULNIS TO W. S. JEVONS

Utrecht, 11 Nov. 1879.[1]

Dear Sir!

The letter for Mr. Van den Berg[2] is, immediately after my receiving it, well and safely remitted to him. He is a very good acquaintance of me, and Secretary of the Company for the "exploitation" of the State Railways. It is because the name *Van den Berg* is very usual (perhaps there are a fourty persons of that name in this city), that your hon. letter, on whose address the initials of the Christian names were omitted could not be delivered.

Since 14 days I received a Lecture entitled *Wealthy and Wise* of Mr. Joseph Hiam Levy of London, a lecture of good stile, but which seemed me to contain no new ideas.[3] Do you know Mr. Levy? He seems to be private lecturer, and perhaps he knows me by your introduction of the Second edition of your Theory of Pol. Ec. otherwise I cannot explain me how Mr. Levy feels himself disposed to send me his copy with his respected compliments.[4]

Truly yours

your obedient Servant
J. d'Aulnis

629.   H. S. FOXWELL TO W. S. JEVONS

St. John's College,
Cambridge.
Nov. 12, 1879.

My dear Jevons,

I am very much obliged to you for the cutting out of Kinsman's catalogue. I ordered three books, and sent for the whole catalogue.[1]

Macleod[2] has been at me again: three hours in three days. If you will

---

[1] The text of this letter has been reproduced as a literal copy of the manuscript.

[2] Probably C. P. J. Van den Berg, author of *De Theorie van het arbeidsloon* (Utrecht, 1879), which was one of the latest publications included by Jevons in his List of Mathematico-Economic Books in the second edition of *T.P.E.*

[3] Joseph Hiam Levy, *Wealthy and Wise. A Lecture introductory to the Study of Political Economy, delivered at South Place Institute, September 30 1879* (30 pp., 1879).

[4] There is no evidence that Jevons knew J. H. Levy, but the latter's lecture contains one reference (p. 27) to Jevons's views on the method of Political Economy as expressed in his Preface to the second edition of *T.P.E.*, so that d'Aulnis's conjecture would seem to have been right.

[1] John Kinsman (b. 1826), a second-hand bookseller in Penzance, Cornwall, who from 1859 periodically published catalogues of books he had for sale. Keynes has recorded that 'Professor Foxwell first caught the affliction of book collecting from him' (i.e. Jevons) – *The Collected Writings of John Maynard Keynes*, volume x, *Essays in Biography* (1972) p. 140.

[2] H. D. Macleod. See Vol. IV, Letter 429, n. 1.

excuse my speaking frankly, I think you have conveyed a rather false impression to him and others of the way in which you speak of him in your preface, and in the new edition of the Theory.

Thus p. 127 you speak of him as using the idea of negative value: which you go on to give (as it seems to me) a real and valuable meaning to – but with Macleod the term is used in an utterly different, and I confess it seems to me, in a ridiculous sense. Cournot seems to think it a joke.[3] I believe that Macleod has scarcely the elements of a mathematical idea in him: he has a smattering of the formulae and phrases, but never seems to put them to any practical use. I believe you agree with me about this: (I know Marshall and Sidgwick do) – but your general tone in speaking of Macleod's mathematical work would not leave that impression on an outsider.

I ought to say that Macleod is by no means satisfied with your notice. He says you cast a vague slur on him without mentioning what are the points in which you disagree with him. *He is thirsting for the fray.*[4] I sincerely trust he won't begin to bore you with a personal exposition of his discoveries and other claims to public recognition, as he does us up here.

One more remark about your preface. It struck me as very strange that in mentioning the names of those who have attacked the Wage fund theory, you omit Thornton,[5] who is to most people the best known, and to whom Mill surrendered: and you include Cairnes, who is regarded here as the sole economist of importance since Mill who dared to defend the theory. I know he modified it slightly: still he objects to Mill's surrender, and seems to me practically on the old ground. Several men up here have also noticed this point.

I believe Sargant also attacked the Wage Fund Theory in 1865.[6] I haven't read him yet. I have just got his book. Marshall learnt and adopted a good deal from him.

[3] Cournot, *Revue Sommaire des Doctrines Economiques* (1877) p. 59: 'M. Macleod a eu une idée qu'il croit lumineuse et qui, nous le craignons fort, ne serait propre qu'à égarer ceux qui la prendraient au serieux'. The idea in question was thus explained by Macleod – ". . . if we denote Property in a product that *has been* acquired as Positive, it is perfectly consonant with the universal practice in Physical Philosophy, to denote Property in a product that is *to be* acquired as Negative.' – *Principles of Economical Philosophy* (1872) p. 177. Macleod did not in fact state 'that there may be such a thing as negative value', as Jevons claimed for him, but merely that 'the whole Science of Economics comprehends both Positive and Negative Quantities'.

[4] This sentence was underlined by Foxwell in the original manuscript.

[5] William Thomas Thornton (1813–80), official of the East India Company and later Secretary for Public Works in the India Office; author of a number of works on political economy including *Over-Population and its Remedies* (1846) and *A Plea for Peasant Proprietors* (1848). His *On Labour; its Wrongful Claims and Rightful Dues* (1869) became well known as the immediate cause of J. S. Mill's 'recantation' of the Wages Fund doctrine. See P. Schwartz, *The New Political Economy of J. S. Mill* (1972) pp. 91–103.

[6] There is no work by Sargant dated 1865; the reference is probably to his *Recent Political Economy* (1867).

Again (p. lii) you speak of the fact that rates of wages follow the same formal laws as rents as "new to those whose economic horizon &c. &c." On this I wd. remark (i) It is very curious to us to find Fawcett, a mere inferior reproducer of Mill, ranked with Mill Ricardo and Adam Smith. (2) That Marshall, who ranks no one above Adam Smith and Mill on the whole, and whose horizon was certainly formed on their writings, brought out that very point in his first set of lectures—which I attended. 1869. I doubt whether you can imagine how much irritation this kind of expression gives to many men here. Very likely you don't care: but I feel that the science suffers whenever there are unnecessary antagonisms and heated feelings braising the chief writers and teachers: and if I could do anything to reconcile them, I should feel it was perhaps worth while living to do so.

I thoroughly agree with that part of your preface where in replying to Leslie and Ingram you give your own views as to the method and probable future treatment of the science.

It is rather curious that Sidgwick thinks that Marshall's theory of Distribution is founded on your theory of Final Utility, while Macleod comes running up to me in triumph to say that you are utterly opposed on all fundamentals. Macleod says your theory is substantially what he published 25 years ago, except that *you carry mathematics too far,* beyond the point at which it can be practically used!!! (This means beyond the point to which H. D. M. can follow you).

After lecturing on Marshall's book,[7] I feel that his defns. and much of his treatment in Bk.I is not so exact or useful as he might have made it. Bk.I is the weakest part. When he comes to pure theory in Bk. II. I think you will like his treatment. It agrees very well with what you say on wages + profit = produce. (p. 291) I should very much like to know how far you would be satisfied to use it as a text-book. As to priority, I think most of Marshall's work was about contemporaneous with yours: his lectures being delivered from 1869–1876 here. I should put down the agreement very much to the fact that you are both thoroughly mathematical in your ideas, if I may be allowed to judge. Marshall always spoke in the highest terms of your book from its first appearance, which might prove either that he was prepared to agree with it, or that he had learnt a good deal from it, or both. Excuse this long note.

Yours very truly,

H. S. Foxwell.

---

[7] *The Economics of Industry* by Alfred and Mary Paley Marshall (1879).

630. W. S. JEVONS TO J. BEAL[1]

> address   Chestnuts
> Hampstead Heath N.W.
> 14 Novr 1879[2]

Dear Sir

I should be much pleased at Mr. Morley's[3] successful candidature or anything conducing towards it; but as regards my name being added to his committee there are the difficulties that I am not an elector of Westminster, and I am not able to incur any pecuniary liability beyond say one or two pounds.

If pecuniary liability does not attach & you still wish non electors names to appear I should be happy to hear from you to that effect.

> I am Dear Sir
> Yours faithfully
> W. Stanley Jevons

James Beal Esq.

631. W. S. JEVONS TO H. S. FOXWELL
[RDF; LJP, 408–9]

> Hampstead
> 14 Novr 1879

My dear Foxwell

Your last letter[1] was one of great interest to me as I much value any such opportunity of getting to know what people think at Cambridge. As regards Macleod I do not wish to enter into any dispute. I have said the most civil things I can of his books, and I see no need to dwell upon his errors because they are not likely to do any harm.

I regret leaving out Mr Thornton's name as regards the wage fund theory. It was an oversight. Cairnes professedly supports the theory but his arguments really tend against it in a deadly manner. He cannot stop at any definite *non competing* groups, & his ideas followed out lead to entire rejection of the theory.

I dare say Sargants' book might have been mentioned also but I forgot it. You will observe that my bibliography only extended to mathematical writers & I certainly never intended on a few pages to sketch the history of Pol. Econ generally in a complete way.

---

[1] James Beal (d. 1891), land agent; Councillor for Fulham in the London County Council, 1889–91.

[2] The original manuscript of this letter is in the Archives of the Greater London Council.

[3] John Morley stood unsuccessfully as Liberal candidate for Westminster in the General Election of 1880. See Vol. IV, Letter 539, n. 9.

[1] Letter 629 above, p. 76.

As regards the analogy of laws of wages & rents, of course I do not know what Marshall gave in his lectures in 1869 as I neither attended them nor [have][2] seen notes unless indeed the answers of some candidates. But I do not remember that they said anything on the matter. My ideas on the subject have been gathered perhaps most clearly from Cournots 'Recherches' which suggests the general method of attacking the subject. However if ever I am able to get thro my large book on Economics I shall take such a very different line of general treatment that there will not be much room for dispute. Many different lines of argument including that of Cairnes converge to something quite opposite to Ricardian doctrines.

As regards Marshall's originality I never called it in question in the slightest degree having neither the wish nor the grounds. On the other hand you seem to forget that the essential points of my theory were fully indicated as far back as 1862 at the Cambridge meeting of the British Assoc[n]. I have no reason to suppose that Marshall saw any printed report of my first brief paper, but of course on the other hand in my book of 18$\overset{71}{7}$0?(Theory of P.E) I could not possibly have borrowed anything from Marshall. But these questions are really of little or no importance now we have found such earlier books as those of Gossen, Cournot, Dupuit, &c. We are all shelved on the matter of priority except of course as regards details and general method of exposition &c.

I have of course got Marshall's book but have really not been able to read it with care, having my head full of Mill, & De Morgan's logic, with some 150 wretched London candidates as well. Now I have got 19 honours candidates in a 2 days exam[n] some of them writing 4 books apiece in 3 hours! From what I gathered in a cursory reading of the 'Economics', together with reliance on Marshall's scientific powers & the careful revision it had undergone, I welcomed the book as getting me out of a difficulty in regard to the Bankers' Institute Examinations for which I have proposed it as the first text book. I hope however the Athenaeum is not right in claiming the book as written on *the lines of Mill* exclusively.[3] I thought there was much divergence. However from considerations which it is difficult to describe briefly I have suggested Mill's Pol. Econ for the Bankers Institute & I even use it in my own class still. Thus however violent may be my attacks on the logic of Mill I cannot be accused of one sidedness. Nor am I inconsistent, for it is one thing to put forward views for rational judgement of competent readers; it is another thing to force those views upon young men by means of examinations. The Mill faction

---

[2] Omitted in the original manuscript.

[3] The review of *The Economics of Industry* in the *Athenaeum*, 8 November 1879, p. 595, contained the following passage: ' "The Economics of Industry" is based on the lines laid down in Mill's "Principles of Political Economy"; its style is clear and incisive and its pages are enlivened by many good illustrations and apt quotations.'

never scrupled at putting their lecturers & examiners wherever they could, but I believe it only requires a little clear logic and a little time to overthrow them.[4]

631A.   W. S. JEVONS TO H. S. FOXWELL
[RDF]

2, The Chestnuts,
West Heath,
Hampstead, N.W.
22 Nov[r] 79

My dear Foxwell

I have read M[r] Bell's[1] letter (returned herewith) with much interest. I see no reason why you should not undertake an edition of the W. of N[s]. The fact is that a year or two ago I was struck with the idea of a really good moderate priced edition, & I proposed to M[r] MacMillan to print a complete text at the same time that we were printing a Students' Edition. But he promptly crushed the idea on the ground that there were Thorold Rogers,[2] Murray's cheap reprint,[3] MacCulloch's[4] & some other old editions. The cheap reprint is what w[d] most stand in your way. I recommend it to my students & find it serves well, but then I give my own comments.

My own feeling would be that a historical & critical edition w[d] be congenial work for you,[5] but then M[r] Bell evidently does not want to add much to the already great length of the text.

I agree with your feeling about the *typography* of the old Bohn's[6] volumes which I am often obliged to use but always with a certain pain. However perhaps M[r] Bell w[d] meet your ideas as much as possible there.

I am a little out of heart about my own Ed. of W. of N. owing partly I expect to your objections but I have by no means abandoned it. Please therefore consider my ideas on the subject as *entre nous*.

[4] The original manuscript ends here, but has a pencilled note added in the handwriting of H. S. Foxwell: 'Not posted – given to me on calling at Hampstead.'

[1] George Bell (1814–90), bookseller and publisher. Entered partnership with F. R. Daldy in 1855, later founded the firm of George Bell & Sons. In 1864 Bell purchased Bohn's Libraries for £40,000. See below, n. 6.

[2] J. E. Thorold Rogers's edition of *The Wealth of Nations* was published in two volumes in 1869 by the Clarendon Press, Oxford.

[3] This was a reprint of the fifth edition published as one of 'Murray's Choice Reprints' in 1874.

[4] McCulloch's edition was originally published by Black & Tait in Edinburgh in 1828, and in Edinburgh and London in 1838, 1849 (reprinted 1855 and 1859) and 1863.

[5] Foxwell appears to have agreed to undertake the edition, but never completed it. See below, Letter 655, p. 106.

[6] Henry George Bohn (1796–1884), bookseller and publisher, published over 600 volumes in a series of classified 'Library' editions in the 1840s and 1850s. Many of these he compiled and edited himself. See above, n. 1.

A history of Pol. Econ. is very much wanted in the English language, which strange to say has not got anything to call such, though it has the richest literature in the world. But to write such a history successfully w^d be a very long difficult task involving much reading & research. I c^d not give you off-hand any advice on such a point. But I must say that I rather incline towards the W. of N. unless you have other literary work in hand I hardly see any objection except the question of type &c., which surely might be overcome.

Private

It occurs to me to ask whether you w^d feel inclined to take an active part in a projected Society for the reprinting of rare & important economic books. [7] I have reason to believe that there w^d be no difficulty in setting such a society up if only there were some one active & energetic enough to meet the correspondence. I have no authority to offer anything as the society does not exist but the train is sufficiently laid & it only wants the match to blow the thing into life. What I want personally is to avoid correspondence & worry while keeping a voice in the choice of books & matter to be published. If you will think the matter over we might find some chance of *viva voce* consideration. The society w^d be of the type of the Early English Text Society, Camden Society &c &c.

Ever yours faithfully
W. S. Jevons

Adam Smith Society.

Private & Confidential

    President

        Wm Newmarch FRS.

    Treasurer

        Sir John Lubbock.

Comm^{ee}.

Cornelius Walford.
R. Giffen [8]

---

[7] There is no record of Foxwell's response to this proposal, but the projected Adam Smith Society did not come into existence.

[8] [Sir] Robert Giffen (1837–1910), assistant editor of *The Economist*, 1868–76; chief of the Statistical Department, Board of Trade, afterwards Controller-General of the Commercial, Labour and Statistical Departments, 1882–97; President of the [Royal] Statistical Society, 1882–4; K.C.B. 1895.

Hodgson
H. R. Tedder.[9]   &c

&c &c

General Editors
R. H. Inglis Palgrave
W. S. Jevons.

Honorary Secretary
H. S. Foxwell.

Assistant Secretary
?   ?

632.   E. HELM TO W. S. JEVONS

Holmacre,
Fallowfield.
Nov: 25: 1879.

My Dear Jevons,

I have been elected President of our Statistical Society[1] for the current Session and am naturally very anxious to have some very good papers. The prospect is not at present at all promising and I am hopeful that my term of office may be distinguished by the reading of a paper from you. Will you kindly take this matter into serious consideration, and give me a favourable reply?

I sent you a copy of the *Guardian* containing a report of my inaugural paper. Yesterday I had a conversation with Mr. Fairchild[2] of the lending house H.B. Claflin and Co. of New York.[3] He has just returned from America and gives me most glowing accounts of the revival of trade there and confirms all my anticipations of its effect on this side the Atlantic. Referring to the *Times* remark that notwithstanding the reported improvement in business there was little increase in the amount of bills

---

[9] Henry Richard Tedder (1850–1924), librarian to Lord Acton, 1873–4; Librarian of the Athenaeum Club, 1874, Secretary, 1889–1922; joint secretary of first International Conference of Librarians, 1877; joint honorary secretary of the Library Association, 1878–80, honorary treasurer, 1889–97, and president, 1897–8.

[1] i.e. the Manchester Statistical Society. Helm was President from 1879 to 1881, but Jevons did not read any paper to the Society during his term of office. Cf. Ashton, op. cit., pp. 138, 171.

[2] Probably Charles Stebbins Fairchild (1842–1924), financier; Attorney-General for New York, 1875–7. He had returned to private business after failing to obtain renomination; Secretary of the Treasury under President Cleveland, 1887–9.

[3] The wholesale company founded by New York merchant Horace Brigham Claflin (1811–85). By the 1870s the volume of business conducted by the firm in various fields had risen to tens of millions of dollars annually.

coming into the discount market he said the orders given out in the various English manufacturing districts which are already very large indeed, would only give rise to bills in January and onwards when the goods which are bought will be made and delivered.

From East Indian merchants who have branch houses in the interior engaged in buying produce – I have very good accounts. One firm tell me they have not had such hopeful prospects with regard to all sorts of crops for many years.

When will the next American panic come? If previous experience is to be relied upon it should not under normal conditions arrive until 1893. [4] But the non cancelling of the greenbacks has given the States an inflated currency, and I fear it is now too late to hope for any contraction.

With kind regards to Mrs. Jevons and yourself.

I am Dear Jevons

Yours very truly,

Elijah Helm.

632A.   W. S. JEVONS TO H. S. FOXWELL
[RDF]

Thanks for
Exam[n] papers.

2, The Chestnuts,
West Heath,
Hampstead, N.W.
6 Dec 1879

My dear Foxwell

I have now found the paper about the box making. The ones I had cost 9/0 per doz. but he expects you to take a good many at that price say $\frac{1}{2}$ gross at least. You must choose the size which best suits your own papers or books. You can have a sample box if you like. Please return the paper. I have been so much interrupted by journies* exam[s], & now by the free skating that I cannot get on with anything.

Yours very truly

W. S. Jevons.

Allen in Euston Rd [1] has a nice copy of 'Thornton on Credit' for 6d. [2] It is a valuable book but having a copy I asked him to keep it for you.

---

[4] In fact the upper turning-point of the cycle came in 1881–2, but was not marked by any acute panic. 'The downturn of the early eighties was slow and quiet. The bubble of overoptimism was pricked in the summer of 1881, and the force of the expansion began to die down in the latter part of the year.' – R. Fels, *American Business Cycles, 1865–1897* (Chapel Hill, N.C., 1959) p. 125.

[1] Cf. below, Letter 706, p. 159.

[2] Henry Thornton, *An Enquiry into the nature and effects of the Paper Credit of Great Britain* (1802).

633.   W. S. JEVONS TO R. H. INGLIS PALGRAVE
       [KCP]

2, The Chestnuts,
West Heath,
Hampstead, N.W.
7 Dec. 79.

My dear Palgrave,

I quite see the position in which Goschen's[1] carelessness has placed you and shall be happy to do what I can in the matter. I am writing for a proposal form and if you can write me out from memory what was inserted in the previous form, if you saw it, it will much assist me. I should like also your idea of a list of supporters in the best order of application, which I can use at my discretion to some extent.

As I have no influence in the Council the eventual election[2] will depend upon Newmarch, Goschen, and Sir J. D. H.[3]

You should have some 6 or 7 names and I will sign about the 7th or 8th.

Yours very faithfully,
W. S. Jevons.

634.   W. S. JEVONS TO R. H. INGLIS PALGRAVE
       [KCP]

2, The Chestnuts,
West Heath,
Hampstead, N. W.
19 Dec. 79.

Dear Palgrave,

I have filled up and sent off the paper to Goschen. After looking carefully thro the proposals for some years back, I came to the conclusion that it was essential to add

Fellow of S.S.[1]

I think also that 'Editor of the Bankers' Magazine, etc.' might too be added, but this might perhaps be done when the paper returns from Goschen. At the end I have said 'distinguished for his acquaintance with

---

[1] George Joachim, first Viscount Goschen (1831–1907), President of the Poor Law Board, 1868–70; First Lord of the Admiralty, 1871–4 and 1895–1900; Chancellor of the Exchequer, 1887–95.

[2] The letter relates to Palgrave's election to Fellowship of the Royal Society. See below, Letter 728, p. 188.

[3] Sir Joseph Dalton Hooker (1817–1911), naturalist; Assistant Director of the Royal Botanical Gardens Kew, 1855–65; Director, 1865–85; President of the Royal Society, 1872–7.

[1] i.e. Fellow of the London [later Royal] Statistical Society.

Econs. Stat and Monetary Science, and for his efforts to promote their scientific study,' leaving out 'attached to science' etc. which seems generally to have a weakening and doubtful effect.

Yours faithfully,
W. S. Jevons.

635.   F. B. EDMONDS[1] TO W. S. JEVONS

72 Portsdown Road,
W.
22 Dec. 1879.

Dear Jevons,

I could not afford time for skating to-day and know nothing of the ice, but seeing that it is now freezing again it is my intention – unless there is some unexpected change of wind here – to go over to Hendon to-morrow afternoon. There was much rejoicing in town this morning but with the mercury in the barometer rounding up again I was doubtful as to the continuance of the thaw. There seems to be a fair prospect just now of the barometer showing a max, above that of the week before last and that was a max. max.

It was with some surprise I read amongst "Notes" . . "Nature"[2] that no less an authority than Mr. Jansen[3] thought the rigour of the present winter might be attributed to the small number of spots and faculae on the sun just now. This would hardly suit my views nor do I think it corresponds with the doleful story of no spots that has become a little stale and belongs rather to last year at any rate and confirms my idea and that of others that the sun spots minimum is past. I never realised this spot maximum before I got hold of Carrington's book[4] and grant that we may not even have the half loaf yet but believe we are quite out of the no bread stage.

The current number of the "Engineer" (19 Dec.) gives a tabular statement of prices of pig iron in Philadelphia for 36 years – 1842 – 78 – lowest, highest and average. It is quoted from the "American Manufacturer" – that publication having compiled it from Mr. Swank's[5] "Statistics of the American Iron Trade."

[1] See Vol. II, Letter 52, p. 111.

[2] 'Notes', *Nature*, 18 December 1879, p. 162.

[3] Pierre Jules César Janssen (1824–1907), French astronomer, noted for his observations of solar eclipses and magnetic phenomena.

[4] Probably Richard Christopher Carrington, *Observations on the Spots on the Sun from November 9, 1853, to March 24, 1861, made at Redhill* (1863). Carrington (1826–75), F.R.A.S. 1851, F.R.S. 1860, an astronomer of private means, built two observatories in Surrey.

[5] James Moore Swank (1832–1914), statistician and historian. Executive secretary of the American Iron and Steel Association, 1873–85, in which capacity he produced an annual report entitled *The American Iron Trade in . . . Practically, Historically and Statistically considered*.

I looked up the par. anent the rumour of starting 2nd class again on the Midland Railway – it was in the London "Figaro".[6] As you surmised Mr. Ellis the late chairman was the individual alluded to as having brought about the present state of things.

Yours very truly,
Frd. B. Edmonds.

636.   W. S. JEVONS TO E. ARBER

2, The Chestnuts,
West Heath,
Hampstead, N.W.
23 Dec 1879

My dear Arber

Best thanks for your letter & papers &c. The proposal is a very practical one but will need much consideration. If not otherwise engaged could you come here about 5 pm on Saturday 27th and after a cup of tea we will go fully into the matter?[1] Afterwards please dine quietly with Mrs. Jevons & self & then we can continue the discussion afterwards if requisite. If you cannot come at 5 please come at 7 to dinner. If Saturday will not do we must find some day that will perhaps after the holydays*. There is no hurry.

I have a certain number of tracts here which you can inspect.

Yours faithfully
W. S. Jevons

636A.   W. S. JEVONS TO THE EDITOR OF *THE TIMES*[1]

LIGHT GOLD COIN.

Sir,

The letter of "Full Weight"[2] seems to place beyond doubt the truth of the assumption which you made in your article of the 19th,[3] that the

---

[6] *London Figaro*, 17 December 1879, p. 3: 'It is rumoured that the directors of the Midland Railway Company intend to restore second-class carriages to their trains. The late Mr. Ellis, we believe, suggested, and, in fact, warmly advocated their abolition and it was effected in opposition to the wishes of several other members of the board.'

[1] Presumably the proposed reprinting society. Cf. above, Letters 597, 625 and 631A, pp. 44, 73 and 81.

[1] Published in the issue of 23 December 1879.

[2] Published in *The Times* on 20 December 1879, p.11. The writer urged Government action to recall all light coin and to penalise those bankers responsible for keeping it in circulation. He cited the example of gold coin held by the West of England Bank, of which more than half was found to be under the legal weight when it was paid into the Bank of England by liquidators.

[3] A long leading article on the deterioration of the gold coinage appeared in *The Times* on 19 December 1879, p. 7.

condition of the gold coinage has not improved in the last ten years. On the contrary, if we are to accept the coin in the West of England Bank as a fair specimen of that in general circulation, it has decidedly retrograded. In 1868 I inferred, from a kind of census of the age of 165,510 gold coins, taken in connexion with the weighing of a certain number of coins, that almost one-third (31½ per cent.) of the sovereigns, and nearly one-half (47 per cent.) of the half-sovereigns, were under the legal weight. In the statement about the West of England Bank the numbers of sovereigns and half-sovereigns are not distinguished; but we are told that more than 65,000 coins out of 129,000 were charged for lightness. This gives just over one-half (50.3 per cent.) as illegally light, which quite corresponds with the facts stated in your article about the insufficient withdrawal of worn coins.

Under these circumstances a general re-coinage cannot be much longer delayed. The present currency of sovereigns and half-sovereigns began to be issued in 1817, and 24 years after it was judged to be indispensable to have a general calling in and re-coinage of the light gold. That operation was completed in 1844, since which year an interval of 35 years has been allowed to elapse without any measure of the same sort. Nor will the state of things ever improve under the present system. On the contrary, it will go on from bad to worse, because the worn coins sink, as it were, into the deep holes of the circulation, and the new issues of full-weight sovereigns swim over the surface, are returned to the Bank of England, or soon disappear by exportation and melting.

Taking the whole gold currency, including part of that circulating in some foreign countries, at £100,000,000, the amount to be re-coined, according to the facts stated by "Full Weight", will be about £50,000,000, and the loss on re-coinage will be about £825,000. Including increased Mint expenses and something for the deficiency of fineness of the older currency, the total expense of the operation will be about £900,000. The Queen's English may be left to take care of itself; but surely the Queen's money, every piece of which bears the Sovereign's image, should be above reproach. Is it not simply scandalous that a person drawing gold coin from one department of State – the Post-office Savings Bank – and unavoidably or unwarily taking it to another department – that of the Inland Revenue – is likely to be mulcted of about 1 per cent. of his money?

Even apart from this impending question of a re-coinage, may I be allowed to point out the imperative necessity which exists for a better appointed Mint? There can be little doubt that we have now passed through the trough of the commercial wave, [4] and in the absence of war,

---

[4] Economic historians now locate the beginning of cyclical revival in 1879 – cf. Rostow, *British Economy of the Nineteenth Century*, p. 210. Again, Jevons did not attempt to reconcile his acceptance of

and of any remarkable series of sunless years and bad harvests such as that
which darkened the commencement of this century, we may fairly expect
between the present time and 1888 a period of growing prosperity. But
experience shows that a burst of trade has in late years been accompanied
by a sudden demand for metallic currency. In 1871–2 the vast amount of
£25,000,000 of gold coinage was issued from the Mint. But it is well
understood that the present antiquated Mint is quite unable to meet such
a sudden demand for gold, and at the same time to continue the striking of
silver and bronze money. Unless the long-projected new Mint be at once
commenced, I venture to predict that you will, after a year or two, be
inundated with complaints about the want of silver currency. Colonel
Tomline's celebrated agitation will be revived in an aggravated form,
and all kinds of evils will be attributed to the remissness of the authorities
at Tower-hill.[5]

> I am, Sir, yours obediently,
> W. Stanley Jevons.

637.   W. S. JEVONS TO J. MILLS
      [TLJM, 340]

> January 1, 1880

Dear Mills—

    Shall we number you among the London statisticians? It is time you
were among us.

    With best wishes for a Happy New Year & a *happy decade* for yourself
and all your family.

> Yours,
> W.S.J.

638.   W. S. JEVONS TO J. MILLS
      [TLJM, 340–1]

> January 7, [1880][1]

My dear Mills—

    The [London] Statistical Society's circular was sent 'by order', and
though I am sorry you do not feel inclined to a more active pursuit of
statistics, I acquiesce regretfully in your decision. I get on but slowly with
Mill's philosophy, having other works on hand. I shall probably have an

---

the crisis of 1878 as confirming his theory of decennial cycles with his acceptance of the fact that
revival had begun in 1879. Cf. Vol. IV, Letter 540, n. 1.

   [5] See Vol. IV, Letter 563.

   [1] The date is misprinted '1889' in TLJM.

article in next Contemporary,[2] which may interest you, & I have many others in contemplation, but they require long hatching.

The revival of trade is interesting to us in a scientific point of view as well as important otherwise. It is curious that in several societies with which I am connected there is a falling off in the current of new members. This I attribute to the fact that the depression of the last few years is only now reaching private incomes in its full intensity. Expenditure is now directed as much as possible to profitable undertakings. I fear we shall have plenty of bubbles, and probably a coal famine in the next three years. Then, perhaps, a temporary revulsion, like that of 1872–73; but I now have complete confidence in the cycle of 10.45 years or thereabouts.[3]

Yours very faithfully,

W. S. J.

639.   W. S. JEVONS TO R. H. INGLIS PALGRAVE
       [KCP]

2, The Chestnuts,
West Heath,
Hampstead, N. W.
17 Jany. 1880.

Dear Palgrave,

Best thanks for the books. The almanack is an excellent book of reference.

The hand book of gold & silver contains a good deal of information but not put together with any clear comprehension of subject.[1]

I am glad to say that I have succeeded capitally with the paper & now have the signatures of Goschen, Lubbock, Guy[2] Galton & Stafford Northcote[3] in this order. I have called once on Dr. Farr who I find lives not very far from here, but found him out. I do not much like posting the

---

[2] See above, Letter 626, n. 3, p. 74.

[3] Jevons seems here to have extrapolated his view of the economic events of the 1870s as a forecast for the 1880s. In fact the next 'coal famine' did not occur until 1899, and the upper turning-point of the next cycle came in 1882. See Rostow, *British Economy of the Nineteenth Century*, pp. 33 and 213.

[1] It is not possible to identify either of the works here referred to with certainty, but the first was probably the *Banking Almanac and Directory* (1880), which was edited by Palgrave.

[2] William Augustus Guy (1810–85), authority on sanitary reform; assistant physician to King's College Hospital, 1842; Dean of the Medical Faculty of the College, 1846–58; Professor of Forensic Medicine at King's College, London, 1858; editor of the *Journal of the London* [later Royal] *Statistical Society*, 1852–6; Vice-President of the Society, 1869–72, and President, 1873–5.

[3] Sir Stafford Northcote (1818–87), created first Earl of Iddesleigh, 1885. Private Secretary to Gladstone, 1841; legal secretary to Board of Trade, 1847; M.P. for Dudley, 1855; Chancellor of the Exchequer, 1874; succeeded Disraeli as Leader of the House of Commons, 1876–80; Foreign Secretary, 1886.

paper any more as loss would be very awkward. I will try to call again but in any case will soon add my signature & give the paper into the R. S.[4]

I fancy your prospects must be very good, but as I explained before I cannot undertake more than the getting up of the paper.

If I meet Hooker I will discuss the matter with him but I flatter myself the proposal form is rightly got up.

> Believe me
> Yours faithfully,
> W. S. Jevons.

The conjunction of two such financial planets as Goschen & Northcote is a portent of success.

640.   F. B. EDMONDS TO W. S. JEVONS

> 72, Portsdown Road,
> W.
> 20 Jan. '80.

Dear Jevons,

I thank you very much for the letter of recommendation and have sent it on to the British Museum this morning. The "Rules" I will retain for a few days.

It seems to me taking Schwabe's[1] sun-spot maximum for 1828 that your views, Piazzi Smyths, and my own (for the interval 1828 – 1870-9) have a close relation, but I am inclined to think that the next spot cycle either before or after must produce a deviation in excess of your average number. However this may be I hope we are all on the right track and I believe yours to be the most difficult work as being a function of so many variables.

Professor Smyth says "We must have therefore each cycle of sun-spots fixed by its own dates alone, and not smoothed away and improved out of creation by being made apparently conformable to others". Just the thought that started me last spring after reading that article in the Times[2] taking your crisis numbers in relation to certain assumed sun spot numbers the values of which have yet to be established.

There seems to be a chance of another turn on the ice at Hendon after all. They were skating – "no person allowed on the ice"

---

[4] i.e. the Royal Society.

[1] Samuel Heinrich Schwabe (1789– 1875), German astronomer; commenced observations of sun-spots in 1826, and in 1843 was the first to put forward the hypothesis of a decennial cycle in their appearance.

[2] 'Sun – Spots and Commercial Panics', *The Times*, 14 January 1879.

notwithstanding – when I passed the Regents Park this afternoon. The ice was very thin and I think they might put a few out of our noble array of policemen to keep boys and idlers from breaking the laws and the ice.

My mother asked me after you called last Friday whether she had not met yourself and wife one Sunday afternoon at the Horticultural Gardens S.K. some years back.

I remain,

Yours very truly,

Fred B. Edmonds.

641.   C. W. FREMANTLE[1] TO W. S. JEVONS

22 January, 1880[2]

PRIVATE

My dear Professor,

I ought to have thanked you several days ago for your letter of the 17th instant, but I have been very busy.

The point of view from which you estimate the gold circulation is a new one to me, and gives a result which is interesting in itself and certainly fortifies us in the belief that the amount actually current in this Country cannot exceed £100,000,000. I am very much obliged to you for calling my attention to this way of calculating it.[3]

I have sent in today a preliminary Memorandum to the Chancellor of the Exchequer on the light gold question, and it remains to be seen whether the Govt. will think it possible to do anything in the matter with the present Mint and a moribund Parliament!

Yours very truly,

C. W. Fremantle.

Professor Stanley Jevons, F.R.S.

---

[1] Hon. Sir Charles William Fremantle (1834–1914), Deputy Master of Her Majesty's Mint, 1870–94; served on the Royal Commissions on International Coinage, 1868, and on Gold and Silver, 1886; represented the British Government at the 1881 and 1889 International Monetary Conventions at Paris.

[2] Written on notepaper with embossed crest, 'Royal Mint'.

[3] The Jevonian method of calculating the amount of gold coinage in circulation was based on two assumptions: that samples taken from the coinage contained the same proportions of coins of different dates as were to be found in the circulation as a whole; and that there was virtually no wastage of recently issued coins, so that the numbers of new coins known to have been issued by the Mint could be used as basis for calculation. See Vol. III, Letters 281, n. 2 and 318; also *The Collected Writings of John Maynard Keynes*, volume 1, *Indian Currency and Finance* (1971) p. 106.

642.   T. H. FARRER[1] TO W. S. JEVONS

1 February, 1880.
Board of Trade,
Whitehall Gardens, S.W.

Dear Mr. Jevons,

Pray come at 3.45 on Wednesday. All my general leaning is in favour of private enterprise. But the difficulty of regulating monopoly is very great.

The Post Office desire the other offices to do nothing in the matter of telephones without their consent – an argument against Govt. monopoly. But, as you say, the telephone will beat the P.O.[2]

Very truly yours,
T. H. Farrer.

Stanley Jevons, Esq.,
The Chestnuts,
West Heath,
Hampstead.

---

[1] [Sir] Thomas Henry Farrer (1819–99), Secretary of the Board of Trade, 1867–86; Vice-Chairman of the London County Council, 1892–8; President of the Cobden Club, 1899; a founder of the Gold Standard Defence Association, 1895; author of *Free Trade Against Fair Trade* (1882), *The State in its Relation to Trade* (1883) and *Studies in Currency* (1898); knighted, 1883; created Baron Farrer of Abinger, 1893.

[2] The issue of state control in trade and industry was an important subject of debate between Farrer and Jevons (cf. below, Letter 685, p. 137). Farrer was more strongly opposed than Jevons to the principle of government control but accepted it in the case of the Post Office as the most appropriate means of providing a public service. In *The State in Relation to Trade*, written three years after this letter, he stated that he was prepared to wait and see whether state control or private enterprise were to prove the more effective means of running the telephone service (second edition (1913) p. 131).

By this date two companies had been established to supply telephones and wires to private subscribers, initially in London. They amalgamated in 1880 to form the United Telephone Company, a development which led the Post Office, anxious to protect its monopoly over telegraphs and to establish a similar monopoly over telephones, to attempt to obtain the necessary amendment to existing legislation. When this failed a High Court action was brought against the telephone companies, the result of which was a judgment favourable to the Post Office in December 1880. Thus a legal monopoly was conferred on the Post Office, enabling it to control the telephone companies through a licensing system. Henry Fawcett, while Postmaster-General (see Vol. III, Letter 190, n. 2) proved reluctant to take up the monopoly, a policy which resulted in confusion and competition between the companies and the Post Office, and it was not until 1911 that the telephone system was finally brought under government control. For details see J. Hemmeon, *The History of the British Post Office* (Cambridge, Mass., 1912) pp. 219–36; H. Robinson, *Britain's Post Office* (1953) pp. 218–20.

643.   W. S. JEVONS TO A. MACMILLAN
    [MA]

2 The Chestnuts,
West Heath,
Hampstead, N.W.
24 March 1880

My dear Macmillan,

I think that nothing has been said about the terms on which you would publish the translation of Cossa's guide to the study of political economy in the translation of which Miss Macmillan has now got on a long way.

I have a note from Professor Cossa suggesting £8 as the price of his copyright for England.[1] This is not a formidable sum. Perhaps however it would be better that you should settle such a point direct with the publishers Hoepli and not thro Cossa and me.

The guide contains a great deal of information quite inaccessible hitherto to English ordinary students. I am a little disappointed about Cossa's style when minutely examined, but that will not so much matter for students' purposes. I think the Cambridge lecturers ought to use the book more or less and if so a fair sale will be secured. My "Studies in Deductive Logic" are very near completion. I shall be writing again about them in a week or two.

Yours faithfully,
W.S. Jevons

644.   L. WALRAS TO W. S. JEVONS[1]

Ouchy sous Lausanne,
Mars 1880

Cher Monsieur,

Je vous dois encore un accusé de réception et des remerciements pour une lettre du 21 février 1879[2] par laquelle vous me faisiez parvenir, au sujet de l'enseignement des sciences morales et politiques en Angleterre, des renseignements précieux dont j'ai tiré bon parti. Un seul mot me suffira comme excuse. Ma femme, dont la santé était sérieusement atteinte depuis deux or trois ans, est devenue dangereusement malade, et je l'ai perdue le 8 juin de l'année dernière. Je n'ai pas besoin de vous dire quel trouble ce triste évènement fait dans mon existence.

---

[1] See above, Letter 610, p. 59.

[1] The original manuscript of this letter is not now among the Jevons Papers, and the text published here follows that given by Jaffé in *Walras Correspondence*, I, 645–7, as based on the draft in Fonds Walras (FW, I, 278/14).

[2] See above, Letter 582, p. 21.

Occupé de soins douloureux, puis parti en voyage avec ma fille pendant les vacances, je n'ai pu m'occuper qu'à mon retour, c'est-à-dire pendant l'automne dernier, de votre *Theory of Political Economy* dont vous m'aviez envoyé la 2e édition. Mais j'en ai fait alors une traduction complète de la première page à la dernière,[3] ce qui est, à mon sens, la seule manière de se rendre véritablement compte d'un ouvrage de cette nature. Je vous avouerai franchement que je n'ai pas trouvé que vous ayez fait de cette publication ce qu'il était possible d'en faire et ce que vous me disiez vouloir en faire dans votre dernière lettre. En faisant précéder votre ouvrage d'extraits de celui de Gossen et en le faisant suivre d'extraits de mes Mémoires, vous auriez fourni paraît-il l'exposition d'un système nouveau des phénomènes économiques. Vous auriez pu alors résumer à grands traits ce système dans une introduction et après celà, mettre en ruines la théorie de Ricardo-Mill. Celà vous aurait demandé plus de travail et vous aurait pris plus de temps; mais il me semble qu'en pareilles circonstances l'essentiel est moins d'aller vite que d'arriver au but. De la façon dont vous avez procédé, vous ne me semblez avoir obtenu aucun résultat frappant et décisif. Faute d'avoir nettement indiqué et défini les éléments du système économique: les *services producteurs* (rente, travail, profit), la *production,* l' *entrepreneur,* le *marché des facteurs,* le *marché des produits,* le mécanisme de l'*enchère* et du *rabais* etc., l'esquisse que vous donnez de ce systeme dans les dernières pages de la Préface est confusé et la critique que vous faites de la doctrine ricardienne insuffisante. J'irai plus loin. Je suis convaincu que quand vous vous déciderez à vous avancer beaucoup plus loin que vous ne l'avez fait encore sur le terrain de l'économique nouvelle, vous modifierez sensiblement vos jugements sur les divers auteurs que vous citez. Ce que vous dites des économistes français: de Condillac, des Physiocrates, de Bastiat, de Courcelle-Seneuil n'est pas d'une justesse bien rigoureuse. Quant à Dupuit, au sujet duquel je vous ai averti, je m'étonne que vous persistiez à lui faire honneur de la courbe d'utilité, quand il est parfaitement sûr et certain qu'il l'a confondue avec la courbe de demande et quand la phrase-même de lui que vous citez[4] (pp XXX–XXXI) accuse entièrement cette confusion. Votre appréciation de la théorie de M. Cournot ne me paraît pas plus exacte ni plus définitive. M. Cournot a presque donné la théorie mathématique de la détermination du prix dans le cas des monopoles; mais il ne l'a pas donné du tout dans le cas de libre concurrence. De tous ces écrivains qui nous ont précédes, un seul, selon moi a eu vraiment un sentiment sûr et profond quoique imparfait du

---

[3] On the fate of this translation, see Vol. IV, Letter 533, n. 6.

[4] 'He [Dupuit] says "nous verrions que l'utilité du morceau de pain peut croître pour le même individu depuis zéro jusqu'au chiffre de sa fortune entière' (1849, Dupuit, *De l'influence des Péages,* etc.,185)'. In the fourth edition of *T.P.E.* this reference is found on pp. xxviii – xxix.

mouvement et de l'équilibre des forces économiques: c'est Gossen. Je suis parvenu tout dernièrement, à force de recherches, à me mettre en rapport avec un neveu à lui, professeur de mathématiques à l'Université de Bonn, le Dr. Hermann Kortum,[5] qui m'a promis de me fournir des détails sur la vie de son oncle. Quand je le saurai, je tâcherai de reprendre pour mon compte et de mener à bien l'oeuvre que vous avez laissée de côté. Je publierai ma traduction de son livre, celle du vôtre (on n'a pas le droit d'abréger des livres de cette importance) et mes Quatre Mémoires, avec une Introduction de nature à bien mettre en relief le chemin parcouru par la science dans ces trois ouvrages.

Mais peut-être prendrai-je le temps d'achever auparavant la rédaction et la publication des deuxième et troisième parties de mon traité d'économie politique, c'est-à-dire des *Eléments d'économie politique appliquée* et des *Eléments d'économie sociale*, auxquelles je travaille toujours et qui avancent sensiblement.[6] En soumettant les questions d'application à notre méthode mathématique, ou en y montrant seulement les conclusions de l'économie politique pure, on les peut renouveler de fond en comble. J'ai traité ainsi la question des billets de banque, et je suis arrivé à des résultats singuliers et intéressants, imprévus par moi dans tous les cas. Avant de les faire figurer dans mon traité, je veux les voir discuter et les examiner un à un à nouveau. C'est pourquoi je les ai consignés dans un Mémoire que j'ai communiqué à la *Société Vaudoise des sciences naturelles* et dont je vous envoie un exemplaire en même temps que la présente.[7] Je serais particulièrement heureux d'avoir votre avis sur ce sujet.

Permettez-moi aussi, en terminant, de vous adresser une petite requête. J'ai donné à une personne de mes [amies] qui a une très belle collection d'autographes la première lettre que j'ai reçue de vous et qui était relative à la priorité de la courbe des besoins et de théorie de la satisfaction moyenne. Cette personne joint ordinairement à ses documents des remarques biographiques sur le personnage, dont ils émanent, et, à cet effet, elle m'a demandé de lui fournir une petite note indiquant les dates essentielles de votre carrière, les fonctions que vous avez remplies, les ouvrages que vous avez publiés. Je vous serais extrêmement reconnaissant de me fournir ces détails quand vous aurez un moment de loisir.[8]

Croyez-mois, Cher Monsieur, toujours tout à vous.

Léon Walras

[5] Karl Joseph Hermann Kortum (1836–1904), Professor of Mathematics at the University of Bonn.

[6] Walras's *Eléments d'économie politique appliquée* was published in 1898, and his *Eléments d'économie sociale* in 1896.

[7] Léon Walras, 'Théorie mathématique du billtet de banque', *Bulletin de la Société Vaudoise des Sciences Naturelles*, 2ᵉ série, 16 (1880) 553–92. A résumé had appeared in *Gazette de Lausanne*, 2–3 December 1879.

[8] There is no evidence that Jevons complied with this request.

P.S. Je ne vous demande pas de me pardonner la franchise un peu brutale avec laquelle je vous donne mon impression sur la Préface de la 2e édition de votre Theory. Cette impression a été très [decidée] et elle ne s'est point affaiblie depuis que j'ai achevé ma lecture. Il m'a été impossible de vous écrire sans vous l'exprimer. Au surplus, lisez Gossen et lisez-moi avec la même attention et le même soin que j'ai mis à vous lire, Gossen et vous, et rendez-moi la pareille si vous le jugez à propos. Vous autres Anglais vous êtes trop pressés. En fait de science, *time is not money.*

645.   W. S. JEVONS TO E. J. BROADFIELD
       [LJN, 410–11]

Athenaeum Club, Pall Mall,
6th April 1880

. . . I shall be much pleased if you can meet my brother in New York, and I am sure that he too will be much pleased. . . .

I congratulate you on the result of your labours in Manchester. I found evidence of your activity now and then in the *Guardian.* As for myself, I feel I can again be proud of the name of Englishman.[1]

I have just been at the declaration of the poll at the University of London.[2] Of course Lowe was very well received, but he made an unfortunate speech, if speech it could be called. He appeared to labour under difficulties the whole time, and was excessively nervous; indeed, he appeared to be breaking down once. I fear that age is telling upon him seriously, and I think he would do well to go to the House of Lords.[3] I hope the papers will not report what he said about the Government doing as much as possible in the first year or two, as they might soon disagree. Too true, no doubt, but not *a propos.* In fact, Lowe was about as happy in his probably final appearance at the University of London as I should be if I went on the stump. Sir John Lubbock, too, appears to like speechifying about as much as I do, and added nothing to the liveliness of the meeting.

We had quite an exciting time on Saturday at Hampstead, and 'Boy' was delighted with the brilliant display of flags in High Street, and the continual procession of cabs and omnibuses along the Finchley Road. We

[1] This letter was written just after the General Election of 1880, in which Gladstone and the Liberals scored a resounding victory: Jevons's sympathies lay with the Liberals. For a full account of the campaign and its outcome, see T. Lloyd, *The General Election of 1880* (1968).

[2] The result of the poll was: Robert Lowe, 1014 votes; Arthur Charles, Q.C., 535 votes.

[3] Lowe was in fact dropped from Gladstone's Cabinet and created Viscount Sherbrooke the following month, but his political career had effectively ended, owing particularly to his failing eyesight.

did our best, but failed.[4] It is said that the city people are too much interested in maintaining the *status quo,* and they live so much in the suburbs now as to make an altogether preponderating vote with the aristocrats and various other foolish people.

All well at home. Our little one, 'Winn,' would please you now, I think.

By the by, I should add that my brother is leaving New York for England towards the end of April or beginning of May, but I hope you will find him still there. . . .

646.   W. S. JEVONS TO L. WALRAS
        [FW] (postcard)

2 The Chestnuts.
11 April, 1880.

I thank you much for your letter of 31 March and for the memoir accompanying it. I shall have pleasure in returning an answer in a little time when I am free from some engagements on hand at present.

W. S. Jevons.

647.   TESTIMONIAL FOR F. Y. EDGEWORTH[1]

Hampstead
10 May 1880.

Having been informed by Mr. F. Y. Edgeworth that he is a candidate for the chair of Philosophy in King's College, London, I have pleasure in saying that I have recently become acquainted with his writings in ethical subjects, and I venture to express the opinion that these writings manifest a distinct and unquestionable genius for the profound investigation of such subjects.

W. Stanley Jevons
Professor of Political Economy in University College, London.

[4] Hampstead, which in 1880 still formed part of the constituency of the County of Middlesex, was held for the Conservatives by the sitting members, Lord George Hamilton and Q. E. Coope. The result of the poll was: Hamilton (C), 12,904; Coope (C), 12,328; Herbert Gladstone (L), 8,876.

[1] Francis Ysidro Edgeworth (1845-1926). After graduating from Oxford in 1869 he spent a period in London attempting to develop a practice at the Bar and became friendly with Jevons, near whom he lived in Hampstead. He became Lecturer in Logic and later Tooke Professor of Political Economy at King's College, London. In 1891 he became Drummond Professor of Political Economy at Oxford, which Chair he held until 1922. First editor of the *Economic Journal*, 1890-1926.

I have corrected an error in the above statement by erasing the word "moral".[2]

7 June 1880. W. S. Jevons.

648.   W. S. JEVONS TO HARRIET JEVONS

> W. Stanley Jevons,
> 2, The Chestnuts,
> West Heath,
> Hampstead, N.W.

5 June 80.

My dearest

I have been very busy to day writing an article for the Cont^y.[1] on the proposed postal notes. I think I can get it & other business done & even down to Buxton on Thursday evening see Morgan[2] on Friday & go on to Birkenhead same evening & bring you all home on Saturday. I want you back very much, I am not very well but up to more than I expected to day. A bit of writing stirs me up for the time. Last night I dined with Cornelius Walford; this evening I took tea with the Thornely's & discussed Norway with Miss T.[3] who seems in great spirits & wants to drive across the Fille Fyeld.

Glad to hear that Boy is so well. Please tell him that the pond at the top is run dry & little boys are running over it.

If there is any difficulty about a bed on Friday night I can sleep at a Hotel. My address on Thursday night will be Palace Hotel Buxton.

There is a nightingale singing in the trees at the back, at least it is what Tom called so at Epsom.

> Ever Yours
> W. S. Jevons

---

² Edgeworth was presumably an applicant for the Chair of Logic and Metaphysics at King's College, London, to which Alfred William Momerie was appointed in 1880. The Chair of Moral Philosophy had been filled in 1879 by the appointment of Joseph Bickersteth Mayor.

¹ For details of this article for the *Contemporary Review* see below, Letter 650, n. 1, p. 101.

² Presumably Dr Morgan. See Vol.IV, Letter 361, n. 2.

³ It is not clear which members of the Thornely family Jevons was referring to here (cf. Vol. I, p. 56, n.9) possibly the family of his cousin Laura Roscoe who had married James Thornely in 1852 See Vol. II, Letter 59, n. 3, p. 141.

649.   F. B. EDMONDS TO W. S. JEVONS

72 Portsdown Road,
W.
13 June '80.

Dear Jevons,

I have made good use of the Museum Library in the endeavours to establish my sun-spot hypothesis and had hoped long before this to have reported progress to you.

My success as yet however has been less complete than I had hoped for – nevertheless I believe I may claim to know more about the sun spot period than any one else does and should very much like to have a chat with you on the subject and get the benefit of your opinion.

I would endeavour to meet any arrangements you might feel disposed to make, and would come to your home – or elsewhere if you give me a rendezvous, morning, afternoon or evening as may suit you best. Without wishing to tie you down to an appointment I think it best to write so that there may be some prospect that my call may not be in vain, and that I may find you with an hour to spare.

Last year you had a little tracing from me that you were good enough to say you would keep in accordance with my request and before writing this I have prepared something of the same series but in a more substantial and complete form, so that you may rely on having something definite to deal with.

Of corroborative evidence I have plenty. Since we met Prof. Wolf has given 1878–9 for the last minimum – exactly my date as it happens – while Prof. Airy in his Reports to the Visitor; lately quoted; gives "about the beginning of 1879" As for the next max., you seemed to think 1882 the date assigned by me – early. Wolf however infers from his numbers that it may be so early as towards the end of next year. There is perhaps no real discrepancy here as 1881 and 1882 happen to be what I call "critical epochs" and a secondary cause in itself of minor importance may under the circumstances determine the max. one way or another. I am still inclined to take the later date of 1882. It does not seem to me that this date is incompatible with your views – "Black Friday" was in 1866 I think – some six years after a max.

I have the more reason for wishing to talk with you on the subject since *my hypothesis does not support* the view *that there was a max. not recognised by Wolf towards the end of the last century* as I had hoped it might – so as to give the 10.6 years mean period or thereabouts†

Hoping that all is well with yourself and family
I remain
Yours very truly
Fred. B. Edmonds.

†I confirm the period of 11 years or thereabouts or tend to that limit.

650.   W. S. JEVONS TO J. MILLS
       [TLJM, 341]

                                                           June 16, 1880
Dear Mills,

I now enclose proof of article,[1] together with proposed postscript & copy of clause.[2] Do you think it well to reprint the latter?

The speech of Fawcett[3] which is in the papers this morning makes the matter worse, and is quite absurd, having regard to the previous history of the measure. He may not intend this & that; but Ministers come & go, while the Department remains.[4]

If you detect anything which is in bad taste or incorrect, or weak, or libellous, and so forth, I shall much like to have it marked. I have a second copy of the proof.

I daresay I have somewhat overstated some points, but there is no good writing about anything unless you get a little warm over it—

                                                    Yours
                                               W. S. Jevons

651.   MARGARET A. MACMILLAN[1] TO W. S. JEVONS

                                               Upper Tooting, S.W.
                                               June 19th [1880][2]
Dear Mr. Jevons,

Two more chapters of Part II are finished, and I hope to be able to revise them and to finish the next (the last but one) before July 1st, when I

[1] This was evidently a proof of the article 'Postal Notes, Money Orders, and Bank Cheques', which appeared in the *Contemporary Review*, the following month: see the full reference in Vol. IV, Letter 502, n. 2.

[2] Government amendment proposing to restrict the currency of postal notes to one month; the clause was Clause 2 of the Post Office Money Order Act 1848 (11–12 Vict. c. 88). Apparently Mills approved its inclusion, for it appeared as a footnote in the article.

[3] *The Times*, 16 June 1880, reported a speech by Henry Fawcett 'at a soirée in Shoreditch Town Hall'. After the general election, in which he was returned as Liberal member for Hackney, Fawcett was made Postmaster-General. In the speech in question he defended the plan to introduce postal notes saying—'It was really a measure for facilitating the transmission of small sums of money, intended to meet a great want on the part of the poor, and not in the least a covert design to introduce a paper currency or to infringe the Bank Charter.'

[4] With 'Ministers' altered to 'Ministries', this phrase is repeated in the postscript to Jevons's article. Cf. *Methods*, p. 323.

[1] Margaret A. Macmillan, elder daughter of Alexander Macmillan by his first marriage to Caroline Brinley; she married Louis Dyer in 1889. In his Introduction to the English version of Cossa's *Guide to the Study of Political Economy*, Jevons described her as 'a former lady student in one of

will send them to you. Chapters II and III are in "slip", and I have finished revising them. I have been able to get some more information with regard to "res fungibiles", which I think makes its bearing on the question of interest quite plain. Perhaps if I copy out the explanation given in my barrister friend's letter, you may find a moment to glance over it and see if you think it will fit,

"The definition (i.e. Ducanjes) is quite accurate, but as it does not refer to the peculiar property of res fungibiles I should omit it as confusion and substitute for your note the following ("A res infugibilis is the subject of a contract or "obligation" which can only be discharged by the return of the thing itself. A res fungibilis is the subject of a contract or "obligation" which can be discharged by the delivery of a similar thing, and must in consequence be always ascertainable by measurement, etc. The commonest instances of res fungibiles were things which perished in use and indeed res fungibiles are generally confounded with things quae usu consumuntur. Austin, Jurisprudence, p. 807. Ed. IV. Mackeldy, § 369–374.")[3] As from their nature and the object of the obligation of which they were the subject they might be replaced by equal quantities and qualities they were called in barbarous Latin res fungibiles because mutua vice funguntur."

The note would be rather long, but I hardly think it could be explained clearly in fewer words.

I shall hardly expect to hear from you about this until your examining work is over, but I thought you might like to know of this new light on the subject.

Believe me,
Yours sincerely,
Margaret A. Macmillan.

---

the excellent classes of Political Economy, conducted under the superintendence of the Cambridge Society for the Extension of University Teaching'.

[2] This letter was written on notepaper embossed with the motto 'Miseris Succurere Disco' and the address 'Knapdale, Upper Tooting, S.W.', of which the first word has been stroked through with pen and ink. Knapdale was the home of Alexander Macmillan.

[3] Cf. Cossa, *Guide*, p. 102. The works cited are: John Austin, *Lectures on Jurisprudence*, fourth edition, 2 vols (1873) II, 807; Ferdinand Mackeldy, *Systema Iuris Romani Hodie Usitati . . . Nunc primum Latine interpretatus est Ernestus Eduardus Hindenberg* (Lipsiae, 1847) pp. 372–8.

652. F. B. EDMONDS TO W. S. JEVONS

72, Portsdown Road,
W.
22 June '80.

My dear Jevons,

I am much obliged to you for your note and I believe I could meet any arrangements you might find it convenient to make within the limit of time mentioned.

I can hardly discuss the spots with any one else and in case the Solar Physics Committee[1] should forestall me it would be some comfort to think you knew I had been well on the road.

Prof. Balfour Stewart evidently means to "do or die". Did you notice a paper of his read before the Lit. and Philos. Soc. of Manchester and given in "Nature" (April last Vol. 21, p. 541)? In this paper he recognises a *long and short inequality* in rainfall and magnetic force.[2]

It may be well for me to say that although my success—as yet at any rate—has not been what I had hoped for, nevertheless *my position is stronger than it was when we last met* and I have no recantation to make. I have purposely avoided directing your attention to the subject until I could get something of a tolerably conclusive character to show you.

As you know I consider it absurd that sun-spots should have no relation to commercial crises and yet be in relation with magnetic force, comparative rainfall etc. — I put magnetic force first because the relation is allowed by the highest authorities but believe that comparisons may cover the whole. It is a question of how and how much for you to deal with if so inclined and although it seems at first sight that my results do not favour your views, yet, the getting rid of the idea of a hard and fast period may lead to progress in the end. At any rate I have sufficient faith in my work to feel it a duty that I should make you acquainted with what seems to bear on yours.

I quite expected to hear that you were busy just now and with a Review article in addition to your Univ. work you must be heavily weighted.

Yours very truly,
Fred. B. Edmonds.

[1] A voluntary body set up in 1879 by the Committee of the Privy Council on Education in response to the pressure to establish an observatory devoted to astronomical physics, which developed as a result of the recommendations of the Devonshire Commission on Scientific Instruction (1871–5). The function of the six-man committee, whose members included J. N. Lockyer, Balfour Stewart and Richard Strachey, was to supervise experimentation with new methods of solar observation and process the results of sunspot research being carried out in northern India. The work which it supervised was carried on by Lockyer in an observatory in South Kensington, which did not receive recognition as the Solar Physics Observatory envisaged by the Devonshire Commission until some ten years later. See Meadows, op. cit., pp. 82–95, 106–17, 129–30; *Parl. Papers*, 1878–9, LVII, 721; 1880; xxv, 805; 1882, xxvII, 401, Cf. Vol. IV, Letter 560, n. 1.

[2] 'On the Long Period Inequality in Rainfall', *Nature*, 8 April 1880, pp. 541–3.

653.   J. D'AULNIS TO W. S. JEVONS

UTRECHT.

23 Juine, 1880.

Dear Sir!

Since long time I wished for the sake of instruction and pleasure, to visit London. Circumstances allow me this year after 10 July to accomplish what till now was a "pium votum". But the greatest pleasure, that I propose myself of paying a visit to England, is to meet with you, sir, with whom I had since 1874 so many scientific and cordial correspondence. Would I have the occasion, when coming in England 12 or 13 July, to find you at home? I remember that a few years ago you wrote me to have been travelling in the summertime in Norway. Perhaps the vacations of the University have commenced at medium July and, I fear, you will at that time have broken up your residence at Hampstead Heath. It would therefore be very pleasant to me when I may have the honour of receiving from you an information, which would disturb my apprehension, and which would give me the security, that I could make at London your personal acquaintance.

For making my plan of travelling I am also conscious to know whether the "Season" at London is opened during the last of July, and whether the theatres give then representations. Would you have the kindness of giving me some information about that matter?

What surprised me most, was to read accidentally in a German book of Prof. Von Mangoldt,[1] entitled Volks-wirth Schaftslehre, Stuttgart a° 1868, p 432, 433 & 146, the principal ideas of the mathematical theory of exchange, viz, a theory of utility, and the indication of the importance of last increments. Von Mangoldt did not make use of mathematical quotations. He was professor at Freiburg (Baden) and died 19 April, 1868, 44 years old. His reputation in Germany is of having had a very judicious but somewhat dry mind,—a thinker more than a poet.

Respectful and hoping for a favourable answer.

I have the honour of being

Dear Sir, your obedient servant,

J. d'Aulnis.

---

[1] Hans Karl Emil von Mangoldt (1824–68), employed in 1848 by the Minister of Foreign Affairs of Saxony to prepare a history of its industry; resigned in 1850 after a *coup d'état;* became editor of the *Weimar Gazette,* 1852, but again resigned for political reasons. His principal work, *Die Lehre von Unternehmergewinn* appeared in 1855; he also published *Grundriss der Volkswirtschaftslehre* (Stuttgart, 1863) and *Volkswirtschaftslehre* (Stuttgart, 1868). Extraordinary Professor of Political Economy at Göttingen, 1858; Professor of Political and Cameral Sciences at Freiburg, 1862.

In economic thought, von Mangoldt's principal contribution was the first systematic study of the 'earnings of management'.

654.   W. S. JEVONS TO J. N. KEYNES[1]

20 August 80.[2]

2, The Chestnuts,
West Heath,
Hampstead, N. W.

My dear Sir

I regret that your letter of 9th July should have remained so long unanswered. It must have come here just after I left for my trip in Norway where I received no letters at all.

I am pleased to know that we shall cooperate in the Scholarship Exam.[n][3] That Exam.[n] will I presume be held as usual some time in November, and unless it be more convenient to you there is no need to prepare the paper until some time in October.

There are always two papers, and the best way will be for you to ask what questions you like in one paper. Being only a Scholarship exam[n] the scope is not limited except by the bounds of Political Economy whatever they may be. The candidates must all be students of my class, & I can set them questions bearing on class work, but they are expected to read independently, so that it is well for you to ask questions at your own discretion.

I well remember the exam[n] in which I had the pleasure of reading your powerful answers.[4]

I send a few copies of previous exam[n] papers and remain

Yours very faithfully
W. S. Jevons.

J. N. Keynes, Esq. M.A.

655   W. S. JEVONS TO H. S. FOXWELL
[RDF; LJP, 414–15]

address for 2 weeks ⎧ Camden Lodge
                    ⎨ Norfolk R[d]
                    ⎩ Littlehampton

9 Sept 80.
My dear Foxwell

I certainly think Caldecott[1] should have the Fellowship & enclose a letter to you which expresses I think the feeling which all the examiners at

---

[1] John Neville Keynes (1852–1949), father of John Maynard Keynes; Senior Moralist, 1875; Fellow of Pembroke College, Cambridge, 1876; Lecturer in Moral Sciences in the University of Cambridge, 1884–1911; Secretary of the Local Examinations Syndicate, 1892–1910; Registrary of the University, 1910–25; author of *The Scope and Method of Political Economy* (1890). Cf. below, Letter 679, p. 133.

[2] The original manuscript of this letter is now in the Marshall Library, Cambridge.

[3] See below, Letter 659, n. 2, p. 109.

[4] See Vol. IV, Letter 453.

[1] Alfred Caldecott (1850–1936), Fellow of St John's College, Cambridge, 1880; Dean, 1889;

London had about his merits. As the London Univ^y Senate discountenance the giving of testimonials upon the ground of the exam^s, I suppose it would be better not to make such a test[1] public. But in your College elections I dare say you manage things without printing pamphlets full of test^ls, & you must use my letter at your discretion. I am glad to hear that he has progressed since the MA degree.

I am now near the end of my arduous 'Studies in Deductive Logic', having sent off the preface, & frontispiece. The printers have been very tedious over it but I hope the proofs will be done in a couple of weeks now. I shall be curious to know what you think of it.

I wish you would get on with your Adam Smith.[2] MacMillan as you have perhaps noticed is bringing out a trans. of Cossa's Guide to P.E. & I have been reading some of the proofs. Cossa remarks on the absence of any really good edition of A Smith or any real attempt to treat his life & works as a whole.

You are quite right in thinking that I hate exam^s, but I hate lecturing even more.

Believe me
Yours very faithfully
W. S. Jevons.

656.   W. S. JEVONS TO J. MILLS
       [LJN, 416–17; TLJM, 360]

Camden Lodge, Littlehamption,
21st September 1880.

. . . It was with much regret that I heard of our friend Dr. Hodgson's sudden death at Brussels.[1] He was so intimate a friend of yours that I feel sure you must have suffered from the loss. My acquaintance with and memory of him was disjointed and occasional, but began a long time ago,

---

Junior Proctor, 1891; University Extension Lecturer, 1880–82, 1886–7; Vicar of Horningsey, 1883–4; Principal of Codrington College, Barbados, 1884 6; Professor of Logic and Mental Philosophy, King's College, London, 1891–1917; Dean, K.C.L., 1913–17; Prebendary of St Paul's, 1915–35.

[2] According to Keynes, 'Foxwell's first project for a magnum opus was the preparation of a definitive edition of Adam Smith. In February 1880 Foxwell wrote to H. R. Beeton "There is no good edition of the *Wealth of Nations* that is one reason why I am going to write one. . . . Jevons is going to publish a selection from Adam Smith for students."

'In September 1880 Jevons was writing to him: "I wish you would get on with your Adam Smith". The work made no progress and eventually Edwin Cannan stepped into the gap' – obituary notice of H. S. Foxwell, *Economic Journal*, 46 (1936) 589–614.

[1] W. B. Hodgson had died suddenly on 24 August 1880 while attending the Educational Congress held that year in Brussels.

when he was head-master of the Liverpool Mechanics' School, and I was a little boy there about ten or twelve years old; but his teaching made a great impression upon me, and I have never forgotten it.

We have been spending three weeks in this quiet but in some respects very agreeable watering-place. There is a good sea-beach for the children, who are in terribly good health, and capital excursions to Arundel, Chichester, and other places of interest and beauty.

The state of trade now interests me very much. I believe we are on the eve of a great though, I hope, a gradual revival. The iron and consequently the coal trade must have a great expansion soon ... The coal trade is said to be very much depressed in Yorkshire and elsewhere; but between ourselves I believe that this is just the last of the ebb, and that a few months will see a different state of things *begin*. My only fear is of too violent an expansion, as in 1871—73, leading too soon to reaction.

Have you ever read Thomas Corbet's book, *An Inquiry into the Causes and Modes of the Wealth of Individuals; or the Principles of Trade and Speculation Explained* (London, 1841; Smith and Elder)?[2] Though badly written, it shows a greater insight into the conditions of safe speculation than any book I ever met with, though he was not aware of the decennial variation of trade. His advice, is, *buy before a rise* and *sell before a fall*. He also points out that a successful speculator must act contrary to the general opinion, as, if he buys that which people are generally buying, it will be already above the chance of safe profit. Sir I. Newton bought South Sea stock when it was nearly at the highest point!

I hope to set fairly to work on my *Principles of Economics* in a week or two, having just completed my laborious *Logical Exercises*. . . .

657.   W. S. JEVONS TO J. MILLS
    [LJN, 417; TLJM, 360—1]

Littlehampton, 23 September 1880

. . . My previous letter, which crossed yours of the 20th, will have told you that I sympathise with you in your loss of so old a friend as Dr. Hodgson. I regret that I had not more frequent opportunity of meeting him, but I remember with much pleasure my visit to his house when I went to Edinburgh for my LL.D. degree.[1] My impression is that Hodgson had great powers, and that his failing was in not making an adequate use

---

[2] The book was divided into two parts—I Trade: II Speculation. Corbet argued that trade is concerned entirely with the present, speculation with movements over time. I have not been able to discover any details of Corbet's biography [Editor].

[1] See Vol. IV, Letter 471.

of them. I know probably all his acknowledged writings, and they are all good, but sadly too few and limited.

. . . I am not a candidate for anything, except for a study where organ—grinders and other nuisances are inaudible. I wish Bell,[2] instead of making such wonderful discoveries as to the conveyance of sound, would turn his attention to the production of sound-proof houses . . .

658.   W. S. JEVONS TO J. MILLS
       [LJN, 417–18]

Hampstead Heath, 3ᵈ October 1880

. . . I return the extract made in Hodgson's hand. It is interesting as showing what he was thinking of, but I have no great opinion of Baden Powell's[1] understanding of any such subject.

Our removal from Littlehampton and work for examinations, etc., have prevented my answering your last letter sooner, and the reasons for a rise in coal and iron are too numerous to be easily stated in a letter. The considerable fall which has taken place since I bought a few weeks since is no doubt disagreeable, but they say it is always darkest before the dawn.

I should have liked you to hear our boy Herbert's singing. He has a sweet voice, and sings all kinds of little songs of his own composition, sometimes quite musical and in form, but hitherto we have not been able to get him to *learn* a note of the piano or of any regular song. He has even no idea yet of singing with the piano, yet I cannot help thinking he has considerable musical tendency; and the question is whether to leave him to educate himself at present. . . .

[2] Alexander Graham Bell (1847–1922), whose invention of the telephone (1872–6) was producing major effects at this date.
[1] It seems more likely that Jevons was referring here to [Sir] George Smyth Baden-Powell (1847–98) than to his father, Baden Powell (1796–1860), Savilian Professor of Geometry in the University of Oxford from 1872 to 1860. G. S. Baden-Powell, colonial administrator and politician who made a study of the economic aspects of colonisation, was M.P. for the Kirkdale division of Liverpool from 1885 until his death; F.S.S. 1879; K.C.M.G. 1888; author of *Protection and Bad Times with special reference to the Political Economy of English Colonisation*, 8 vols (1879) and *State Aid and State Interference*, 8 vols (1882).

659.   W. S. JEVONS TO J. N. KEYNES

2, The Chestnuts,
West Heath,
Hampstead, N. W.

22 Oct 1880[1]

My dear Sir

I now enclose the Joseph Hume papers[2] – I am sure all your questions are perfectly suitable & to the point, but as I must select out of the abundance you have given, I wd name those numbered 2 – 11 inclusive. I have given a question which may replace No 1 and I have also taken a hint from 12.

If you agree to this selection it will not be necessary to rewrite; the printers will no doubt return your paper & we can easily mark off those not to be printed.

My own paper actually refers somewhat but not exclusively to the subject treated in the class. Please say if you have any objections to the questions.

Could you kindly give me a precise reference to quotation from Mill in your No. 5?[3] I cannot find the passage at the moment. It is theoretically an important one.

Excuse delay in my writing but I have made so many exam[n] papers the last 2 weeks, about a dozen papers in all, that I am quite weary of the work, especially as I had only just finished my work in Deductive Logic which is exam[n] from beginning to end, question & answer.

The exam[n] you see is still a month off. There are only 3 candidates yet, so not much reading.

With thanks for setting so many excellent questions.
I am yours faithfully,
W. S. Jevons.

[1] The original manuscript of this letter is now in the Marshall Library, Cambridge.

[2] J. N. Keynes and Jevons were Examiners for the Joseph Hume Scholarship at University College London in November 1880. This Scholarship in Political Economy of £20 a year was tenable for three years. The paper comprised two parts, containing ten and nine questions respectively. See *University College, London, Calendar for the Session 1880–81*, pp. 154, 182–3.

[3] Jevons was probably referring to the question which became number four in the first part of the paper: 'Illustrate Mill's statement that "cases of extra profit analogous to rent are more frequent in the transactions of industry than is sometimes supposed" '. No reference to the quotation was supplied in the paper. It is in fact the opening sentence of section 4 of chapter v in book III of Mill's *Principles*, 'Of Rent, in its Relation to Value'. Jevons's failure to identify the quotation is curious since he had referred to this very section of Mill's *Principles* in the Preface to the second edition of the *Theory of Political Economy*, written in May 1879. Cf. *T.P.E.*, fourth edition, p. li.

660.   UNDATED FRAGMENT OF A LETTER FROM W. S. JEVONS
TO T. E. JEVONS
[LJP, 419]

[October 1880]

. . . for their visit,[1] though I am glad to remember that except in the case of Rex[2] there was not very much room for improvement.

I have been a good deal upset the last few days about the professorship. It is impossible to relinquish the employment of 18 years without some perturbation of spirits, & when I introduced my deputy to a well filled class room I had some pangs of regret. But I am nevertheless sure that the step was not only wise but indispensable. It is quite impossible for me to go on with trying fixed duties when I have so much literary work on my mind.

People in general are probably quite unaware that you cannot control or moderate work on a large book, because the contents are in your head & cannot be got rid of except by writing them out. Thus every obstruction to their delivery aggravates the burden.

However in the course of 2 or 3 years I hope to have ready a very novel & complete treatise on P.E. which will elucidate most of the ins & outs of trade & industry.

As my London Examinership terminates practically in 6 weeks time I hope to be vastly more free for the future.

I am glad you have seen Henny, & find her at any rate not much changed for the worse. Improvement is not to be looked for.

I fully intend to go about a good deal, & shall often go to the Crystal Palace for the Saturday afternoon concerts.

Saying farewell to you all with much regret in which Harriet equally joins

I am
Your affect. Brother
W. S. Jevons

[1] T. E. Jevons and his family had spent the summer of 1880 in Europe, their last visit before Jevons's death. Jevons and his brother had toured Norway during July and August. See LJ, pp. 412–14.

[2] Reginald Jevons (1872–1907), eldest son of T. E. Jevons.

661. H. RYLETT TO W. S. JEVONS

Moneyrea,
Comber, Co. Down. Oct. 28/80.

Dear Mr. Jevons,

Many times of late I have been on the point of writing to you, for I have a good deal to say of one sort or another, but the pressure of other duties has so borne upon me that I have had no time – & now I have not time enough to say all I shd like. Your exceeding kindness, however, in sending me your new book "Study in Deductive Logic" compels me to write at least to thank you very sincerely for your gift.

I have no doubt you are nauseated with the Irish question – but the English people will have to face the problem. The chief difficulty is that the English people are so densely ignorant on the subject and as the P.M. *Gazette* says cannot be got to listen. I get the *Scotsman* often – & occasionally the *Glasgow Herald;* now & then a Sheffd paper and a Manchester paper, but whatever paper I get the leading columns betray the crassest ignorance of the very elements of the Irish Question. I get the *Times* Weekly Edition, & the *X^{tn} World*[1] – and here too the same ignorance prevails. I get several weeks after date the P.M. *Budget,* & now, since the change of Editor, that is the only paper I see that talks sensibly on the matter.[2] Of course I see the B'fast morning paper "*Northern Whig*", and herein, as also in the *Scotsman* I see the utterances of public men on the same question & these all betray the same blank ignorance. What can be done? I was in Glasgow lately and went to see the Editor of the *Herald* I had a long conversation with him on the question. He thought he understood the matter, but I showed him that his understanding amounted to ignorance, and he closed at last by suggesting that I shd write as I had prop^{sed} certain letters to his paper on the question. I had a similar understanding with the Manchester *Examiner,* and so did not hurry on with the *Glasgow Herald* work. I wrote three letters each of 2 cols for the *Examiner*. Two have appeared but as to the third I have as yet no news.[3] So I think when I get into November a little way I shall start the

---

[1] The *Christian World,* established in 1859, was a liberal religious newspaper representing all shades of Evangelical opinion. It was published twice weekly by James Clark & Co. of Fleet Street and contained political as well as religious news.

[2] The *Pall Mall Budget* was a condensed edition of the *Pall Mall Gazette.* Frederick Francis Greenwood (1830–1909), founder of the *Pall Mall* in 1865 and its first editor, had resigned six months earlier due to political differences with the proprietor, George Smith of the publishing firm of Smith & Elder, and his radical Liberal son-in-law, Henry Yates Thompson, who took over the paper shortly after the General Election of April 1880, Rylett evidently found the more uncompromisingly pro-Gladstone editorial policy of Greenwood's successor, John Morley, more to his taste. Cf. J. W. Robertson Scott, *The Story of the Pall Mall Gazette* . . . (1950) pp. 236–42.

[3] Rylett's first two letters to the *Manchester Examiner and Times,* both on 'The Irish Land Question and signed 'An Irish Clergyman' were published on 21 and 30 September 1880 respectively. The first

work for the Glasgow *Herald*. But these papers I wrote for the Examiner only as it were opened the question. I begged for time & space but I presume the Examiner people do not think my ideas or contributions sufficiently valuable. The Broadfields wrote to me once or twice upon the subject – spoke rather highly of my first letter, and sent me a communication they had received upon the subject. I rather expect that the *Glasgow Herald* after this lapse of time will not give me space.[4] The difficulty is that I have no means of getting into any paper that will reach the people who need to be convinced. There is unquestionably enormous wrong being daily & hourly inflicted upon the Irish people by the landlords as a whole. Landlordism as you once said in a letter to me is an enormous *burden*. That is just it. Landlordism *is a burden,* and a burden too grievous to be borne. Hence those who bear it rebel. Their civilly uttered protests prove to be of no avail & they are forced to adopt coarser modes of expression. In England it seems to excite horror that people sh^d refuse to pay rent–or as some journals say "refuse to fulfil the conditions of their contract or bargain" – and being evicted shd then urge their neighbours not to take the vacant farm. And yet this is plainly reasonable & just. The rent in the first place is *not* a matter of contract in the sense in wh. it is so in England. Generations ago doubtless in regard to each particular farm, there was a contract, but in Ireland to day such a thing as freedom of contract is unknown. The truth is there is licence of contract on the part of the Landlord & no liberty at all on the part of the tenant. The tenant seeing that he cannot carry his *interest* in his farm with him, must remain whether the rent is increased little or much. True he may sell, but if he sells his interest the landlords for the most part choose the purchaser & raise the rent – whereupon the selling tenant gets so much less for his interest. Then this happens: the Landlord class as a rule get a return in the shape of increased rent, upon capital which they do not invest, which is not theirs but the tenants. The rent being increased now a days violates the first principle of tenant right inasmuch as it is based upon the increased value of the farm as a letting concern consequent upon the improvements in tillage buildings drains fences etc which the *tenant* has made, and has ceased to be a share of profit in the strict sense or a natural increase owing to the increased value of *land alone*. So every increase of rent is an appropriation of tenants' property. The practice of the Downshire Estate illustrates this. In every case of sale it is well known that

---

sought to explain the disadvantaged position of the Irish tenant farmer in comparison with his English counterpart and contained vivid illustrations of the abuses and hardships to which Irish tenants were subjected by corrupt landlords. The second letter consisted of a detailed examination of the provisions and efficacy of the Land Act of 1870 with regard to the relations between landlord and tenant. Rylett concluded by declaring his intention of continuing the discussion on a subsequent occasion, but no further letters were published.

[4] No letters from Rylett appear to have been published in the *Glasgow Herald*.

the rent will be "readjusted" i.e. an increase of 5/- or 10/- per acre will be demanded. Upon what save the capital invested by a tenant is such an increase based. There is therefore all over Ireland at this time a wicked – I can use no other term – violation of the law that every man is entitled to a just return upon his own invested capital & not to any return upon the capital invested by another. The landlords here are entitled to a fair return upon their invested capital – their originally invested capital, but not to a fraction of return upon capital invested by tenants according to immemorial custom. Or as you are fond of scriptural illustrations there is I may say throughout the country a violation of the law that whatsoever a man soweth that shall he also reap – in as much as the landlords without contributing as a rule anything to the improvement of the land keep rich & even get richer, while the tenants who do contribute to the improvement keep poor & even get poorer, and abandon their homes in despair, leave their native shores with curses in their hearts & maledictions on their lips. And yet there is throughout this country a fulfilment terribly real of this same law of sowing & reaping – England has sown thickly the seeds of injustice & is now appalled at the result.

Now, if a man refuses to pay rent on the ground that it is exorbitant and is evicted by reason of being in arrears I maintain that he is perfectly justified in dissuading his neighbours from taking his land, and more than that, seeing there is no freedom of contract at present existing I maintain that that is the only legitimate way of bringing the landlord to his senses. In the first place the evicted man has left behind him generally an amount of value far exceeding his arrears of a *reasonable* rent. In persuading his neighbours to refrain from taking his land is his only means whereby he can prevent the landlord from pocketing the excess of value over arrears. What we want in Ireland is something like this: a state of law which shall give the tenant a voice in the determination of the rent: at present all power is on the side of the landlord – a tenant needs to be armed with the power of putting his capital in his pocket, & walking off if he is not content with the rent. The peace and prosperity of Ireland are to be realised & that not slowly when England extends to this country what she herself enjoys viz freedom of Contract. Given this the law of supply & demand wd work freely and the Irish Question w^d cease to exist. Freedom of contract and the law of supply & demand would mean for Ireland Revolution, certainly, in the eyes of the Landlord class; but in the eyes of the People Regeneration w^d more accurately describe the result. Rents w^d go down to their natural level *for Ireland*, – for the natural level *for Ireland* differs from that which w^d be natural for England. In this way: the rent w^d not be determined alone by such a consideration as what w^d it be worth a man's while to pay? Could he pay so much, say £1 per acre & still make a good living & put money "past" him. Other considerations w^d

come in, such as, what will I give over & above say the £1, for the privilege of possessing land (this is the burning desire of your genuine Irish Tenant farmer) &, then, what will I give over & above, again, for the satisfaction of dwelling on the land my father lived on, & his father & so on back for several generations. The natural level of rent w^d be determined therefore not only by purely commercial principles but also by certain sentimental considerations. The Landlord w^d benefit by these considerations for a time, but only for a time. The long reign of injustice in the land has eaten the heart out of the people, & even here in the north I know hundreds of farmers with whom these sentimental considerations are already having less weight. Were they but free to depart they w^d be off to America tomorrow. Give freedom of contract & supply demand – constitute a fair *market* – enable a man to get his fair market-value for his interest in the soil, and you need have no fear of subdivision – which seems to be a sort of Irish bogey to the English people, and it is but a bogey, for the figures show that the tendency is strongly in the direction of farms of about 50–60–70 acres & upwards – the smaller ones are going gradually out of existence. Let a man get his fair market value for his farm & he will not *sub*divide; he will divide from his country & go to America. Of course they w^d not all go, but so many w^d go that the rents w^d come down still further – landlords w^d be willing to sell *their* interest and all over Ireland you would find the unusually thrifty & smart farmers putting money "*past*" them, as they say, *marrying* – having children, educating them properly, and living a far more decent life than they at present live, and as the crown of all you would see them purchasing the fee simple – & thus you w^d have a peasant proprietory gradually established, not *all over* Ireland, but widely spread enough to give stability to the country. Education w^d make headway – now it makes none worth talking about. Religion w^d take the place of a narrow dogmatic fanaticism & superstition.

How this freedom of contract is to be secured I confess it is exceedingly difficult to say. I fear the only way to do this great right is by doing what may seem to some to be a little wrong – But seeing that the Landlord clan have had it all their own way for so long it can scarcely be a very great wrong even if any that the tenants sh^d have things a little *their* way now. I have published in a paper for which I occasionally write (the *Inquirer*) [5]

---

[5] The *Inquirer*, a weekly religious newspaper founded in 1842, advocated a liberal viewpoint in both political and religious affairs. Rylett's contribution, which was unsigned and ran to two columns, was published in the issue of 2 October 1880, p. 643. Under the heading 'The Land Question in Ireland', he explained the lack of impact made by Liberal Christianity in Ireland in terms of the social condition of the country, particularly with regard to the effects of the landlord–tenant relationships. The main body of the article consisted of a brief reiteration of his analysis of the 'Irish Question' similar to that given in this letter, including the three points listed below.

something like what I think is necessary, but the idea is far from perfect:
you may be able to mend it.

1. If a Landlord wants to raise the rent, & the tenant objects to pay,
   let the landlord either buy the tenant out at the valuation implied
   by the increased rent or find another tenant ready to do so and
   willing to pay the increased rent.

2. If a tenant wants to lower the rent, & the landlord objects, let the
   tenant either find a tenant willing to pay the present rent &
   purchase his interest at the valuation implied by the amount of
   rent he himself w^d be willing to pay, or sell to the landlord at the
   same valuation.

3. Enable the Landlords to offer their interests for sale also i.e. free
   the land from primogeniture & entail.

It might be argued that this w^d be to put the shoe on the other foot & to
give license of contract to the tenant & not freedom of contract to both
landlord & tenant – but I do not think it w^d practically be so. The
landlord w^d always have *the land;* and that was all that was ever his: the
buildings, drainage, fertility etc are the tenant's, and the only way of
preventing these from being appropriated piecemeal by raisings of rent is
by some such plan as I have sketched.

But really I must pause, for no doubt your chronic Irish nausea is
returning by this time & you will be glad to see the last line of this letter. I
dont think I have written to you since the change of government. That
was a sort of clean sweep that did my heart good. The Salford job was well
done. I take some little credit to myself for the defeat of Charley & Walker
& the triumph of Arnold & Armitage.[6] I with one or two others got the
Party completely reorganised on the Brummagem basis when I was a
student of yours at Owens.

I see you are going to issue a students Wealth of Nations. How in the
world do you get through so much work? It is always a matter of
amazement to me that some men seem equal to any amount of work –
while I get through so very little, and sometimes dont write one sermon a
week & then seldom a good one.

I imagine that if the storm wh. is raging here at this time [Thursday
after.] & has been raging this two days, gets a touch at London there will
be mischief done to some old chimneys. It is what we call a Scutcher – a
term descriptive of a process in the preparation of flax. Most of the crop is
secure however – only here & there a farmer or two with potatoes still in
the ground.

---

[6] The General Election held the previous April had resulted in a Liberal victory in Salford. The
results of the poll were: B. Armitage (L), 11,116; Arthur Arnold (L), 11,110; Sir W. T. Charley (C),
8,400; Walker (C), 8,302.

By the way, I have got married again[7] I think since I last wrote to you
& that alone will perhaps be a sufficient excuse for my long silence. My
wife's fortune happily is in herself — she is an excellent wife, and is a great
comfort to me.

With all kind regards & renewed thanks for your exceeding kindness to
me.

Very sincerely yours

Harold Rylett

662.   W. S. JEVONS TO R. HARLEY[1]
      [LJN, 420–1]

Hampstead 15th November 1880

. . . Thanks for your suggestion about the possible infinite number of
exceptions.[2] You are obviously correct, and I will introduce your remarks
if we ever come to a second edition, which I fancy we shall do in a little
time.

I am very sorry to hear that M'Coll[3] is so ill. I fear his lot is not a
prosperous one. As regards my resignation, you will perhaps feel it
difficult to understand what a millstone upon my health and spirits the
work of lecturing has been. Sometimes I have enjoyed lecturing,
especially on logic, but for years past I have never entered the lecture-
room without a feeling probably like that of going to the pillory. Now that
I have been able to get rid of the burden I shall probably be much better.
I shall never lecture, speechify, or do anything of that sort again if I can
possibly help it. Apart from special reasons, too, I find that the pressure of
literary work leaves me no spare energy whatever. Besides the *Logical
Exercises* just finished, I have a large treatise in political economy in full
progress, a bibliography of logic in hand, the analysis of *Mill's Philosophy*
on my mind, a student's edition of the *Wealth of Nations* in preparation,
besides a new edition or two, and various minor articles and things of that
sort. It may seem impossible and absurd to attempt so much at a time

[7] Rylett, a widower, had married Louisa Boucher of Moneyrea in his own church on 6 June 1880.

[1] Robert Harley (1828–1910), Professor of Mathematics and Logic, Airedale College, 1864–8;
Minister of the Congregational Church, Brighouse, 1854–68; Leicester, 1868–72; Vice-Master of
Mill Hill School, 1872–81; Principal of Huddersfield College, 1882–5.

[2] Cf. Jevons, *The Principles of Science,* chapter XXIX, 'Exceptional Phenomena'.

[3] Hugh MacColl (1836–1909), logician and mathematician; began his studies in Glasgow;
Member of the London Mathematical Society; taught in Oxford and later at Boulogne-sur-Mer,
where he lived for over forty years, until his death. Author of numerous papers and *Algebraical
Exercises and Problems* . . . (1870); *Symbolic Logic and its Applications* (1906); *Men's Origin, Destiny and
Duty* (1909), as well as two novels, *Mr. Stranger's Sealed Packet* (1889) and *Ednor Whitlock* (1891).

with any advantage, but the fact is, it is difficult if not impossible to help it. You will easily see that under the circumstances it is much the most wise thing to throw up all interfering engagements as far as possible. Of course I suffer a loss of income, though less than might be supposed, as the professorship only yielded about £70 a year. This will perhaps, too, be made up to me in time, as my books occasionally pay some profit, though little compared with the labour they cost.

By the by, I had intended to introduce, with your permission [in the *Studies in Deductive Logic*], Stanhope's syllogistic table as a kind of logical puzzle, but it was eventually crowded out with other matter, which I am keeping either for a future new edition or for the bibliography. I intend the latter to form a kind of guide to the materials for a history of logic in recent times. . . .

663.　W. S. JEVONS TO H. S. FOXWELL
　　　[RDF; LJP, 421]

address　　Hampstead
30 Nov. 80.

My dear Foxwell

I ought to have answered your previous interesting letter, but unfortunately I have not yet overcome the pressure of exam^s & other matters & I find I cannot undertake anything like prompt & regular correspondence. My health has been so distinctly worse during the summer & autumn that I thought it best to take a decided step about the professorship. With the doctors' help and freedom from harassing engagements I hope soon to be more up to par, though I can never again be really strong as I was 10 or 12 years ago.

As regards your proposed application I am glad to hear of it, and my best wishes will be always with you. I should have asked you to become my deputy now, but that I thought it would complicate matters in event of your applying for the professorship.

As regards the appointment of a successor, I wish to have as little to do with it as possible. It is not unlikely that I may positively refuse to have any voice in the matter at all. In any case I think it best not to give any testimonials at all, & having already answered Mr Keynes to this effect, you will see that I must carry out the same principle in your case. I could easily name one or two others likely to apply but until they actually do so it might be better not to name them. As the election will not be for some 5 months hence it is too soon to speculate upon the list of applications, and I hope that in any case you will appreciate the difficult position I might get into if I made any promises on the subject. Nor would I wish you to suppose that I shall have any voice in the decision.

I am glad to hear you are getting on with the Adam Smith.[1] I have just got rather over head & ears in the History of P.E in the 18th century & hope to have an article soon ready which may interest you upon the Mr Cantillon who is quoted by Smith.[2]

Believe me

Yours very faithfully

W. S. Jevons.

664.   W. S. JEVONS TO T. E. JEVONS
        [LJN, 421–2]

Hampstead, 5th December 1880

. . . It is excessively kind of you to have rushed in at the right moment and bought me those interesting old notes, which are a most important addition to my collection. They must be an almost if not quite unique lot, and added to the previous American and other notes make such a collection as probably hardly any one else has. I was much pleased also to hear that you were comfortably and prosperously settled.

I have not been very happily engaged of late; my resignation of my long-accustomed work of lecturing being a thing which could not be effected without some regret and dejection of spirits. Moreover, I have come unwillingly to the conclusion that my health is really suffering. . . . I am now quite up to the writing point, and I have nearly completed the series of heavy examinations which oppress me at this time of year.

My *Deductive Logic* has been decidedly successful, I think, 572 copies having been sold in the first month, whereas only 800 or 900 copies of the *Elementary Lessons* were sold in the first two months, though at nearly half the price. The book has been rather favourably reviewed by the

---

[1] see above, Letter 655, n. 2, p. 106.

[2] This is the first reference to the research which resulted in the publication of Jevons's paper 'Richard Cantillon and the Nationality of Political Economy' in the *Contemporary Review*, 39 (1881) 61–80. This article, which revived interest in the work of Cantillon after a lapse of a century and led to the general recognition of his quality as an economist, was reprinted in *Principles*, pp. 155–83, and in the Royal Economic Society edition of *Essai sur la Nature du Commerce en Général*, edited with an English translation and other material by Henry Higgs (1931). Hereafter, it is referred to as Jevons, 'Richard Cantillon'.

The current state of knowledge on the life and work of Cantillon is set out in the edition of his *Essai* by A. Sauvy, published by the Institut National d'Études Démographiques, Paris, 1952. Cf. also J. J. Spengler, 'Richard Cantillon; First of the Moderns', *Journal of Political Economy*, 62 (1954) 281–95, and 406–24; reprinted in Spengler and Allen, *Essays in Economic Thought* (1960) pp. 105–40.

Athenaeum,[1] but I have not yet seen any other notice of importance. However, I find myself pretty well independent of Reviews.

Of late I have been completing an article for the *Contemporary* of January, on a curious point in the history of Political Economy. Now that I am fairly launched on a purely literary life, I hope I shall get into a method of steady but moderate work. I fancy that the excitement and pressure of lecturing and other engagements often did me great harm.

Our children are very well and happy. We had a fine run on the Heath this afternoon. . . .

665.   W. S. JEVONS TO H. S. FOXWELL
        [RDF; LJP, 422–3]

2, The Chestnuts,
Branch Hill,
Hampstead, N.W.

5 Dec 1880.

Dear Foxwell
    Would it be giving you too much trouble if I were to ask you to look into the Cambridge University Library & examine whether they have got the following books?
    Philip Cantillon – Analysis of Trade. London 1759   8°
    Essai sur la Nature du Commerce en General.
    Traduit de l'Anglois. London (Paris) 1755   12mo.
    (ascribed to Cantillon).
    I am writing an article on them for the *Contemporary,* which will I hope give you a high idea of their interest, & as Cantillon is one of the few quoted by A Smith,[1] the search will probably be well worth making with regard to your own literary work.
    I have copies of the books but so far do not know of any other copies in the country & if they are in Cambridge I should like to mention the fact.
    I hope you will be able to get on steadily with your Adam Smith.
                        Believe me
                    Yours very faithfully
                        W. S. Jevons.

P.S. If there are any other entries in the Catalogue connected with the name of Cantillon or Phillipe de Cantillon they might be of interest, but I have already searched out almost every available item referring to him.

---

[1] A two-column, unsigned review of *Deductive Logic* was published in the *Athenaeum* on 13 November 1880, p. 636.
[1] *Wealth of Nations,* book I, chapter viii.

666.   W. S. JEVONS TO H. S. FOXWELL
        [RDF] (postcard)

Hampstead.
12 Dec 80.

Best thanks for your kindness in asking after Cantillon's book. I am glad to know the result which is in time for the article. But I asked you to inquire under the mistaken idea that there was no copy in the British Museum.[1]

W. S. Jevons.

667.   R. GARNETT[1] TO W. S. JEVONS

British Museum.
Dec. 30, 1880.

My dear Sir,

I am greatly obliged to you for the present of the Contemporary Review containing your article,[2] which I have read with extreme interest. In rescuing an eminent name from oblivion you have pointed out a nest of errors in our catalogue, which must be throughly revised. I am not, however, quite convinced that our attributing the book to Philip instead of Richard Cantillon is one of them. Grimm's[3] testimony is a strong argument, but so is the ascription of the book to Philip in the English edition. Either Grimm or the English edition must have been misinformed, and it seems to me at present difficult to feel certain which of them it was. A search among the wills of members of the Cantillon family at Somerset House might throw some light upon the point, and I think it would be worth your while to make it.

I have been endeavouring to determine the original language of the Essay, and have noticed one circumstance which makes me think it was English. Near the bottom of page 422 the French text has "Les achats et ventes de capitaux si *venimeux*." This is a palpable error, unless *venimeux* bears a sense which I have been unable to find in the dictionaries. I suspect that the right word is "enormes". Now it seems less probable that the French word "enormes" should be misprinted "venimeux" than that

---

[1] Foxwell apparently reported that there was no copy in the Cambridge University Library. Cf. Jevons, 'Richard Cantillon', *Principles of Economics*, p. 157.

[1] Richard Garnett (1835–1906), Assistant in the Library of the British Museum, 1851; editor of the British Museum Catalogue, 1881–90; Keeper of Printed Books, 1890–9.

[2] See above, Letter 663, n. 2, p. 118.

[3] Friedrich Melchior Freiherr von Grimm (1723–1807), *Correspondence Littéraire, philosophique et critique de Grimm et de Diderot, depuis 1759 jusqu'en 1790*. In 'Richard Cantillon' Jevons quotes from the Paris edition of 1829, 1, 332–41: cf. *Principles of Economics*, p. 159.

"enormous" in an English MS should be misread "venomous" and translated accordingly.

I hope you will find opportunitity for another paper on Cantillon, especially with reference to his views on foreign commerce and on Banking, which seem to have an historical as well as economical interest.

Believe me, my dear Sir,

Yours very truly,

R. Garnett

668.   W. S. JEVONS TO R. GARNETT

31 Dec. 1880.

Dear Mr. Garnett,

Thanks for your remarks about Cantillon. The mistake you point out is a curious one and tends in the direction you indicate, but unless more like errors can be found it is rather a slight ground of argument.

I think I must look up the wills when next I pursue the subject, but these searches take up much time.

I should attribute little importance to the occurrence of 'Philip' on the title pages of the 1759 version, because it is altogether a base production. But I cannot imagine why the name Philip Cantillon or Phillippe de Can^n became current on the continent. There is a mystery in the matter that needs a good deal of resolving.[1]

I may be partial to the subject but it strikes me as a very pretty literary problem.

However I generally find that when a subject is stirred, light is thrown upon it after a time, and it is possible we may have some hints from the Continent.

With best thanks for your invaluable assistance in the matter,

I am

Yours faithfully,

W. S. Jevons.

[1] In his article 'Richard Cantillon' Jevons surmised that 'Richard and Philip were brothers, and carried on their merchant's and banker's business in close correspondence. But I do not know how to explain the fact that literary reputation became attached to the name Philip Cantillon.' Subsequent researches by Henry Higgs led to the now accepted view that Philip was probably a first cousin of Richard Cantillon. See Jevons, 'Richard Cantillon' and Henry Higgs, 'Life and Work of Richard Cantillon', pp. 339 and 377 respectively in *Essai sur la Nature du Commerce en Général* . . . (1931). Cf. also J. Hone, 'Richard Cantillon, Economist – Biographical Note', *Economic Journal*, 54 (1944) 96 – 100.

669.   R. GARNETT TO W. S. JEVONS

January 1, 1881

My dear Sir,

Since I wrote to you, Mr. Miller,[1] whom we consulted respecting the typography of the "Essai", has been looking into the English version, and has arrived at the conclusion, in which I agree with him, that no claim of authorship is therein made on behalf of Philip Cantillon. He appears simply as the arranger of, and extractor from, R. Cantillon's papers. If this is the case, your ascription of the authorship to the latter is undoubtedly correct.

Mr. A. Miller finds that the English word where the French text has "venimeux" is "prodigious", which might very well have been rendered by "enormes", though the misprint would be prodigiously enormous!

There is a long review of the English version in vol. 20 of the Monthly Review.[2] I have not your article by me, and do not remember whether you mentioned it.

I remain, my dear Sir,
Yours very sincerely,
R. Garnett

670.   W. S. JEVONS TO T. E. JEVONS
[LJN, 423]

Athenaeum Club, 8th January 1881

. . . Thanks for your letter recommending me to read the article of Dr. Brunton,[1] which I will do as soon as I have found the periodical. I believe it is in the London Library.

We are pretty straight now at home baby having quite recovered from a rather sharp attack, which made us uneasy for a day or two..

In the January number of the *Contemporary* you will find a rather long article of mine on a point in the history of Political Economy. I am now

---

[1] Arthur William Kaye Miller (1849–1914) superintended printing of the General Catalogue of Printed Books, British Museum, 1890; Assistant Keeper of Printed Books, 1896, and Keeper, 1912.

[2] A review by William Kenrick (1725?–79) of Philip Cantillon's *The Analysis of Trade* appeared in the *Monthly Review, or, Literary Journal* (First Series), 20 (1759) 309–15. Jevons made no reference to this review in his article.

[1] It has not proved possible to identify this article. It may have been one of the numerous publications of Sir Thomas Lauder Brunton (1844–1916), an eminent physician who wrote on social questions such as alcoholism and vivisection in which Jevons was interested, also on the relations of religion and science, notably *The Bible and Science* (1881).

hard at work on an article on 'Free Libraries' for the next *Contemporary*. [2]

About 800 copies of my *Studies in Deductive Logic* were sold to the end of the year, which is more than half the edition of 1500. About 260 of these went to America.

. . . I had a very pleasant run about the Heath with Herbert and Winn for about an hour this afternoon, and then came to dine here and go to the *Damnation of Faust*, which Hallé [3] is giving over and over again at St. James' Hall with much success. Dinner ready! . . .

671. M. A. HICKSON[1] TO W. S. JEVONS

January 18th, 1881.
3, Church Street,
Tralee.

Sir,
I have read with considerable interest your article on the Nationality of Political Economy in the Contemporary Review for this month. But you are altogether mistaken in the genealogy of your hero, if as tradition (and I believe correctly) asserts he Richard Cantillon was one of the three sons of Robert Cantillon a Kerry man born in 1700. This Robert is said to have had three sons. 1. Richard author of the Essai connected with the O'Briens Lords Clare and the De Bretueils in France v. 2nd vol. of Archdall's Lodges Peerage[2] ed. 1789 p. 33. 2. Philip a merchant in Paris. 3. Robert a merchant in Limerick who had a daughter married to the uncle of Daniel O'Connel M.P. (v. Burke's Landed Gentry.) So far tradition and I believe authentic tradition. Now as to the Cantillons of North Kerry or Clanmaurice from whom the above claim descent. The original name of the owners of Ballyhigue was not Cantillon at all but de Cantilupe — The first of them in Ireland was the son of Mabella sister of Raymond Le Gros and niece of Maurice FitzGerald. This Raymond de Cantilupe came with his uncle and granduncle to Ireland in 1172 all three companions in arms of Strongbow and he Raymond de Cantilupe had a grant of Ballyhigue from his uncle Raymond Le Gros, ancestor of Lord Lansdowne. The name is spelt indifferently in the Exchequer

---

[2] 'The Rationale of Free Public Libraries', *Contemporary Review*, 39 (1881) 385–402; reprinted in *Methods*, pp. 28–52.
[3] Hallé did much to encourage public recognition of the music of Berlioz in England. This was one of several occasions on which he brought his orchestra from Manchester to London to perform major works by Berlioz. See Vol. II, Letter 167, n. 4, p. 458, and below, Letter 678, n. 1, p. 131.
[1] Mary Agnes Hickson (1826–99), local historian of County Kerry. Author of *Ireland in the Seventeenth Century*, 2 vols (1884) and *Selections from Old Kerry Records, Historical and Genealogical* (1872).
[2] Mervyn Archdall and John Lodge, *The Peerage of Ireland*, 7 vols (1872) II, 33–4.

records relating to Kerry from 1172 to 1620 and in other documents of that time Cantil*upe*, Cantel*ou*, Caunt*elo*, C*o*ntlon, Cantlon, Cantyl*one* until late in the 17th century it settled into Cantillon the form it still retains. If your hero then was of the Ballyhigue stock as I have no doubt he was he was the direct descendant of the old English conquerors of Ireland in 1172 and the cousins of the FitzMaurices ancestors of the Earl of Kerry husband of Sir W. Petty's daughter — He had English, Welsh, Norman and a little Irish (native) blood and his nationality is best described as Anglo Irish.

I am Sir,
Yrs. truly,
Mary Agnes Hickson.

P.S. The mother of Mabella de Cantilupe was the daughter of Sir Adam de Kingsley of Cheshire. (v. Archdall; Lodge's Peerage, vol. 2. p. 182). The Carew MSS at Lambeth will also give you some information about the Cantillons formerly de Cantilupes of Clanmaurice in North Kerry.

672.   J. K. INGRAM[1] TO W. S. JEVONS

Cantillon[2]
Trinity College Library,
Dublin.
Janr. 21, 1881.

My dear Sir,

My friend Leslie gave me credit for more knowledge on the subject of Cantillon than I really possessed. I knew nothing of him but what I had seen in Lavergne's "Économistes Français".[3] After reading what he says of him, I searched the Catalogue of our Library in the hope of finding something more about him, but without success. By your thorough examination of the subject, you have now made it your own. I read your article, I need not say, with much interest. I will now return on it, and look more closely into it, since that is your wish; and if there be any special

---

[1] John Kells Ingram (1823–1907), Fellow of Trinity College, Dublin, 1846; Erasmus Smith's Professor of Oratory in the University of Dublin, 1852; Regius Professor of Greek, 1866; Librarian of the University, 1879, and afterwards Vice-Provost. An exponent of Auguste Comte's philosophy of Positivism, Ingram was known in Economics as a supporter of the historical method, as expounded in his Presidential Address to Section F of the British Association, 1878, 'The Present Position and Prospects of Political Economy' (see Vol. IV, Letter 539).

[2] Written on the top right-hand corner of the original letter, apparently in the handwriting of W.S. Jevons.

[3] Louis Gabriel Léonce de Lavergne (1809–80), *Les Economistes Français du XVIIe siècle* (1870).

point, which my position here might enable me to discover or verify for you, I shall be happy to try.

I must not close this letter without acknowledging the very kind mention[4] of my British Association Address in the new edition of your work on Political Economy. I can honestly say that there is no one from whom such a favourable judgment could give me greater pleasure.

Believe me,
Yours very truly,
John Kells Ingram.

W. Stanley Jevons, Esq.,

673.   M. A. HICKSON TO W. S. JEVONS

Sir

I am very glad that any information I have been able to give you about the Cantillons has been of use or interest. The mistake you made as to their origin was most excusable in fact inevitable for any one who had not studied the genealogies of our remote little county a subject in which you could take little interest. The name sounds Spanish and there was much intercourse between certain districts in this country and Spain in old times but Ballyheigue was not one of them. The Kerry tradition always has been that the family were originally De Cantilupes but I did not half believe it until within the last four or five years when I searched the State Papers for proofs and obtained ample proofs that the tradition was true. I enclose some notes giving extracts from the Exchequer Records and Patent Rolls.[1] I would observe however that I do not at all know whether the author of the "Essai" was of the Kerry stock. I never heard of the work until I read your interesting paper but I am sure that the Richard Cantillon who was burnt according to Archdall Lodges Peerage Vol. 2 p. 34 edition 1789 in his house in London and whose wife was the grand-daughter of O'Brien Lord Clare, was a Kerry man and the cousin of the FitzMaurice decendants of Sir W. Petty and well acquainted with him and them. The Kerry tradition is that both Richard and Philip Cantillon lived in Paris but this is likely to be a mistake. The MSS of Sir George Carew, Earl of Totnes in the Lambeth Library contains some information about the Cantillons and FitzMaurices and Mr. Sweetman's

---

[4] 'The question [of economic method] has been further stirred up by the admirable criticism to which it was subjected in the masterly address of Professor J. K. Ingram, at the last meeting of the British Association'. – *T.P.E.*, Preface to the second edition, pp. xiv – xv. Cf. reference in n. 1 above.

[1] These notes are not now among the Jevons Papers.

Catalogue of the Irish State Papers between 1172–1400[2] ought to contain more.

> I am Sir in haste
> Yours very truly,
> Mary Agnes Hickson.

January 25th 1881.
3 Church Street,
TRALEE.

P.S. I send you also an unbound copy of a small contribution[3] of mine to Kerry history printed for private circulation a few years ago and shall be glad if you think it worth your acceptance. At pages 34, 37, 43, 50 and 244, 296 you will find notices of the Cantilupes or Cantillons. When these were written however I had not yet verified or found verifications of the tradition as to the original name and merely noticed the tradition

673A.   W. S. JEVONS TO J. K. INGRAM

> 2, The Chestnuts,
> Branch Hill,
> Hampstead, N.W.

30 Jan 1881.[1]
My dear Sir

Accept my best thanks for your answer of 21st Inst. I have in the last few days received such full particulars about the Cantillon family in earlier times that it would be quite needless for you to trouble yourself further about that matter.

There still remains much mystery about the Continental life of Richard & Philip Cantillon, and the production of the 'Essai', but I should not think of troubling you further.

> Believe me
> Yours faithfully
> W.S. Jevons.

J.K. Ingram Esqe LLD.

[2] *Calendar of Documents relating to Ireland preserved in Her Majesty's Public Record Office, London, 1171–1301*, edited by H. S. Sweetman, 4 vols (1875–81). The reference to '1400' appears to be an error, since the fifth volume of the *Calendar*, covering the years 1302–7, was not published until 1886.

[3] *Selections from Old Kerry Records, Historical and Genealogical, with Introductory Memoir, Notes and Appendix* (1872).

[1] Reply to Letter 672, above, p. 124. The original manuscript of this letter is now among the Ingram Papers in the Public Record Office of Northern Ireland.

674. M. A. HICKSON TO W. S. JEVONS

January 31st 1881.
3 Church Street,
Tralee.

Dear Sir,

We ought to be very grateful to you for your kind wish to com-
memorate illustrious or great Irishmen but it is only fair to your own
country, for I suppose you are an Englishman, to observe that Berkely,[1]
Hutcheson[2] and Cantillon, had as much English blood as Irish in their
veins. Indeed down to 1620 and even later about twentyfive years before
the Cantelupes or Cantillons forfeited Ballyheigue that family was in the
eyes of the law not Irish at all, but English, although it had been settled
here for nearly five hundred years. The Cantillons could hardly have held
Ballyheigue in Elizabeth's reign or earlier if they had been what the law
termed "mere Irish", it was as natives of Ireland of English descent and
name that they held their ground until 1649 when as *Roman Catholics* they
had to leave Ireland. The strife of that year was a religious not a racial
one. The inhabitants of Ireland at the present day are all of the same
mixed race but the religious difference remains and separates them much
and it endeavours to revive the old racial strife for its own purposes.

We really are in race all west Britons *whatever our agitators pretend to the
contrary* and I hope that while generously doing justice to Richard
Cantillon's talents you will not fail to lend the aid of your valuable pen to
crush this *pretence* and to make it known that he was a man of the mixed
race with as much English as Irish blood in his veins.

I am Sir,
Yours truly,
Mary Agnes Hickson.

P.S. A friend tells me that in Eyton's[3] Antiquities of Shropshire there are
notes on the barons of Cantilupe which may help to elucidate the lineage.
Giraldus[4] does not give the name I believe in his list of the conquerors of
Ireland but this was because they did not play a foremost part but

---

[1] So mis-spelt by Mary Agnes Hickson. George Berkeley (1685–1753), philosopher, Dean of
Derry, 1724; Bishop of Cloyne, 1734; author of *The Querist* (1735), from which his reputation as an
economic thinker mainly derives.

[2] Francis Hutcheson (1694–1746), born in County Tyrone, the teacher of Adam Smith, and his
predecessor in the Chair of Moral Philosophy at Glasgow; author of *An Inquiry into the Original of our
Ideas of Beauty and Virtue* (1725) and *A System of Moral Philosophy*, posthumously published in 1755.

[3] R. W. Eyton, *Antiquities of Shropshire*, 12 vols (1854–60).

[4] Giraldus Cambrensis (c.1146–c.1223), Norman-Welsh ecclesiastic and author, whose *Topog-
raphia Hibernica* (c. 1188) and *Expugnatio Hibernica* (c. 1189), compiled as a result of a visit to Ireland in
the service of Henry II in 1185, comprise one of the most important sources of Irish history during the
early Norman period.

followed Raymond Le Gros. It is to the Exchequer Records we must look for the names of those who settled on his Kerry lands his followers and relatives all of course could not be given in Giraldus' list.

675.   J. K. INGRAM TO W. S. JEVONS

Trinity College Library,
DUBLIN.
Febr. 7, 1881.[1]

My dear Sir,

Within the last halfhour a young man named Leopold Albert Cantillon[2] has come to my room to announce his intention of attending my lectures during the coming term. He has told me (on my inquiry about it) that he is of French descent, and that his eldest brother's name is Richard Talbot. He lives in the County of Cork. He has promised to ascertain the particulars of his descent and to give them to me.

I find that we have in this Library a book by "John Nickolls, Jun."[3] It is entitled "Original Letters and papers of State addressed to Oliver Cromwell, concerning the affairs of Great Britain from the year 1649–58, found among the political collections of Mr. John Milton." The date is 1743, London. In our Catalogue the "Remarques sur les avantages . . . etc."[4] is given as a translation from the English of *the same* John Nickolls; but that may, of course, be a mistake.

Believe me,
Yours very truly,
John K. Ingram.

W. S. Jevons, Esq.

[1] No further reply by Jevons to this letter is now among the Ingram Papers.

[2] Leopold Albert Cantillon was in this second year at Trinity College Dublin at this time. He appears to have left in 1881 without taking a degree. (*Trinity College, Dublin, Calendars, 1880, 1881.*)

[3] John Nickolls (1710–45), antiquary, collector of prints, books and letters. Nickolls came into possession of a number of letters once owned by John Milton, which formed the basis of the work referred to by Ingram: these were subsequently returned to Milton's former secretary, Thomas Ellwood.

[4] *Remarques sur les avantages et les désavantages de la France et de la Grande Bretagne, par rapport au commerce et aux autres sources de la puissance des états.* Traduction de l'anglois du Chevalier John Nickolls. (Leiden and Paris, 1754). The translation was a pretended one, and the entry in the T.C.D. catalogue therefore was a mistake: the work is now attributed to Plumard de Dangeul. Cf. *Catalogue of the Kress Library of Business and Economics through 1776, Supplement,* S. 2053.

675A. W. S. JEVONS TO H. S. FOXWELL
[RDF] (postcard)

> 2, The Chestnuts,
> West Heath,
> Hampstead, N.W.
> 10 Feb. 81.

Thanks for note. I have got Condorcet's Vie de Turgot from London Lib (1786) & find the mathematical note at pp. 162–169 vol. 1. It is very difficult to follow & I cannot do so as yet. The mark $\int$ is equivalent to Σ as used by later math[s] that is mere summation of a finite number of terms.[1] I shall of course insert in Bibl' when I have an opportunity of reprinting.[2] The 'Vie' seems well worth reading. I am finding out a good deal more about Cantillon, & a real living C[n] has turned up.

> W. S. J.

676. W. S. JEVONS TO R. H. INGLIS PALGRAVE

> 2, The Chestnuts,
> Branch Hill,
> Hampstead, N.W.
> 20 Feb. 81.

My dear Palgrave,

I enclose a couple of letters which I should be glad if you will look over when you have leisure, if indeed that ever comes.

This Mr. Pownall was a student of mine a good many years ago[1] and he has since proved himself useful in Manchester and become Hon. Sec. of the Stat. Soc. there. All the statements in his letters are I believe accurately true and dependable and I believe he could make a valuable inquiry of it if assisted. Perhaps when you have time you would kindly say

(1) Whether you approve the inquiry generally
(2) Whether you would be prepared to assist him by a few words in the *Econ.* or Bankers' Mag. or by printing the circular at length in the Mag.

---

[1] For an account of Condorcet's analysis, which concerned the replacement of indirect by direct taxation, see R. D. Theocharis, *Early Developments in Mathematical Economics* (1961) pp. 70–1. Theocharis describes the use of the sign $\int$ as a sign of summation of finite quantities as 'the only innovation' in Condorcet's mathematics.

[2] The reference was inserted by Mrs Jevons in the third edition of *T.P.E.*, p. 278.

[1] G. H. Pownall is recorded as having received the Cobden Club Prize in the Senior Evening Class in Political Economy for the Session 1875–6. During that period he was employed by the Union Bank of Manchester Ltd. Cf. above, Letter 584, n. 1, p. 25. See *Calendar of Owens College for 1876–7*, p. 123.

(3)   Whether you think it might be better to apply to the Bankers' Institute of which Pownall is an associate.

I am so deeply engaged in my large pol. econ. and other writing that there is no chance of my undertaking such a work, yet it ought certainly to be done.[2]

Best thanks for the books which you sent which are an acceptable lot. The Bankers' Almanack[3] is as usual excellent. I only note that the table of foreign monies is antiquated, the Norwegian and Danish money having been completely altered some 5 years ago.

Hoping you are all well,

I am,

Yours faithfully,

W. S. Jevons.

Wilkinson[4] has a good opinion of Pownall I believe and gave him a position in his Ann St. Bank.

677.   W. S. JEVONS TO R. GARNETT

21 Feb. 1881.

Dear Mr. Garnett,

Thanks for your note with extract from the Pall Mall Gazette sent some weeks since.

I have been to the Probate Court Registry this morning and have found the will of Philip Cantillon. It was not proved until 1772; he left London to live in Ghent where he died. I found Richard Cantillon's will a week or two ago. It occurs three times over in the registry not being finally proved until 1761, but neither Philip nor Richard mention each other. There are also wills of R. Cantillon's daughter the Countess of Stafford and of Bernard Cantillon(?) but I have not seen them yet. I have now an

---

[2] The enquiry to which Jevons refers, to which both he and Palgrave lent their support, resulted in the publication of one of Pownall's best-known early papers, 'The Proportional Use of Credit Documents and Metallic Money in English Banks', *Journal of the Institute of Bankers*, 2 (1881) 629–64.

Pownall had mentioned an investigation of this kind in a letter to Jevons in March 1879 (see above, Letter 584, p. 25) and was in fact carrying out research similar to that planned by Jevons in 1876 (see Vol. IV, Letters 461 and 464). In his circular, dated 26 March 1881 and published in *The Economist*, the *Bankers' Magazine* and the *Journal of the Institute of Bankers*, Pownall states that Jevons had originally suggested the line of enquiry which he was proposing to follow, namely to estimate the total banking transactions in the country. The circular was followed in each case by examples of two forms he proposed to be completed by bankers, designed to show aggregate receipts, form of receipts and the mode of disposal of cheques and bills.

[3] *The Banking Almanac and Directory* (1881). Edited by R. H. Inglis Palgrave.

[4] Thomas Read Wilkinson (1826–1903), who had succeeded William Langton as managing director of the Manchester and Salford Bank in 1876; entered the bank as a junior clerk, 1841; chief cashier, 1854; sub-manager, 1861; general manager, 1873; F.S.S. 1875; President of the Manchester Statistical Society, 1875–7.

order to search free of expense, but there is so much red tape at Somerset House that it is a difficult thing to get much done.

A certain Mrs. Mary Anne Hickson of Tralee has sent me abundant information about the earlier history of the family which it seems was really that of the *de Cantilupes* a Norman name.

I have a great deal of reading to do at the Museum presently.

Mr. G. L. Gomme,[1] Hon. Secretary of the Folk Lore Society &c tells me he often visits the Library but does not know you. He is a very able man and few would make better use of your advice.

I am, Yours faithfully,
W. S. Jevons.

678.   W. S. JEVONS TO T. E. JEVONS
       [LJN, 424–5]

Athenaeum Club, 17th March 1881

. . . I was much pleased to get your recent letter, and learn that you were so cheerfully and pleasantly employed.

It was a mistake not to tell you that I had heard Berlioz's *Damnation de Faust.*[1] It not simply pleased me, but surprised and excited me more than any music I had previously heard. It was a complete revelation of new musical power. The Sylph's ballad I had previously heard at the Crystal Palace, and I considered it to be, especially in the few last notes, almost magical. The Amatory duet is the most intensely-feeling piece of vocal music I know. Lately Hallé brought out the *Childhood of Christ* at St. James Hall, and I took Harriet to hear it. Though not nearly so striking as *Faust,* it has passages of great beauty, and the 'Adieu des Bergers' is permanently running in my head.

Two nights ago I went to a concert of Lamoureux,[2] the late conductor of the Grand Opera, Paris. We had three hours of almost entirely new music, some of it fine and delightful. A duet of Berlioz, a nocturn,* struck me as exquisite and original in a high degree; the orchestra keeping up a

---

[1] [Sir] George Laurence Gomme (1853–1916), editor of the *Antiquary,* founder and sometime secretary of the Folklore Society; Statistical Officer and afterwards Clerk to the London County Council. Gomme and Jevons shared an interest in the antiquities of the Hampstead area.

[1] Cf. above, Letter 670, p. 123. The implication of this sentence seems to be that Jevons had written another letter, which has not survived, to his brother between 8 January and 17 March and that this did not contain the comments which Tom Jevons expected on Hallé's performance of the *Damnation of Faust.*

[2] Charles Lamoureux (1834–99), French violinist and conductor: established Nouveaux concerts (later called 'Concerts Lamoureux') at Paris, 1881, and did much to popularise the music of Wagner in France. In 1881 Lamoureux presented concerts at St James's Hall, London, on 15 and 22 March.

low humming and chirping to represent the sound in the woods at night, in apparent independence of the melody.[3] A man who could strike out such original ideas must have been a great musical and poetical genius; but his history was a sad one on the whole. I am thinking of getting some of his books to read[4] . . .

We are in a state of prolonged crisis in England and Europe at present. To-day it is reported that an attempt was made to blow up the Mansion House last night,[5] and the nerves of the old gentlemen of the Athenaeum seem to be slightly shaken by the news. I am busily engaged in various inquiries. This morning I went to Somerset House and finished my search for the wills of the Cantillon family. I have found those of both Richard and Philip. I have an article on hand about 'Museums' for the *Contemporary*,[6] and am thinking of printing a volume of collected essays before the end of the year.[7] I have also engaged to write a book on *Trades Unions* for a series of Macmillan's.[8]

Harriet and I recently took a week's tour to Brighton, Lewes, Canterbury, and Tunbridge Wells. I think Harriet enjoyed it much, especially Canterbury; but the weather was very unfortunate, and I was not very well. While we were away, John and Lucy came to Hampstead and took care of the children. They like the opportunity of seeing them by themselves, I think, and 'Boy' and Winn took to them greatly. The children are getting on very well, and 'Boy' is much engaged in making boxes . . .

[3] The programme of the concert given on 15 March included three works by Berlioz: Jevons appears to have been describing the Duo from *Béatrice et Bénédict*.

[4] Louis Hector Berlioz (1803–69), suffered ill-health, bereavement and lack of success with his music. He was author of many works on his own and others' music, as well as his *Mémoires*, published posthumously in 1870. See J. H. Elliott, *Berlioz* (1967).

[5] A bomb consisting of a box containing about forty pounds of gunpowder was discovered in a recess in the wall of the Mansion House shortly before it exploded on the night of 16–17 March 1881. The incident, which received wide coverage in *The Times* on 18 March and subsequent days, was thought likely to have been connected with the situation in Ireland and agitation concerning the Coercion Bill.

[6] 'The Use and Abuse of Museums', *Methods*, pp. 53–81. According to Mrs Jevons, in the Preface to *Methods*, this essay 'was chiefly written in 1881, for the *Contemporary Review*, but was laid aside from the pressure of other work', and consequently not published before Jevons's death.

[7] Jevons had planned both the collections of papers which subsequently appeared as *Investigations* and *Methods*, before his death, but *Investigations* appears to have been the first to be undertaken. See LJ, p. 424.

[8] *The State in Relation to Labour*, English Citizen Series (1882). Cf. below, Letter 685, p. 137.

679.   W. S. JEVONS TO J. N. KEYNES

2, The Chestnuts,
West Heath,
Hampstead, N.W.

25 March 1881.[1]

Dear Mr. Keynes

I quite understand your withdrawal from the U.C.L. professorship competition. I noticed that you have been appointed to a Secretaryship in connection with the Extension Syndicate,[2] & I should doubt whether with pressing work in Cambridge it w^d be worth your while to travel twice a week to London. At any rate it is a matter for your own inclinations to decide. As to your claims compared with those of Foxwell or other Candidates, it is of course needless for me to attempt to form any estimate now.

                    I am
                Yours faithfully
                W. S. Jevons.

680.   W. S. JEVONS TO A. MACMILLAN
       [MA]

2 The Chestnuts,
Branch Hill,
Hampstead, N.W.
5th April, 1881.

My dear Macmillan,

On turning over this evening the adver. sheets in your magazine I was surprised to see "The Theory of Political Economy" with Mr. Sidgwicks name to it. At first I thought there must have been some typographical mistake but it would really seem as if Mr. Sidgwick proposed to bring out a book with the exact title of mine.

Surely this is very undesirable and will give rise to mistakes and misapprehensions. It would be absurd of me to propose to write a book called "The Methods of Ethics" and a similar objection may be taken to his choice of the words of my title. There would not be a similar objection to Philosophy of P.E. or Theory of Economics or anything which is not

---

[1] The original manuscript of this letter is now in the Marshall Library, Cambridge.

[2] During 1881–2, J. N. Keynes acted as Assistant Secretary to G. F. Browne, Secretary of the Cambridge University Local Examinations Syndicate, 1870–92. After Browne's resignation in 1891, the Syndicate decided to appoint two secretaries of equal standing, to be responsible respectively for 'lectures' and 'examinations': Keynes was appointed to the latter post in March 1891.

identical. No doubt if you just mention the matter to Mr. S. he will at once modify the title but I write rather in haste for fear of the printer getting forward with the work.[1]

Believe me,

Yours faithfully,

W. S. Jevons.

681.   W. S. JEVONS TO T. E. JEVONS
[LJN, 425–6]

Hampstead, 18th April 1881

. . . I was much pleased to get your letter a few days ago, and to learn that all was well with you. We are getting on fairly well . . . I am myself, indeed, far from being so well as I could wish, but I propose to take life very quietly for the future, and with care in diet hope to improve. I have just written this morning the first few pages of the finished draft of my treatise on *Economics*,[1] but the main part of the book is hardly more than sketched out, and I hardly like to think of the years of work it must yet take before being completed.

On Saturday I am going to take Harriet to hear Berlioz's *Faust* – her first visit. I shall be curious to know whether it strikes me as much as at first. About a week ago we went to hear his *Romeo and Juliet,* and there was much beauty in it, as well as in the rest of the very long concert. But neither *Romeo* nor the *Childhood of Christ* have the startling power of *Faust.* I hope to hear a good deal of Wagner this spring under Richter's[2] conducting . . .

Many bubbles are now being put forth in England, and they will probably increase very much in the next few months, but I do not think there is any ground for a crisis just yet. It will take a year or two for the investment in their companies to tell upon the abundant free capital of the country.[3]

We have now apparently got safely through the Fenian plots and other

---

[1] Sidgwick's work appeared in 1883 with the title *Principles of Political Economy.*

[1] In view of Jevons's statement in his letter to T. E. Jevons of 30 March 1882 – 'I am now going to make a new start with the large book on *Political Economy*' (see below, Letter 723, p. 180) – it is not certain that this 'finished draft' was the same as the opening pages of *Principles of Economics* (1903).

[2] Hans Richter (1843–1915), conductor successively at theatres in Munich, Budapest and Vienna, became known to English audiences during the Wagner concerts of 1877, when he shared the duties of conducting with Wagner himself (see Vol. IV, Letter 488, n. 3). His London concerts continued successfully until 1897, when he moved to Manchester to become director of the Hallé orchestra.

[3] It is interesting to note that this passage implies a 'capital shortage' theory of the crisis rather than a 'sun-spot' theory.

difficulties, and I hope that Gladstone has succeeded in steering into smoother waters. His spirit in making peace with the Boers was wonderful.[4] . . .

682.   W. S. JEVONS TO A. MACMILLAN
       [MA]

2, The Chestnuts,
Branch Hill,
Hampstead, N.W.
1 May 1881.

Dear Mr. Macmillan,

I have now got on sufficiently with my large treatise on Economics to be thinking of the form it will take. It will naturally take some years to complete but it might be possible to begin printing before the end of this year. Before that time we shall I hope have opportunities of discussing the matter fully but in the meantime I should be much obliged if you would have a specimen page set up. My ideas are described in the enclosed paper.

As regards the printer I have a pleasing recollection of the way in which Maclehose[1] at Glasgow knocked off my Political Economy primer, and it was altogether well done. If you see no objection I should like to contemplate putting this book into Maclehose's hands, and therefore I suppose you will ask him for specimens.

The book will in any case be a long one, two vols. of 500 pages each or more. Possibly the first vol. might be published separately when ready. Certainly I should like to go on with the printing without waiting for the completion of the M.S.[2]

As it is in all probability the largest work I shall ever write I am rather anxious about its 'get up'.

Does the sale of "Studies in Deductive Logic" progress satisfactorily?

---

[4] Gladstone's second cabinet, formed in April 1880, faced two dominating problems: Ireland and South Africa. Gladstone was opposed to coercion in Ireland and on 7 April 1881 had introduced measures for land reform which eased the situation to some extent, despite a continuing series of dynamiting outrages in London caused by Irish revolutionaries. Cf. below, Letter 699, p. 150. In South Africa the Boers had revolted against the government imposed on the Transvaal after its annexation in 1877. British forces were defeated at Majuba Hill in February 1881 and largely as a result of this Gladstone restored the independence of the Transvaal republic under the Pretoria Convention of 1881. See Ensor, *England 1870–1914*, pp. 68–9, 71–7.

[1] The *Primer of Political Economy* was printed by Robert Maclehose at the University Press, Glasgow.

[2] The fragment of the *Principles of Economics* actually published ran to only 151 pages.

The London Statistical Society would like to have a copy of Cossa's Guide presented. They had a careful review of the book.[3]

Yours faithfully,

W. S. Jevons.

683.   W. S. JEVONS TO MRS LUCY HUTTON
[LJN, 427]

Hampstead, 14th May 1881

. . . I must write a few lines to wish you many happy returns of to-morrow. My memory for birthdays is indeed so bad that I should hardly have been likely to remember it had not the children been so very busy preparing you surprises. I hope that Herbert's remarkable letter will reach you safely. It has been the result of very anxious care on his part and of some little trouble on my part.

I have been on duty now with the children for three days, while Harriet was away, but am thinking of dissipating a little in town now. I have not even seen the Academy. I sent you a day or two ago a copy of the *Contemporary,* with my article on 'Bimetallism'.[1] After you have quite done with it I shall be glad if you will post it back, as I like to have a spare copy of articles. I also sent you a copy of the *Biograph,* with my 'Life' in it.[2] The article is little more than a reprint of what appeared in the *Owens College Magazine* shortly after I left Manchester, having been written, I believe, by my successor Adamson. Please keep this. I am writing pretty steadily at my large book on Political Economy, and it absorbs all my strength and almost all my thoughts just at present . . .

684.   W. S. JEVONS TO H. S. FOXWELL
[RDF; LJP, 428]

2, The Chestnuts,
Branch Hill,
Hampstead, N.W.

17 May 1881.

My dear Foxwell

I only heard yesterday at College that the Council had finally appointed you my successor. I now congratulate you on the result which

---

[3] *JRSS,* 43 (1880) 705–7.
[1] 'Bimetallism', *Contemporary Review,* 39 (1881) 750–7; reprinted in *Investigations,* pp. 317–29.
[2] *The Biograph,* v, no. 29 (May 1881) 426–34.

was however from the first a foregone one. There were 2 or 3 other candidates whose claims we were bound to talk over but there was nothing to put in serious competition to your services & claims.

I have now the pleasure to hand you the key of office, being the key of a drawer in the professor's room marked No 6 where you may keep any papers or other articles you need. I handed my key of the door to my deputy – you will obtain one from Mr Brown the assistant secretary when you need it.

There is in the .professors room a large roll of diagrams chiefly consisting of illustrations of my statistical papers. They are of no further use to me & if not preserved by you must go as 'waste'. Before they are destroyed you may as well look at them & see whether they are ever likely to be useful to you. Considerable use might be made of diagrams in P.E. but I have never had energy enough to carry the use far. Now lecturing is a thing of the past with me. I regret in some ways the laborious & sometimes exciting & pleasing hours I have had, but my nervous framework was not framed for the platform.

I am making nice progress with my large work on Pol. Econ^y as far as my health will allow.

I was sorry not to be at home when you called. I hear of you at the booksellers occasionally & fancy you must be getting a good collection of economic books.[1]

I have given up all hope of cataloguing my books & trust to my memory & sight but if I could work for longer hours I should like to make a card catalogue.

> Believe me
> > Yours faithfully
> > > W. S. Jevons.

685. H. CRAIK[1] TO W. S. JEVONS

> Hillside,
> Nottinghill Square, W.
> May 17. [1881]

My dear Mr. Jevons,

Mr. Farrer (whose name I thank you much for suggesting) gives me hope that he may join the Series.[2]

[1] Quoted by Keynes in his 'Centenary Allocution' of 1936 as 'a remark which has remained *à propos* any day in the fifty-five years since then' – *The Collected Writings of John Maynard Keynes*, vol. x, *Essays in Biography* (1972) p. 140.

[1] [Sir] Henry Craik (1846–1927), first baronet, civil servant and politician; educated at Glasgow University and Balliol College, Oxford; Examiner in the Education Department, 1870–85; Secretary of the Privy Council Committee for Education in Scotland, 1885–1904; C.B. 1887; K.C.B.

He asks me "How Mr. Jevons would be disposed to divide the subjects of Trade and Labour e.g. where the state interferes with Industrial Undertakings for the benefit of the Labourers employed in them as it does in the case of shipping. If he has thought of this I should be glad to know the result."

My own idea would be that the subject named by him would possibly be touched upon by you as one instance where men were protected in their labour by the state: I think it would certainly be touched upon by Mr. Farrer as one instance where trade was regulated for the general benefit of the State. A little cross reference might be necessary: but I do not see that confusion need arise.[3]

Would you be so kind as to let me hear your view of this?

Thanking you again for your kind assistance and suggestions,

Sincerely yours,

Henry Craik

W. Stanley Jevons, Esq.

686.   W. S. JEVONS TO J. MILLS

[LJN, 429]

Hampstead, 19th May 1881.[1]

. . . Thanks for the copy of your letter on Bimetallism,[2] which I have read with much interest. It is a strong and pointed argument against

---

1897; M.P. for the Universities of Glasgow and Aberdeen, 1906–18, and for the combined Scottish Universities from 1918 until his death. Author of a number of works including *The State and Education* (1883), published in the English Citizen Series, *A Century of Scottish History* (1901) and *Impressions of India* (1908), as well as contributions to the *Quarterly Review* and other periodicals.

[2] The English Citizen Series, published by Macmillan, of which Craik was General Editor. The fact that Jevons was preparing *The State in Relation to Labour* at the time appears to have encouraged Farrer to agree to contribute a similar work on Trade to the Series. According to his Preface: 'When first asked to write on the Relations of the State to Trade, I saw with pleasure that Mr. Stanley Jevons was to write on the Relations of the State to Labour, and hoped that we might consult with one another on the line to be taken and on the distinction to be made between these two kindred subjects . . .' Cf. above, Letter 642, p. 93.

[3] In *The State in Relation to Labour* Jevons dealt with the Factory Acts, Trades Union Legislation and the Law of Industrial Conspiracy. Farrer in *The State in its Relation to Trade* included a chapter (chap. XVII) on 'Interference of the State with Special Trades in order to secure Health and Safety'. Commenting on the Factory Acts, the Mining Acts, and a large part of the Merchant Shipping Acts, he wrote 'these cases have been already discussed by Mr. Stanley Jevons in his *Treatise on the Relation of the State to Labour* [sic] and I therefore need only make a general reference to them' (p. 154).

[1] This letter is also published in TLJM (pp. 353–4), where the date is given as 19 June 1881. The original manuscript is not now in the Jevons Papers. Apart from the discrepancy noted below (n. 5), the TLJM version does not have the passage beginning 'As to coal'. However, Mrs Mills added the following note of her own: 'This letter is a valuable addition to the convincing reply given to an attempt made at the Brussels Congress to show that Mr. Jevons had changed his views on the subject of bi-*versus* mono-metallism.'

[2] Mills's letter, dated 11 April 1881 and signed 'M', was published in the *Manchester Examiner and*

Cernuschi and his school. [3] I had not seen the letter before, and if you sent me an *Examiner* I must have accidentally failed to notice the letter.

Grenfell's extract is probably quoted from Giffen's paper in the Statistical Journal, March 1879, vol. xiii, pp. 36–68, [4] an important paper, but I have not found the precise passage.

I do not think the subject of Bimetallism is worth much powder and shot. The whole thing will collapse at the next meeting of a conference. [5] My own impression is, that the French Government are heartily sick of their double standard, and are putting up Cernuschi that they may conveniently recede under cover of his absurdities.

As to coal, I certainly made a mistake of six months, and I have had some unhappy half-hours over some of my shares, but I do not plead guilty to more than six months' error as yet. There is a great future coming. Moreover, the Coal Question is going to be verified in a manner which no one would have believed. With coal so cheap, and pits working half time, the output is only some twelve millions behind the calculated amounts, or about 8 per cent which will readily be made up in a single brisk year! . . .

---

687. J. H. NORMAN[1] TO W. S. JEVONS

Scinde Punjaub & Delhi Railway Co.,
Gresham House,
Old Broad Street,
LONDON. E. C.
23 May, 1881.

Sir,

Permit me to send you a table which I prepared when in India 6 years ago on the current coins of the principal countries of the world, showing the relative proportion of gold and silver in such countries as have a coinage of both metals. [2] You will notice that there are 15 differences in 22

Times, 12 April 1881, p. 4.

   [3] Henri Cernuschi (1821–96), Italian politician and economist exiled to France after the 1848 revolution in Lombardy, was at this time a director of the Banque de Paris and the leading French advocate of bimetallism. In 1881 he published *Le Bimetallisme à Quinze et Demi nécessaire*.

   [4] R. Giffen, 'On the Fall of Prices of Commodities in Recent Years', *JRSS*, 42 (1879) 36–68. The volume number is given wrongly as 'xiii' in LJ, p. 429.

   [5] In TLJM this sentence reads 'The whole thing will collapse at the great meeting of Conference.' Since there was an International Monetary Conference in Paris in 1881, this reading may well be more nearly correct.

   [1] John Henry Norman, a foreign-exchange dealer, and author of various pamphlets opposing bimetallism published between 1882 and 1895.

   [2] Accompanying the manuscript letter is a printed table entitled *Table of the Principal Current Coins*

countries named and the extremest between Portugal which has 14.09 of silver to 1 of gold and the Argentine Republic which has 17.65 of silver to 1 of gold is something more than 25 per cent = On my return to England I attempted to complete this table but could get no assistance either at the Mint or at the Foreign Office I expressed the hope in a note I wrote to Sir Louis Mallet[3] before he left for Paris that at the Conference the additional necessary information would be afforded

Allow me to thank you for your powerful advocacy of principles of currency which I believe to be sound on the simple ground that as the laws governing the cost of the precious metals are the same as those governing the cost of other substances the attempt to establish parallel lines of cost being unnatural must break down and in the long run create infinitely more mischief than any present benefit which the establishment of bi metallism could confer.

You will notice that the cost of silver coinage in India is 2 & $\frac{1}{10}$ per cent in America it is $\frac{1}{5}$ of 1 per cent, the India office proposition does not meet this, but as I read Lord Hartington's[4] answer in the House of Commons he is prepared to make the proportions the same as exist in the U.S.A. and France $15\frac{1}{2}$ to 1. Now as in India at present it is 15 to 1 33.33% more silver must be put into each rupee or some other adjustment to the disturbance of values.

I am Sir,
Yours very faithfully,
J. Norman.

4 Cannon Place, Hampstead.

---

and Metallic Currency in use in India, China, Japan and Java: Also the Coinages of the Chief European Countries and the Americas. The table is dated January 1875 and signed 'Norman Brothers, Exchange Brokers' with the legend 'We are sorry that we cannot obtain in Calcutta the necessary information to complete this table.'

[3] Sir Louis Mallet (1823–90), entered the Board of Trade 1847 and was assistant commissioner responsible for drawing up the tariff under the Anglo-French treaty of 1860. Member of the Council of India, 1872, and permanent Under-Secretary of State for India 1875. Mallet, an advocate of bimetallism, was the Indian delegate to the International Monetary Conference at Paris in 1881 and shortly before the date of this letter had caused some stir by a speech there which some construed as committing the British Government to support of bimetallism.

[4] Spencer Compton Cavendish (1833–1908), Marquess of Hartington, 1858–91, subsequently eighth Duke of Devonshire; Leader of the Liberal Party, 1875–80; Secretary of State for India in Gladstone's second cabinet, 1880–2; Secretary of State for War, 1882–5. Hartington, answering questions in the Commons on 20 May 1881 about Mallet's speech, explained that different instructions had been given to the British and Indian delegates: those to the latter included the following passage: 'in the event of your being pressed on the subject, or your seeing reason to think it desirable that such a declaration should be made, you are authorized to agree, on the part of the Government of India, that, for some definite term of years, not exceeding ten, it will undertake not to depart, in any direction calculated to lower the value of silver, from the existing practice of coining

688.   O. J. LODGE[1] TO W. S. JEVONS

17 Parkhurst Road, N.
24 May 81.

Dear Prof. Jevons,

I went to Manchester and saw the Principal using your note and everybody nearly except Roscoe who was away. I enclose a copy of my application.[2]

Faithfully yours,
Oliver J. Lodge.

689.   J. H. NORMAN TO W. S. JEVONS

4 Cannon Place.
26 May, 1881.

Dear Sir,

Allow me to explain that the play in the Indian exchanges at the same price of silver in London is 6 per cent the 14 per cent is made up of 8% the difference between 62^d & $57\frac{1}{2}^d$ troy in London = India is only just gradually emerging from the use of cowries an african shell as currency & no more requires gold than Britishers do diamonds as currency = To change the currency of India to gold would cost at least £30,000,000 sterling if justice is to be done between man & man which Col Smith's scheme[1] would not effect = A thought which I should like to see worked out is this, Have we no conclusive demonstration that in international trade gold & silver exchange with other articles at the cost of production? would not the Australian & Indian trades furnish this evidence? I am

---

silver freely in the Indian mints as legal tender throughout the Indian dominions of Her Majesty. Such a declaration must, however, be conditional on the acceptance by a number of the principal States of an agreement binding them, in some manner or other, to open their mints for a similar term to the coinage of silver as full legal tender in the proportion of $15\frac{1}{2}$ of silver to 1 of gold, and the engagement on the part of India would be obligatory only so long as that agreement remained in force'. – *Hansard,* third series, CCLXI, 956, 20 May 1881.

   [1] [Sir] Oliver Joseph Lodge (1851–1940), physicist; Demonstrator at University College London, and Lecturer in Physics and Chemistry at Bedford College, 1876–81; Professor of Experimental Physics in University College, Liverpool, 1881   1900; Principal of Birmingham University, 1900–19; knighted, 1902.

   [2] Lodge at this time was an applicant for a Chair of Applied Mathematics at Manchester, which had been created to supplement the Chair of Physics held by Balfour Stewart. He was unsuccessful, Arthur Schuster being appointed to the new Chair.

   [1] John Thomas Smith, 'East Indian Currency and Exchange', *Westminster Review* (New Series), 59 (1881) 506–27. Smith's scheme, which he had previously published in a pamphlet entitled *Silver and the Indian Exchanges discussed in Question and Answer* (1880), was one for the suspension of silver coinage and the gradual introduction of a gold standard in India.

disposed to think myself that they would = There is no question that a sound metal basis is of the first importance to the internal transactions of a country & that currency should suit the genius and requirements of the country, the adjustments of international transaction are of secondary signification & I cannot but think that if the whole East with Russia as at present clung to the silver standard & the rest to gold that it would be much better for the world than any attempt by governments – at bimetallism which an intelligent people might not follow = [2]

     Believe me   Yours faithfully,

                  J. H. Norman.

690.   L. H. COURTNEY TO W. S. JEVONS

                           House of Commons,
                              7th July, 81.

My dear Jevons,

    I am very glad you consent to be nominated as an ordinary member of the Club [1] – I do not doubt we shall elect you on the first opportunity next Session. I hope your rest by the sea will do you good permanently as well as give pleasure now. We shall want you often at our meetings.

                Very faithfully yours,
                Leonard Courtney.

691.   W. S. JEVONS TO T. E. JEVONS
     [LJN, 430–1]

                    Bulverhythe, Hastings, 8th July 1881

. . . I was pleased to get your cheerful letter some weeks since. I was so much below par, and so occupied with examinations and other matters, that I could not well answer before. We are having a quiet holiday here, and for the first four days of our visit enjoyed delightful weather. Then came a heavy thunder-storm, lasting the greater part of the night, and now we have cool winds. The children are very well, and enjoy grubbing about the shore very much. Harriet is also enjoying herself fairly, but

   [2] While most Indian civil servants and merchants were at this time opposed to the idea of a gold standard for India, the alternative which generally found support with them was the introduction of bimetallism. Norman's suggestion that the East should retain a silver and the West a gold standard would not seem to provide any necessary remedy for the problem which was then at the core of the debate – the fall in the value of silver and the consequent depreciation of the Indian exchanges.
   [1] The Political Economy Club, of which Jevons became an ordinary member in 1882. See *Political Economy Club, Centenary Volume,* VI (1921) p. 364.

seems to feel maternal cares. I am in an extraordinary weak state, and was quite knocked up the other day by walking to St. Leonards and back, two miles each way. I sleep quite twelve hours out of the twenty-four which seems to do me more good than anything else at present. I have now written to take passage by the *Domino* to Bergen on the 26th July. Will[1] will be my companion for a part of the trip . . .

After my holidays I have to write a brief popular book on *Labour* for Macmillan, and then I hope to have a clear fling at my large *Political Economy*. The attempted assassination of the President[2] created a great sensation in England. We have of course, all particulars here in the papers, besides telegrams in the St. Leonards News-room when I can get there. One can imagine the Emperor of Russia saying to himself, 'Ah, it is not only we autocrats that get shot'[3] . . .

The census reports in England, together with the coal statistics, are wonderfully bearing out my Coal Question, and my opponent, Price Williams,[4] finds the ground entirely cut from under him. Possibly I may next write to you from some retreat in Norway . . .

692.   W. S. JEVONS TO L. WALRAS[1]
[FW; LJP, 431]

2, The Chestnuts,
Branch Hill,
Hampstead, N.W.

My dear Sir,

I have received with much pleasure the copies of your two memoirs which you have been so kind as to send to me. They both treat of subjects interesting to me and I hope in a little time to study them carefully. I am at present however taking relaxation for the improvement of my health and in a few days I leave home for Norway to spend 5 or 6 weeks there perhaps. My recent application to study has a good deal injured my health and I have on this account resigned my professorship of Pol. Econ.

[1] His cousin, William Edgar Jevons. See Vol. II, Letter 32, n. 1, p. 58.

[2] James Abram Garfield (1831–81), twentieth President of the United States, was shot by an assassin on 2 July 1881 and died in September of that year.

[3] Emperor Alexander II of Russia (1855–81) had been assassinated the previous March in a bomb attack on his carriage in St Petersburg.

[4] Richard Price Williams (1827–1916), civil engineer; M.Inst.C.E. 1861; F.S.S. 1877; carried out statistical enquiries on coal and maintained that the rate of increase of coal production was showing a progressive diminution. See his paper 'The Coal Question', *JRSS*, 52 (1889) 1–39; also *The Coal Question* (1906 edition) pp. x, 279. Price Williams also contributed papers on population to the Statistical Society.

[1] The original letter has no date, but Walras has written on it in pencil '20 juillet 1881'.

at University College. My future address will therefore be exclusively at Hampstead as stated above for the future.

I have been making considerable progress with my large treatise on Economics which will go over the whole field of the subject. I have also promised to write a small popular treatise on the subject of "labour"

In a former letter you told me you had learned some particulars of the life of Gossen. I wish that you would either publish these yourself or send me the facts that I may publish them in your name in some English journal. [2]

I regret that I am so bad a correspondent but my strength is overtaxed by the work I have on hand.

I am glad to say I think the Math. view of Economics is making much progress in England and is fully recognised by those competent to judge.

Believe me

Dear Professor Walras

Yours faithfully,

W. S. Jevons.

693.   L. WALRAS TO W. S. JEVONS
[FW]

Ouchy sous Lausanne,
6 août 1881 [1]

Cher Monsieur,

J'ai appris avec peine par votre dernière lettre que l'état faible de votre santé avait été la cause du retard que vous aviez mis à m'écrire. Je désire vivement que vous arriviez le plus tôt possible à terminer vos travaux urgents afin de pouvoir prendre le repos qui seul vous permettra de vous rétablir. Je suis, comme vous, très fatigué, aussi ai-je récemment arrêté le programme de ce qui me reste à faire pour élucider et exposer complètement une théorie et en dehors de quoi je suis résolu à ne plus rien entreprendre.

J'apprends avec plaisir que l'économique mathématique fait de sensibles progrès en Angleterre. J'espère qu'elle va d'ici à peu de temps pénétrer en Allemagne. Il vient de paraître dans ce pays une traduction

---

[2] Although in a letter of March 1880, Walras had informed Jevons that he was in touch with Gossen's nephew, Karl Joseph Kortum, it was not until 29 July 1881 that Kortum sent Walras the promised biographical details of Gossen, which formed the basis for Walras's 'Un économiste inconnu, Hermann-Henri Gossen', *Journal des Economistes*, fourth series, 30 (1885) 68–90. See Jaffé, *Walras Correspondence*, 1, 644 and 708–9.

[1] The original manuscript of this letter is not now in the Jevons Papers. The version published here follows that given by Jaffé (*Walras Correspondence*, 1, 710) and based on the draft in Fonds Walras, FW1, 278/15.

de mes quatre mémoires sur la théorie mathématique de la richesse sociale; et tout semble annoncer que cette publication sera bien accueillie.

Au moment où votre lettre m'est parvenue le Professor Kortum, de Bonn, ne m'avait pas encore envoyé les renseignements qu'il m'avait promis sur la vie et la carrière de son oncle Gossen.[2] Mais sur l'envoi de la brochure allemande et du Mémoire sur le prix des Terres,[3] il s'est enfin exécuté. Je viens de recevoir de lui, cette semaine une lettre et une notice biographique que je vais utiliser immédiatement; et dès que mon travail sera terminé j'aviserai au moyen de le publier.[4] Aussitôt qu'il aura paru, vous en aurez un exemplaire.

Agréez, Cher Monsieur, l'expression de mes sentiments bien dévoués.

Léon Walras

694. W. S. JEVONS TO THE COUNCIL OF THE LIVERPOOL
UNIVERSITY COLLEGE

2, The Chestnuts,
Branch Hill,
Hampstead, N.W.
21 Sept 1881.

Mr. F. Y. Edgeworth M.A. having informed me that he is about to become a candidate for the professorship of Logic, Mental and Moral Philosophy and Political Economy in the University College, Liverpool,[1] I have pleasure in stating that I well know him to be an ardent sincere and talented student of several branches of these sciences. [He is and has for some time past been engaged in the public teaching of Logic & economics, but in this respect he will doubtless adduce more direct evidence than I have the means of giving].

I have no hesitation in saying that his published works on old & new Ethics, and on Mathematical Psychics[2] are among the most remarkable and original contributions to the Social Sciences which the past few years

---

[2] See above, Letter 692, n. 2, p. 144.

[3] L. Walras, 'Théorie mathématique du prix des terres et de leur rachat par l'Etat', *Bulletin de la Société Vaudoise des Sciences Naturelles*, 2ᵉ série, 17 (1881) 189–284.

[4] As noted above, Letter 692, n. 2, Walras's article on Gossen was not published until after Jevons's death.

[1] University College, Liverpool, was founded in 1878. The College, consisting of an establishment of seven Chairs, received its Charter in October 1881 and opened for classes in January 1882.

Edgeworth's application was unsuccessful. The first holder of the Chair of Logic, Mental and Moral Philosophy and Political Economy, from 1881 to 1910, was John MacCunn (1846–1929).

[2] F.Y.Edgeworth, *New and Old Methods of Ethics* (Oxford, 1877); *Mathematical Psychics: An Essay on the Application of Mathematics to the Moral Sciences* (1881).

have produced. I expect to see other works of equal ability and greater talent proceed from an investigator of such unquestionable power.

I believe that Mr. Edgeworth will confer honour & advantage upon any collegiate body which places him upon its staff.

W. Stanley Jevons.

695.   W. S. JEVONS TO MRS LUCY HUTTON
[LJN, 433–4]

Stoneleigh, Malvern Wells,
Monday, 26th September 1881

. . . We got here in pouring rain on Saturday, but yesterday it turned out fine, and we had a beautiful view from part of the hills, which we all, excepting baby, ascended without difficulty.

. . . A curious discovery which I recently made among my books will perhaps interest you. In looking over a series of volumes of pamphlets which I bought a year or two ago, I discovered that the first few volumes were collected by my grandfather Roscoe,[1] and had lists in his handwriting; two or more subsequent owners had continued the series, and one had made a note about 'Roscoe', which first drew my attention to the fact. I have only, however, got a portion of the series, other volumes having been sold before I met with the set. The volumes include copies of some of W. Roscoe's own pamphlets. One of the subsequent owners was named Benson.

. . . Yesterday we saw some of the Welsh mountains in the extreme distance, and I fancy we could almost see as far as Rhayader. The Clee hills were quite plain . . .

696.   W. S. JEVONS TO T. E. JEVONS
[LJN, 434]

Malvern Wells, 2d October 1881.

. . . It is quite time I wrote an answer to your and Isabel's[1] pleasant letter of 28th August. Please thank Isabel very much for her addition to your letter.

We have got moderately pleasant lodgings here, and the strolls over the

[1] See Vol. I, pp. 4 5
[1] T. E. Jevons had married Isabel Seton, daughter of an American naval officer, in New York on 19 April 1870.

hills in fine weather are very enjoyable. The children are in high feather, and find endless amusement with blackberries, wells, streams, and other peculiarities of the place. 'Boy' has walked with me to the top both of the Worcestershire and Herefordshire Beacons, which are at nearly equal distance, without showing signs of fatigue . . .

My health is, I hope, steadily improving after its long depression, and I have been able to write steadily for a few days at my new book on *Labour*, but I have to bear up as well as I can against depressing influences.

. . . In England there is no fear of a real crisis for many years to come. There will probably be ups and downs, but for the present a decided *up* is in progress. It is possible that, as in 1873, there may be an intermediate *check* rather than real collapse in 1883 or 1884, but there is no present prospect of any such thing.[2] If peace be maintained there will probably be an unprecedented period of prosperity for the next seven years. I do not say that the same will be the course of events in the United States, for you move so fast that there may be an earlier check. But remember that the same causes which acted in 1873–74, namely, a breakdown of prices and rents inflated by the previous influence of paper money, does not now exist. I do not like the excited and violent tone of American politics, and the prevalence of 'corner' and extravagant speculation. . . .

696A.   W. S. JEVONS TO H. S. FOXWELL
        [RDF]

2, The Chestnuts,
West Heath,
Hampstead, N.W.
13 Oct. 1881.

Dear Foxwell

I have been requested to act with you in examining for the Ricardo Scholarship.[1]

It has always been usual in these exams[s], I believe, for each exam[r] to set one paper, so I suppose it will suit you if I send a paper, say at the end of this month, or early next month.[2] Hoping that you like your new work so far, & have a satisfactory class, I am

Yours very faithfully
W. S. Jevons.

[2] Cf. above, Letter 638, n. 3, p. 90.
[1] Cf. Vol. IV, Letter 435, n. 1.
[2] See below, Letter 699A, p. 151.

697.   W. S. JEVONS TO T. E. JEVONS
       [LJN, 435–6]

Hôtel de Normandie, Rue St. Honoré,
Paris, 30th October 1881.

. . . You will perhaps like to hear a little about the visit which Harriet and I have managed to pay here, leaving the children in the care of John and Lucy, who have kindly taken our places at home. We have now been here nearly two weeks, staying one night in Boulogne – where I wished to see a brother logician, an English tutor there resident[1] – and another night in Amiens. We were very much pleased with the cathedral at the latter town. It is a charming work of architecture – perhaps the most beautiful church, on the whole, that I ever saw.

Then after buying a few very cheap and valuable French books we came on to Paris, where we have enjoyed ourselves ever since. We have not been to the theatre at all, as I never succeed in finding the way into a French theatre, but we have had concerts, grand dinners, and above all the Electric Exhibition. The latter alone was worth coming from London to see, being indeed the most beautiful and enjoyable exhibition I have ever seen – and I have seen nearly all the great exhibitions in London and Paris in and since 1851. The various rooms, lighted by different species of electric light, and the innumerable applications of electricity in all modes, are most interesting. We have spent four evenings in the building (the Palais de l'Industrie), and have by no means exhausted it. Yet it is an exhibition of moderate dimensions, and does not exhaust the visitors. They are going to try to repeat it at the Crystal Palace, but I do not think they can equal what the French have had the genius to originate.[2] On three evenings we have dined at the Grand Hôtel,[3] which you probably

---

[1] Probably Hugh MacColl, who was living at 73, Rue Siblequin, Boulogne-sur-Mer, during 1881. Cf. above, Letter 662, n. 1, p. 116.

[2] The first International Electrical Exhibition was held in Paris between August and November 1881, to coincide with the first International Electrical Congress. The main object of the Congress was the advancement of the new technology: discussions included the adoption of a universal system of electrical and magnetic measures and of international signals for use at sea, also the construction of submarine cables. The delegates were appointed by their governments, and proceedings were held in private between 15 September and 5 October 1881. Highlights of the Exhibition included an electric railway to convey visitors from the Place de la Concorde to the Porte de l'Est of the Palais de l'Industrie, and telephonic transmission of operatic performances. Similar exhibitions were held subsequently at the Crystal Palace and in St Petersburg and Vienna. Detailed reports of the Exhibition appeared in *Nature*, vol. 24, between May and November 1881; see also T. P. Hughes, 'British Electrical Industry Lag: 1882–1888', *Technology and Culture*, 3 (1962) 27–44.

[3] The Grand Hôtel, Boulevard des Capucines, was described in Baedeker as one of the three largest hotels in Paris, 'magnificent edifices . . . each containing 600–800 rooms . . . managed somewhat in the same style as the large American hotels . . . replete with every comfort . . . In favourable seasons about 300 guests, including many from other hotels, frequently dine at the tables

know. It is rather expensive work, but they are the most enjoyable dinners I have ever had, resembling first-class banquets, without any of the worry of speechifying or the ridiculous twaddle and etiquette of dinner parties. Properly speaking, I believe we ought (that is to say, musical people) always to dine to the sound of music; it produces a placid and exhilarated tone of body and mind, highly conducive to digestion and general wellbeing.

A large part of my time has been taken up in book-hunting on the banks of the Seine. I have secured almost a trunk full of books on economics, of much scientific and historic value, but often at ridiculously low prices. I am going, by degrees, rather fully into the history of Political Economy in France during the eighteenth century, and book-hunting is in the end the easiest and cheapest way of acquiring the means. We return home on 1st November. Do you remember our changing money at Piccadilly Circus at the rate of 24 fr. = £1? I went there and changed some at 25.20 – the full rate! . . .

698. W. S. JEVONS TO H. S. FOXWELL
    [RDF; LJP, 436]

2, The Chestnuts,
Branch Hill,
Hampstead, N.W.

3 Nov. 81

My dear Foxwell

I now enclose draft of the exam^n paper for Ricardo Scholarship. It is to be distinctly understood that though candidates are obliged to attend the class of P.E. before being admitted, the exam^n is not restricted to the course of instruction. The outside examiner, who in this case happens to be myself, is especially at liberty to ask any questions coming within the sphere of economics. But according to clause 3 of the regulations the papers of each examiner are to be submitted to the other for his approval.

I am sorry you were disappointed about the lot of French Economic books at Allen's.[1] They were certainly a desirable set.

I have just been on a bookhunting visit to Paris, & have returned with more than 100 French economic works – I have met with the original editions of Vauban's Dixme Royale,[2] Boisguilleberts Detail de la

---

d'hôte . . .'. Dinner, including wine, cost between six and eight francs at the Hotel du Louvre and charges at the Grand Hotel were similar. The cost was four francs at the Hôtel de Normandie. See *Paris and its Environs*, sixth edition (1878) pp. 4–6.

[1] See below, Letter 706, n. 3, p. 159.

[2] Sebastian Le Prestre Vauban (1633–1707), *Projet d'une Dixme Royale* (1707).

France,[3] Le Trosne's works,[4] & a few others, besides plenty of recent economic publications.

Hoping that you get on pleasantly with your work I am
Yours faithfully
W. S. Jevons.

699.   W. S. JEVONS TO H. RYLETT
[LJN, 436]

Hampstead, 6th November 1881.

. . . Though there may have been much to sympathise with in the earlier efforts of the League,[1] all my sympathy with the League ceased as soon as they began to work against the new Land Act.[2] I look upon that Act as the greatest concession that could be made, and one which is a sufficient step towards setting Irish affairs right. Every real friend of Ireland will be found as a supporter of the action of that Act, and the new Court created by it. I do not mean to say that no further reforms are needed. There may be plenty to be subsequently done – the repeal of the Whiteboy Acts, the Consolidation of the Irish Railways, and a good many minor reforms. But these will follow, and they will not be hastened by the intense ingratitude to Mr. Gladstone shown by those who ought to have been his truest followers.

There can be no doubt that for many years past the fondest hope of Mr. Gladstone has been to redress the wrongs of Ireland, and to restore her to all possible prosperity. If he has made any mistake, it was in the decision of his Cabinet to endeavour to govern Ireland without any extraordinary powers. If I recollect aright, he allowed the Coercion Act of the Tory Government to lapse when he might have insisted on its re-enactment.

The milder policy would probably have succeeded had good harvests occurred in the subsequent years. But the failure of harvests, and the rejection of the Eviction Bill, frustrated his efforts to maintain the milder course.[3]

---

[3] Pierre le Pesant de Boisguillebert (1646–1714), *Le Détail de la France* (1695).

[4] Guillaume François Le Trosne (1728–80), *De l'ordre social, ouvrage suivi d'un traité élémentaire sur la valeur, l'argent, la circulation, l'industrie, le commerce intérieur et extérieur* (1777).

[1] The Irish Land League, founded in 1879 by Michael Davitt. See below, Letter 737, n. 1, p. 196.

[2] The Land Act (Ireland) 1881, Gladstone's second major Irish Land Act, which conceded the 'three Fs' – fair rent, fixity of tenure, and freedom of sale – demanded by the tenant interest since 1850. The Act did not satisfy Davitt and the other leaders of the tenants in 1881, who were then advocating peasant proprietorship.

[3] '. . . though the leaders constantly urged the methods of peaceful persuasion a penumbra of outrage surrounded the League from the very beginning. All the old ruthlessness of agrarian vendettas reappeared and intimidation, cattle-maiming, burnings and shootings, spread through the

I am sure that no one can possibly regret more than Mr. Gladstone the necessity of reverting to coercion;[4] but coupled as it is with such a noble gift as the new Land Act (not to speak of earlier reform, such as the disestablishment of the Irish Church), I am quite unable to understand how you can be found among his opponents.

Thanks for the copy of Henry George's pamphlet on the 'Irish Land Question.'[5]

I have already got his book on *Poverty*.[6] . . .

699A.   W. S. JEVONS TO H. S. FOXWELL
            [RDF]

2, The Chestnuts,
West Heath,
Hampstead, N.W.
13 Nov. 81.

My dear Foxwell

I did not know that your lecture lasted so late as 8.15. By all means come on Tuesday morning; I have a good deal to say. If you could come at 12 o'clock or so & stay lunch it wd be very convenient & I could push on a little before hand with my book on Labour which I have to get done. But if you have nothing else to do in the morning pray come as soon as you can. We can settle the paper then I should suppose.[1]

Yours very faithfully
W. S. Jevons.

---

country-side. Usually . . . these crimes were closely related to the progress of evictions. Thus, in 1877, 463 families were evicted and the number of outrages was 236; in 1878, evictions numbered 980 and outrages 301; in 1879, the comparable figures were 1,238 and 863. And in 1880, at the very height of agitation, when over 2,000 families were driven from their homes outrages totalled 2,590.' F. S. L. Lyons, *Ireland Since The Famine* (1971) p. 160.

[4] In October 1881 Parnell, the leader of the Irish Party, had been arrested on the orders of the Viceroy of Ireland, Lord Cowper.

[5] Henry George (1839–97), *The Irish land question: what it involves and how alone it can be settled. An appeal to the Land League* (1881).

[6] Presumably George's *Progress and Poverty* (1879).

[1] Presumably Jevons had in the meantime sent Foxwell the draft examination paper for the Ricardo Scholarship promised in his letter of 13 October 1881 (above, Letter 696A, p. 147). The final version of the paper settled at the meeting between the two men was as follows:

RICARDO SCHOLARSHIP IN POLITICAL ECONOMY.
I.

1. Estimate the position and importance of the Physiocratic writers in the history of Political Economy.

2. Describe the principal schools of economists which have been recognized in this country or

abroad during the last half century. How far would you say that the Historical is inconsistent with the Ricardo – Mill School?

3. What is the relation which mathematical analysis has indicated between utility, value, and labour? Give some account of the mathematical methods of Cournot and Gossen.

4. Examine carefully into the economic meaning of the term Luxury.

5. Describe briefly the main features of the existing Factory Legislation of the United Kingdom. Analyze its principles, and conclude with an expression of opinion as to the economic validity of legislative restrictions upon the hours of labour of adult men.

6. Under what circumstances is it desirable to establish Courts for the fixing of rates of wages, rents, or other pecuniary claims?

7. How far do the principles of the division of labour apply to retail trade? In your answer advert to the case of several large cooperative stores and to certain large private establishments which seem to aim at becoming "universal providers."

8. What is the existing law as regards the application of revenue to the reduction of the National Debt? What are, in your opinion, the comparative advantages of terminable annuities, fixed statutory payments, application of surplus revenue, reduction of interests, or other possible methods for the reduction of the Debt?

II.

1. Carefully define the terms *competition* and *freedom of contract*.
Give and classify the principal limitations imposed in this country, whether by law, custom, or public opinion, on the absolute freedom of contract.

2. Give a systematic account of the chief causes of the differences of wages in different employments; and examine how far the progress of society is likely to remove or lessen these differences.

3. State carefully, and in a general form, the law of Diminishing Returns. To what economic phenomena, other than those of agricultural production, does the principle apply? Mention the chief parts of economic theory which are based upon it.

4. State the different inferences which might be drawn from each of the following circumstances. How far could they be found existing simultaneously in the same society?

    (a)   A low rate of business profits.
    (b)   A high rate of interest.
    (c)   A high price of Consols.
    (d)   A low rate of discount.

5. Adam Smith tells us that "our ancestors . . . endeavoured to hinder as much as possible any middleman of any kind from coming in between the grower and the consumer."
What examples are there in our own times of attempts to supersede the middleman? and what objections would commonly be brought against him? Give Adam Smith's defence of the middleman in the corn trade; and discuss the question when, and in what degree, middlemen are economically advantageous.

6. What is meant by the incidence of taxation? Examine the conditions under which taxes, whether direct or indirect, can be shifted by those on whom they are first levied to the shoulders of the consumer; and notice at the same time the degree in which they can be so transferred.

7. "No one class of producers is entitled to protection on account of a rise of wages, because a rise of wages affects equally all producers; it does not raise the price of commodities because it diminishes profits; and if it did raise the price of commodities, it would raise them all in the same relative proportion, and would not, therefore, alter their exchangeable value" – RICARDO.
Notice and criticize the assumptions involved in this reasoning.

8. Most economists of the 18th century advocated competition as tending to bring about an equitable distribution of wealth. The socialists of the 19th century attack it on the very ground that it makes such an equitable distribution impossible.
Try to account for this difference of opinion; and give your own judgement on the matter.

                 H. S. FOXWELL,⎫
                              ⎬ *Examiners.*
                 W. S. JEVONS,⎭

—Extract from the *Calendar of University College, London,* 1882–83, pp. 178–9.

Point out the connection which exists between the business of banking and the doctrine of probability, and investigate precisely the nature of the principal risks & difficulties to which bankers are subject.[2]

700.   R. HAMILTON TO W. S. JEVONS

28 Nov. 1881.

Dear Professor Jevons

Many thanks for your note. I am very glad to learn by it that it is good work & not bad health that is keeping you so much at home. I have made a few slight additions to my paper on Money & barter, & added as an appendix an analysis of an *"international transaction"*[1]

It is very interesting to find a record of a "Clearing house" in the 17th. Century,[2] but I quite agree with you that there would be no reason to be surprised at finding an account of one in Babylon. Perhaps the following personal recollection of business as carried on in Liverpool some 30 years ago[3] may have some interest for you in this context.

The Banks there in those days charged a small commission on their accounts & did not lay themselves out for "cashier's" work. Hence, in every large office there was a responsible clerk as "Cash Keeper" – periodical (generally weekly) "pay" or rather "settlement" days were the custom in every trade – by custom Bills of Exchange *with a Bank's Endorsement,* were received, less discount, in the settlements, there was no real difficulty in getting notes or coin but these were more handy & served the end required.

The Head of the businesss, who managed its finance in the broader sense, of course had to provide any *balance* required for payment, or appropriated to use any balance to be received, but all the work of adjusting the cross receipts & payments was the routine business of the Clerks. They had to run about, meet each other on Change & elsewhere & arrange their respective sets off with as little trouble as they could, & now & then would be a little bothered when things went cross, but that

---

[2] This sentence in Foxwell's handwriting is on a separate piece of paper accompanying the letter. Apparently a suggested question, it did not appear in the published examination papers.

[1] Rowland Hamilton, 'Money and Barter', *Journal of the Institute of Bankers,* 3 (1881) 1–21.

[2] The original 1875 edition of Jevons's *Money and the Mechanism of Exchange* contained the assertions that 'the Clearing House appears to have been first created just a century ago' (p. 264) and that 'the London Clearing House is entirely the birthplace of the system'. Ferraris in 1878 had drawn his attention to Rota's claims that the system originated earlier in Tuscany (see Vol.IV, Letter 565), and this may have been in turn pointed out by Jevons to Hamilton.

[3] There does not appear to be any record of Rowland Hamilton's banking career in Liverpool in the 1850s. In the first paragraph of the paper referred to in n. 1 above, he stated '. . . my first practical knowledge of business was obtained in one of the great merchant banking houses, whose transactions extended to every quarter of the globe'.

was all "in the day's work". There was no such paying & receiving large sums of money backwards & forwards as Professor B. Price imagines to have been necessary in "pre Clearing House" days. [4]

So it must have been in every large market & the perfection of the mechanism of the Clearing House is the outcome of expedients which are *obvious* enough to those who have to encounter these difficulties in detail.

I remain
Y^r vy faithfully
Rowland Hamilton

701.   W. S. JEVONS TO T. E. JEVONS
       [LJP, 437]

Hampstead
12 Dec. 1881 [1]

My dear Tom

I was much pleased with your last letter written soon after your return home. It showed you to be well & happy & with plenty to do. The Geological discovery was well worth making & in America there must be much more field for such things than in this well scanned country. [2]

We were very sorry however to hear that Rex was feeling the ague again. He certainly requires care.

Our little ones are all quite well at present, I am glad to say, & Lucy Cecilia [3] has just begun to walk about the room. She is a cheerful happy little thing & completes the trio nicely.

Harriet is suffering from headache today & has complained several times lately, but she is well & strong on the whole.

I have been working under pressure for a week past to finish our article for the Contemporary on "Married Women in Factories." [4] It treats of infant mortality, & I hope you will like the view it takes.

I am getting towards the end of my book on the State in relation to Labour, but it involves a great deal of reading & thinking.

---

[4] Probably a reference to Bonamy Price's *The Principles of Currency* (1869) pp. 119–20, in which he argued that the creation of a number of clearing-houses in the large towns, and particularly London, would greatly reduce the number of banknotes in circulation.

[1] Written on notepaper embossed 'Athenaeum Club, Pall Mall' – 'Hampstead' written in ink by Jevons.

[2] In the absence of the letter from T. E. Jevons I have been unable to establish what his geological discovery was [Editor].

[3] Jevons's younger daughter, born 8 April 1880.

[4] See below, p. 161.

Baynes[5] wanted me to undertake a long article on Pol. Econ. for the Encyclopaedia Brit^a., with handsome remuneration of £3 per page; but after some hesitation I have declined.

I want to get on with my large book on Economics, which will never be finished, if I take up every task offered.

I am also intending to bring out a reprint of all my principal articles & papers on money, &c, under the title "Investigations Concerning Currency & Finance." I hope that it will make a nice volume. You see that I have plenty on hand, but I often feel very unequal to it.

The Coal & iron Trades are getting on favourably & I am a good many hundreds of pounds on the right side already. But I shall hold for a year or two at least as we are only at the beginning yet. I have had great luck with John Brown & Co, which have had a run of large orders for steel armour plates since I invested two lots in them. I expect to be making 10 per cent pretty nearly all round before long, but the shares do not rise rapidly at present. Investors have still got the idea that coal & iron are dangerous. After a good dividend or two they will probably come round & make a run on them when I shall clear out.

I am just going to buy a piano but am much perplexed between the makers who are all so good.

With best love to Isabel

Ever your affect brother

W. S. Jevons.

702. C. J. WILLDEY[1] TO W. S. JEVONS

11 Theresa Terrace,
West Hammersmith,
London W.
19 Dec: 1881

Dear Sir,

In the summer you kindly pointed out strong objections in my *parcel post scheme*,[2] and said you hoped you should hear more of it.

---

[5] Thomas Spencer Baynes (1823–87), Professor of Logic, Metaphysics and English Literature in the University of St Andrews from 1864 until his death. He superintended the ninth edition of the *Encyclopaedia Britannica* from 1873.

[1] Charles John Willdey (b. 1844) entered the Civil Service in London in 1863 and spent his career as a clerk in the Post Office. He had been promoted from third-to first-class clerk in 1875 and retired in 1904. No further details of his career, or of the proposed scheme, appear to have survived.

[2] Jevons had written an article advocating 'A State Parcel Post' in the *Contemporary Review*, 34 (1879) 209–29; reprinted in *Methods*, pp. 324–52. At this time the high charges made by railway companies for parcels traffic were a frequent cause of complaint. The Post Office first undertook the carriage of parcels in August 1883.

The objections (border jealousies in a separate one for England) have been I think removed; and I enclose the whole for your perusal of it, or of such part as you may think worth while. I should also be glad if you would return it when convenient, as I think I will submit it to Mr. Fawcett,[3] as soon as possible.

I remain

Dear Sir

Yours truly,

C. J. Willdey.

W. S. Jevons, Esq.

P.S. You said "Why do you not publish something of the sort?" – I am not able to do that, as officials of the post office may not write to journals about the business of the department.

You are welcome, however, to extract such matter as you may wish.

703. W. S. JEVONS TO F. Y. EDGEWORTH
[LJN, 439]

Hampstead, 26th December 1881

. . . I have read your remarks on capital[1] with care and interest; you will excuse my saying that you seem to be still deep in the fallacies of Mill. I fear you have not yet approached to a comprehension of my theory of capital as involving solely the element of time. I now see that the whole theory of the matter is implied in the expression for the rate of interest as given on p. 266 of my 2d edition [*Theory of Political Economy*].[2] Some of my other expressions may be misleading. Indeed, as long as you speak of 'capital' instead of 'capitalisation', I think you are pretty sure to go wrong. However, the matter is too difficult to discuss in a letter, and I hope in a short time to try and write it out more fully and satisfactorily.[3] . . .

---

[3] Henry Fawcett was at this time Postmaster-General. See Vol. III, Letter 190, n. 1.

[1] It seems probable that these remarks were unpublished, although no paper or letter by Edgeworth on capital survives in the Jevons Papers. Edgeworth's *Mathematical Psychics* (1881) and other works published before this date do not contain any passages to which Jevons's criticism could reasonably be considered to apply.

[2] *T. P. E.*, fourth edition, p. 246.

[3] Jevons had partly written out this piece, intended to be chapter xxv of his *Principles of Economics*, at the time of his death. It was published by H. S. Jevons as appendix 11 to the fourth edition of *T.P.E.*, pp. 294–302.

704.   W. S. JEVONS TO R. H. INGLIS PALGRAVE
       [KCP]

Private   2 The Chestnuts,
                                         Branch Hill, Hampstead, N.W.
                                                  29 Dec 1881.

My dear Palgrave,

Thanks for the copy of "Economist" with Rylett's letter.[1] It reads as an interesting *exposé* of an educated Land Leaguer's ideas.

I should like very well to receive a copy of the Economist which at present I only see casually in town. I shall be happy to write a letter now & again when anything occurs.

I enclose a reply from Henry Craik the Editor of the Citizen Series.[2] I thought it best in the first instance not to mention your, or your brother's name, but merely to describe the book I thought your brother might undertake & say that if desired I could suggest a writer intimately acquainted with the subject. My idea, perhaps yours, is that the practical working of the H. of C. with the private bill legislation & a great deal more might furnish material for a wholly new & original book. You have probably observed however that "The Legislature & the Electorate" is already in the list, but I hardly see how it can treat of the H. of C. adequately.

I enjoyed my visit to you as much as the state of my health wd. admit, but was suffering at times from nervous pains & disturbances. These incapacitate me so much from going into society that a quiet retired life seems to be absolutely essential to me. I was at one time in hopes that I might really recover from the great break down I suffered about ten years ago when lecturing full swing at Owens College and writing the Principles of Science at the same time. A year's relief from lecturing then partially restored me, but the excitement & worry of life in London during the past few years has again been too much for me. For nearly a year & half too, causes for the gravest anxiety with regard to my health have made themselves apparent, though I cannot undertake at present to define them. Altogether I am hemmed in with difficulties with which it requires much patience & resolution to cope.

Thank Mrs. Palgrave for her kindness not only at home but in providing me so well with refreshments for the journey. I got home comfortably before 7.30 p.m. without any difficulty or delay.

---

[1] *The Economist*, 24 December 1881, pp. 1589–90. Cf. below, Letter 737, p. 197.
[2] This is no longer with the manuscript.

I hope you will come & spend a night with us here occasionally when the weather is a little better, if a time could be found convenient to you.

Believe me,

Yours very faithfully,
W. S. Jevons

705.   W. S. JEVONS TO A. MACMILLAN
[MA]

2, The Chestnuts,
Branch Hill,
Hampstead, N.W.

1 January 1882

Dear Mr. Macmillan,

The time seems to have come when it would be suitable for me to reprint the series of papers and pamphlets which I have written on currency and allied subjects during the last 20 years. I find that they fall into convenient and nearly consecutive order. With a page of about 320 words they will make a nice sized volume of about 350 pages, in addition to an introductory chapter or preface of some length, and a certain number of diagrams in lithography. The latter will add a little to the cost, but will much increase the interest of the book.

As there is likely to be a good deal of controversy in April and May about the Bimetallic question and other currency topics, it might be well to have it out then, if you can get a printer who will really be brisk.

In the case of a book of this sort the arrangement would I presume be the usual one of half profits to me and no risk, though I do not suppose that there is any risk in the matter.

The title I propose (if you think it a good one) is "Investigations in Currency and Finance". There are too many "Essays", and "Papers" and the like already.

If not ready in April or May I should make a point to defer publication until November.

The first part of the copy which has needed only slight revision will be ready to send to the printer in a day or two, and after supplying a few gaps, the remainder will all be ready before the printer is likely to need it. If you accede to my proposal kindly say whether I shall send the copy direct to the printers whom you name or to Bedford Street.

The diagrams seem to be the only troublesome part of the book. I enclose a specimen in order that you may see their general character. It would add much to the appearance of the book if they could be coloured, especially hand coloured. But I suppose that this would be too expensive. There would be about twenty diagrams of the size of the page and one or two rather larger folding ones. Perhaps the better way would be to leave this question open until some day I could discuss it with you in Bedford Street, showing you the drawings.[1]

The MS for the "State in relation to Labour" is nearly ready, but as I am not very well I suppose I need not hurry.

With best wishes for a happy and prosperous New Year.

Believe me,

Yours faithfully,

W. S. Jevons

706. W. S. JEVONS TO H. S. FOXWELL
[RDF; LJP, 439]

Hampstead Heath.

1 Jany 1882

My dear Foxwell

I find that I have Playfairs book on the Decline of Nations,[1] a good copy. Also the "Essai sur les Causes du declin du Commerce, 1757".[2] Entirely at your convenience you can send the other books in a parcel by rail or parcel Company addressed to me care of

Mr Allen

Bookseller

432 Euston R^d [3]

This avoids the difficulty of delivery at Hampstead.

You must send me a full statement of all you paid for the books including binding.

---

[1] In the Preface to the first edition of *Investigations*, which was published by Macmillan in 1884, Mrs Jevons explained the reasons why Jevons did not carry these intentions into effect: 'The state of his health, combined with the pressure of other work, obliged him to proceed more slowly than he had hoped to do, and he therefore postponed the publication until the autumn. When he laid the book aside, hoping to resume work upon it in the autumn, he had seen all but the last two papers through the press; but the manuscript of the concluding one ["Sir Isaac Newton and Bimetallism"] was still unfinished, and the Introduction, which was to have been a long and full one, bringing up the results of the papers to the present time, was hardly commenced.'

In the volume as finally produced the collection of papers occupied 360 pages; in addition to two large folding diagrams (black-and-white reproductions of those originally published by Edward Stanford for Jevons in 1863) there were eighteen diagrams in the text with the graphs tinted in blue.

[1] See Vol. IV, Letter 355, n. 2.

[2] *Essai sur les causes du déclin du commerce étranger de la Grande Bretagne*, 2 vols (1757), a translation by J. P. Gua de Malves of Sir Matthew Decker's *An essay on the causes of the decline of the foreign trade, consequently of the value of the lands of Britain, and on the means to restore both* . . . (1744). The work went into several editions, the second appearing in 1750 (cf. below).

[3] Thomas Allen, a bookseller at this address during the 1870s and 1880s.

The books will be a valuable addition to my library.

I enjoyed my visit to Cambridge[4] as much as my weak state of health will allow. Unfortunately I suffer from neuralgic pains in the back which generally come on when they are least wanted.

I am getting my book on Labour nearly done. Then I have a collection of papers on Money on hand, & my large political economy looming faintly in the distance.

Hoping to hear soon of your A. Smith—

I am

Yours faithfully

W. S. Jevons.

Best wishes for a happy New Year.

I have two copies of 2nd Ed. of "An Essay on the Causes of the Decline of Foreign trade &c 1750 but I think you had it.

I have Josiah Child,[5] but I want Malynes[6] and all the other books set aside.

707.   C. J. WILLDEY TO W. S. JEVONS

11 Theresa Terrace,
West Hammersmith,
LONDON W.
3rd January, 1882.

Dear Sir,

I beg to acknowledge the receipt on Thursday, of my paper.

The two objections you point out I have considered.

As far as that one goes which considers the charge prohibitory for short distances so as to leave in the field the existing concerns, it will be remembered that this would be only in so far as they can deliver, which is over a very limited space and population, the latter not being half within any given sufficient radius even for all these enterprises put together.

As for the objection in the difficulty of rural delivery, my father (superintendent of the Paddington District) and myself both agreed with you, but on further examination I find the difficulties lessen, owing to the numerous places of call of the carts carrying the bags from head offices: these places are more numerous than railway stations, and the P.O. could do at least as much near them as R^{lys} do near their stations. Moreover

---

[4] Jevons had visited Foxwell in Cambridge on 19 December 1881. See LJ, p. 438.

[5] Sir Josiah Child (1630-99), *A new discourse of trade, wherein is recommended several weighty points relating to companies of merchants. The act of navigation. Naturalization of strangers. The balance of trade. And the nature of plantations, and their consequences in relation to the kingdom, are seriously discussed . . .* (1693).

[6] Gerard de Malynes (1586?-1641), *The Centre of the Circle of Commerce. Or, a refutation of a Treatise intituled The Circle of Commerce, or the Balance of Trade, lately published by Edward Misselden* (1623).

they lie in the villages with the populations round them. In the Rugby delivery without counting the head-office itself; of 33000 people, some 14000 must live within 5 minutes walk of where a cart stops to leave a bag (and parcels). The carts also thread through many more.

In the towns there would be no difficulty; nor with collections.

Thanking you for noticing this difficulty, which I am getting over: so as to send Mr. Fawcett something as good as I can make it.

I remain

Yours very truly
C. J. Willdey

W. S. Jevons, Esq.

Infant Mortality

The high death rate among children under one year old became a matter of increasing public concern towards the end of the nineteenth century, as medicine and the social sciences developed. The combination of factors that were responsible – disease, ignorance and faulty feeding habits – came to be recognised as affecting all social classes, though the problem was obviously more acute among the industrial working classes. The large body of data that was built up from numerous sources made grim reading and indicated that there was less difficulty in illustrating the scale of the evil than in devising methods of dealing with it.

Infant mortality was the last major social issue to which Jevons was to turn his attention and his concern can therefore be seen within the context of increasing agitation among social reformers, which eventually resulted in a new body of legislation to replace the framework provided by the Poor Laws, which had virtually broken down by the end of the century.

In January 1882 his article 'Married Women in Factories' was published in the *Contemporary Review*, 41 (1882) 37–53, reprinted in *Methods*, pp. 156–79. This paper was largely based on facts and figures derived from the experience of Manchester; but Jevons had undertaken to prepare a paper on the subject for the Nottingham meeting of the Social Science Association to be held in September 1882. The relevant correspondence among Letters 708–18 below relates to his preparation of this paper and reaction to the article in the *Contemporary*.

708.   F. J. MOUAT[1] TO W. S. JEVONS

12 Durham Villas
Kensington W.
4 Jany 82

Dear M[r]. Jevons

I have not sooner answered your note of the 1st Jany because I wished first to find out where a fair type of the workhouse system of dealing with the infants of working mothers was to be found.[2]

I have ascertained that an excellent example exists at the Kensington Workhouse in Knight's Lane close to me. If you can therefore kindly meet me at the workhouse in question, or at my house – 12 Durham Villas close to the High Street station of the underground railway at 12 o' clock on Friday or Saturday next – whichever you may prefer, I shall be happy to show it, and the people who work it will explain it to you.

Kindly let me know quickly that I may make arrangements accordingly as I shall in all probability be compelled to leave town next week on public duty.

I do not know where the private (charitable) creches are to be found – but they ought certainly to be seen by you. I have always refused to countenance them, as wrong in principle, and as doing a [?][3] work in an incorrect manner.

Very truly yours
F. J. Mouat.

Stanley Jevons Esq.

P.S. My house is within 5 minutes' walk of the High St station.

[1] Frederick John Mouat (1816–97), who had retired from India in 1870 after a long and distinguished career in the army medical service in Bengal; Inspector-General of the Local Government Board in England, 1870–88; Secretary of the [Royal] Statistical Society, 1873–6; Honorary Foreign Secretary, 1876–81; President, 1890–2; author of several works recounting his travels among the islands of the Indian Ocean, and *Hospital Construction and Management* (1883), as well as numerous papers.

[2] The amount and type of relief provided by workhouses varied considerably from one parish to another. In cases of parental destitution, or of extreme neglect and cruelty, children were usually taken into the workhouse to be cared for and educated while the parents sought work. In these circumstances, infants were generally cared for by other inmates, usually without responsible supervision, and sometimes with tragic results. Cf. *Report from the Select Committee of the House of Lords on Poor Law Relief*, 1883 (363) xv.

[3] This word is illegible.

709.   W. S. JEVONS TO J. E. THOROLD ROGERS

2 The Chestnuts,
West Heath,
Hampstead, N.W.

10 January, 1882.[1]

My Dear Sir,
    The enclosed document[2] explains itself so fully that I feel sure I need add nothing more than that we have good promises of aid from Sir H. Maine,[3] Fawcett, Courtney and others. I shall be much obliged if you will sign and return the copy as early as possible.
                            I am, Yours faithfully,
                                    W. S. Jevons.
Prof. Rogers, M.P.

710.   W. S. JEVONS TO THE EDITOR OF THE *MANCHESTER GUARDIAN*

MARRIED WOMEN IN FACTORIES.

Sir,
    It is out of the question that I should attempt to answer the letter of Mr. W. Darbyshire,[1] who writes from the Great Ancoats Post-office. Obviously he has never seen the article which he so freely disposes of. Had he done so he would not have needed to ask "Does Mr. Jevons call a widow with young children a married woman for the purposes of his proposed enactment?" He would have known that this class of women, as well as unmarried child-bearing women, were considered, and that I expressly point out that it is child-bearing women, not married women, that the proposed reform must deal with. Mr. Darbyshire, judging from a few extracts from my article, has formed his own theory of what I put

---

[1] The original manuscript of this letter is now in the possession of Dr M. A. T. Rogers.

[2] The document in question apparently related to the proposal of R. H. Inglis Palgrave for Fellowship of the Royal Society. Jevons wrote a virtually identical letter, on the same day, to H. S. Foxwell. See below, Letters 725 and 728, pp. 183 and 188.

[3] Sir Henry James Sumner Maine (1822 88), jurist; Regius Professor of Civil Law, Cambridge, 1847–54; first Reader in Roman Law and Jurisprudence in the Inns of Court, 1852; legal member of the Council in India, 1862–9; Corpus Professor of Jurisprudence, Oxford, 1869–78; Master of Trinity Hall, Cambridge, 1877; Whewell Professor of International Law, Cambridge, 1887; K.C.S.I. 1871; F.R.S. 1874. His principal works were *Popular Government* (1885) and *International Law* (1888); one of the foremost contributors to the *Saturday Review* from 1855.

[1] It has not proved possible to trace any biographical information about W. Darbyshire.

In his letter, published in the *Manchester Guardian* on 7 January 1882, Darbyshire accused Jevons of ignorance of the subject on which he wrote and asserted that any legislation to prevent women with young children from working would lead simply to an increase in infanticide.

forward. Great though his acquaintance with the factory population may be, it is hardly equal to that of the various medical officers of health, medical commissioners of enquiry, members of Parliament, factory inspectors, coroners, and other persons whose evidence I carefully cite. And though I mainly depend on the knowledge of those men whose special business it is to know the facts, I am not quite so ignorant of a factory population as he supposes, having lived thirteen years at Manchester, and lost no opportunity of becoming acquainted with the subjects about which I have the temerity to write.

In answer to Mrs. Jacob Bright's trenchant letter [2] I would again point out that her quotation of my proposed remedy is incomplete. Though I propose to aim at the "ultimate" complete exclusion of mothers of infants from factory work, I carefully qualify this in the paper by explaining that intermediate or transitional measures are indispensable. These measures would probably resolve themselves into the permission of such labour, provided that the children were disposed in well-appointed *crèches*. Judging from what I have been able to see of the nursing-rooms of the large London workhouses (with the kind assistance of Dr. Mouat, the Poor-law Medical Inspector) it is clear that no practical obstacle exists as regards the management of such *crèches*. Manufacturers, no doubt, will raise insuperable objections to the stoppage of work involved in the mothers leaving their employment for twenty minutes in the middle of each morning and afternoon spell; but the evidence which I have cited shows that the operation of the present factory law, in separating mothers from their infants, is inhumane and prejudicial to the interests of the people in the highest degree. Your correspondents do not appreciate the teaching of those silent dark figures which are added up in Somerset House, and which prove, as registered facts alone can prove, the evils of the present state of things.

The chief motive of Mrs. Bright's criticism seems to be contained in her concluding references to women's rights to vote. I am to a great extent of the same opinion as Mrs. Bright; at any rate, I think that every woman who can vote for municipal elections ought to have a parliamentary vote; but I fail to see the precise bearing of this question upon that which I have treated. As to the grievance so strongly brought out, both by Mrs. Bright and Mr. Darbyshire, that a married woman can now only establish a claim for support upon her husband by enrolling herself as a pauper, and thus inducing the Guardians to prosecute her husband, this is certainly

---

[2] Jacob Bright (1821–99), younger brother of John Bright, married Ursula, daughter of Joseph Mellor, a Liverpool merchant, in 1855. Her letter, published in the *Manchester Guardian* on 4 January 1882, emphasised the weakness of the legal position of married women which Jevons's proposed legislation would do nothing to alleviate and concluded with a plea to give women the right to vote, as the only ultimate solution.

one of the defects of existing legislation which ought to be remedied. It would necessarily be one of the chief points of the inquiry into the treatment and condition of very young children in the manufacturing districts, which it is the real purpose of my article to advocate.

Two or three of your correspondents object that instead of interfering with the labour of industrious mothers we should decrease the temptations to intemperance among the husbands. I answer that nothing can possibly tend more to drive a husband to the public-house than to have a wife coming home tired from the factory, and beginning perhaps to do the housework and prepare the meal, when she ought to have all things comfortable and cheerful for him. The present system tells doubly in favour of intemperance, for it leaves the husband with his wages to spend at the public-house, and it destroys the counter-attraction which should be found in a well-kept home. I do not altogether agree with Mr. T. C. Horsfall[3] that "homes" are at present physically impossible. Small and unsanitary though the dwellings may be, it is difficult not to see that a well-kept small dwelling differs *toto cœlo* from an ill-kept one. Now, whether women are to have votes or not, there can be no doubt that the proper place of a good housewife is in her house.

A great deal of stress is laid by your correspondents on the need for diminishing the number of public-houses. Without denying this need, I may point out that the statistics collected by the Select Committee of the House of Lords on intemperance,[4] especially Mr. J. H. Poynting's[5] remarkable tables, failed to establish any relation between the numbers of public-houses in different towns and their rates of intemperance. But upon one point the witnesses were unanimous. The Lords say (Report, 17th March, p. xii.):— "All the evidence indicates that, speaking generally, the increase of intemperance is mainly due to the rapid rise of wages, and the increased amount of leisure enjoyed by the manufacturing

---

[3] In his letter published in the *Manchester Guardian* on 4 January 1882, T.C.Horsfall declared: "Homes" for all workpeople who have not most exceptional power of resisting temptation must be impossible till physical cleanliness is less nearly impossible, . . . and till there is some other place of recreation than the public-house, and till there is not a drinking place at every street corner . . . till in short the middle classes . . . make physical and moral welfare possible for the people of towns.'

[4] *Fifth Report of the Select Committee of the House of Lords on Intemperance*, 1878–9 (113) x, 504. In appendix R to the *Fourth Report*, 1878 (338) xiv, 580, John Dendy and J. H. Poynting produced statistical evidence of the pattern of drunkenness throughout the country, based on Police Reports in 1876. Their results appeared to show a higher incidence in northern England and a direct link between drunkenness and the denisty and rate of increase of the population. No direct connection between the number of public-houses and the incidence of drunkenness in various districts was proved.

[5] John Henry Poynting (1852–1914), Professor of Physics at Mason College, Birmingham, from 1880 until his death, was the son of a Unitarian minister in Manchester and a former student at Owens College. In 1878 he had become a Fellow of Trinity College, Cambridge, where he worked with J. Clerk Maxwell in the Cavendish Laboratory. During the period in which this paper was prepared, Poynting was working under Balfour Stewart as a demonstrator at Owens College.

and mining classes." There are many towns in the southern half of England where there are the utmost facilities for obtaining drink, and yet intemperance is comparatively slight. The opposite state of things holds in the northern half of England, where wages are higher. It is easy to declaim about the poverty of the people and the difficulty of paying 4s. 6d. for house rent, and then keeping "chubby children." But a careful review of undoubted facts shows that there are more healthy children and less drunkenness where there are lower earnings. The inference is that high wages are not conducive to the good of a certain part of the manufacturing population while their state of civilisation is at its present standard. Now of all the ways of earning higher family earnings the worst undoubtedly is that of sending the mother to the mill. Although I am quite aware of the necessity of licensing reform, and have had the opportunity of giving in a previous number of the *Contemporary Review* [6] my idea of the manner in which it should be attempted, I venture to think that such reform does not touch the root of the evil.

With the greater part of Dr. Anna Dahm's [7] letter it is impossible not to concur warmly. While hoping with her that "twenty-five years hence we shall already see a generation of women grow up who will need no policeman to tell them that their place is not in factories," I may point to the evidence that such is not the case with the present generation. The factory system has been growing for about a hundred years, and in respect of child-bearing women it has undoubtedly been allowed to diverge from a sound state of things. Some motive force must be required to set right the accumulated errors of a century. What might have been readily checked at the beginning has now assumed formidable dimensions, and there is no clear evidence to show that it will ever be mended except by the temporary intervention of the policeman.

I quite accept Mr. T. C. Horsfall's explanation of the fact that the Sanitary Association do not look upon the establishment of *crèches* as a "remedy", and that they are perfectly well aware of the value of a mother in her right place. I will only express in conclusion the hope that that Association will take a somewhat bolder course, and will urge the necessity of a Government inquiry into the whole question of the treatment of children under the school age. Now that the long fight over the Factory Acts, and the bitter struggle over the Elementary Education Act are practically over, there is a chance of some legislative care being

---

[6] 'Experimental Legislation and the Drink Traffic', *Contemporary Review*, 37 (1880) 177–92; reprinted in *Methods,* pp. 253–76.

[7] Anna Dahms, eleventh woman to be registered as a medical practitioner in Great Britain, in 1878, having graduated from Paris the previous year. She is recorded as practising at various addresses in Manchester and London from 1905 to 1917 and at this date was physician to the Ancoats Dispensary for Women and Children; later became Medical Officer for the Post Office and Resident Medical Officer in the New Hospital for Women, London.

extended to that very numerous and most helpless class of all the population, the very young. They have never been authoritatively "inquired into" except by the very ineffective Committee which evolved the Infant Life Protection Act.[8] Through the assistance of Mr. Edward Herford,[9] I have shown the futility of that Act, which served merely to allay whatever public attention was drawn to the subject eleven or twelve years ago by correspondence in your columns or elsewhere. I will endure patiently any amount of criticism on the detailed proposals of my paper if only it be conceded that sufficient grounds are therein disclosed for a comprehensive inquiry concerning infant mortality.

I am, &c.,

W. Stanley Jevons.

Hampstead, N. W., 10th January, 1882.

711.   W. S. JEVONS TO A. SCHUSTER

2 The Chestnuts.
12 January, 1882.[1]

Dear Professor Schuster,

I thank you for the copy of your Introductory Lecture[2] which I have read with interest and pleasure.

It occurs to me to ask you whether you have ever met with any facts confirmatory of your idea about the cycle of good wine harvests.[3] Without denying the possible or even probable truth of the coincidence assumed to exist, I must say that I have examined a long series of prices of wine in Italy published in the Annali di Statistica of the Italian Govet. Stat. Dept. without finding any trace of periodicity. One wd. have expected any periodicity manifested in France and Germany to be still more distinct in Italy which approaches more to a semi-tropical climate.

[8] The Infant Life Protection Society had been formed in 1870 by, among others, Sir W. T. Charley and George Hastings, to bring pressure to bear to end the abuses of 'baby-farming'. The matter was brought before the House of Commons, resulting in the *Report of the Select Committee on the Protection of Infant Life*, 1871 (372) vii, and finally in the Infant Life Protection Act, 1872, which required the registration and inspection of all persons receiving infants under one year old.

[9] Edward Herford (1815–96), elder brother of W. H. Herford; Manchester City Coroner, 1853–95. A Unitarian, and a solicitor by profession, he played a prominent role in the public and intellectual life of the city for over sixty years: he was a founder of the Manchester Statistical Society, before which he presented numerous papers.

[1] The original manuscript of this letter is in the Schuster Papers, Royal Society, London.

[2] A. Schuster, 'The Influence of Mathematics on the Progress of Physics': introductory address delivered at Owens College, Manchester (Manchester, 1881), in which Schuster gave an account of the development of a number of physical theories to illustrate the growing importance of mathematics as an aid to the scientist.

[3] Cf. Vol. IV, Letter 491, n. 4.

I am probably going to reprint my paper on the subject, and may add some remarks on this point.

I do not know whether you have pursued your ideas about the matter in interplanetary spaces. I am inclined to think that it is to that matter rather than to any direct effect of the planetary motions that we are to look for an explanation of the solar cycle.[4]

> I am,   Yours faithfully,
>
> W. S. Jevons.

712.   W. S. JEVONS TO F. J. MOUAT

> 2, The Chestnuts,
> Branch Hill,
> Hampstead, N. W.
> 15 January 1882.

Dear D[r] Mouat

The Infant Mortality Question is beginning to assume a more practical appearance than I had ventured to hope. An active correspondence is proceeding in the Manchester Guardian, some portions of which I enclose. Yesterday, however D[r] Ransome[1] wrote on behalf of the Manchester & Salford Sanitary Assoc[n] to say that they accepted my challenge and were ready to urge a gov[t] inquiry, if I had any suggestions to make. This is rather awkward for me as I am not really prepared to do more than the literary part of the work.

I therefore venture to trouble you & ask whether you can give me any hints as to the right way of proceeding. Might it not be possible to induce the Statistical Society, the Social Science Assoc[n], & perhaps some of the medical assoc[s] to join the Manchester Societies in asking for a Royal Commission. The Home Secretary is so interested in juvenile delinquents that he might perhaps be induced to take up the whole subject of the treatment of children, & I think that the public are quite prepared to sympathise at any rate as regards older children.

It is a great thing that D[r] Ransome publicly assents to such an idea, & his name will carry much weight in the north. I feel sure that the "Manchester Guardian" having once taken the matter up, will go thro with it, and the opportunity is altogether one not to be lost.

[4] For a later account by Schuster of his views on this question, see his *The Progress of Physics during 33 years (1875–1908)* (Cambridge, 1911) pp. 137–8. The suggestion there mentioned by Schuster 'that finely divided matter is being projected outward from the sun' could be regarded as an anticipation of later ideas about the now well-established phenomenon of the solar wind.

[1] Arthur Ransome (b. 1834), M.D., M.A., F.R.S., Lecturer in Medical Jurisprudence, Owens College, Manchester, 1876–8; Lecturer in Hygiene, 1876; author of many works on hygiene and disease, including a number of pamphlets for the Manchester and Salford Sanitary Association in the 'Health Lectures for the People' Series.

I repeat however that I am in far too weak a state of health to incur labour or responsibility, and if anything is to be done, I shall take an early opportunity of repeating my usual policy of resignation.

I hardly know Mr George Hastings[2] personally, but he was interested in the former inquiry about Infant Life & it is possible he w^d lend the weight of the Social Science people. If you w^d bring support from the Statistical Society & the medical people, there might be little difficulty in getting sufficient pressure to bear. But I am much afraid that the infants alone would not command sufficient sympathy & that it would be necessary to bring the juvenile delinquents, industrial school victims, kidnapped arabs, canal boat children & others to our assistance.

Thanking you much for the aid you have already given me I am

Yours very faithfully

W. S. Jevons.

713. W. S. JEVONS TO R. H. INGLIS PALGRAVE

Hampstead 19 Jan 82

My dear Palgrave,

I dare say it will please you to see that Leslie was able to send you his thanks for your kind assistance.[1] Last night we heard that his doctor wishes to send for his friends so that I fear there is little chance of his recovery. The memorial was to be sent into the Treasury today by Reilly[2] but additional signatures could be transmitted afterwards.

---

[2] George Woodyatt Hastings (b. 1825) barrister and ardent social reformer, Liberal M.P. for Eastern Worcestershire, 1880 – 5, and for the East Division of Worcestershire, 1885 – 92: his political career was brought to an end by a financial scandal; General Secretary of the National Association for the Promotion of Social Science (Social Science Association), 1857–68; Chairman of the Council, 1868 – 82; Vice-President, 1883 – 6. Cf. Vol. II, Letter 115, n. 9, p. 322.

[1] Jevons and Palgrave were among the forty signatories of a memorial to Gladstone presented in January 1882 and requesting a Civil List pension for Cliffe Leslie on the ground that Leslie had 'unhappily suffered for several years from a painful and dangerous malady, giving at times ground for apprehension that he may be physically incapacitated for the discharge of the duties of Professor, when the periods for his attendance at the [Queen's] College [Belfast] come round'. Emile de Laveleye and Erwin Nasse wrote in support of the memorial, which was primarily sponsored by Fawcett, Sidgwick and Foxwell. It had just been laid before Gladstone when Cliffe Leslie died (see below, Letter 715, p. 171). Foxwell's printed copy of the memorial and related correspondence is in the Goldsmiths' Library, University of London.

[2] [Sir] Francis Savage Reilly, Q.C. (1825 – 83), eminent parliamentary draftsman, who for many years shared Chambers in Lincoln's Inn with Cliffe Leslie. Educated at Trinity College, Dublin; called to the Bar, 1851; for many years counsel to the Veterinary Department of the Privy Council; member of the Statute Law Commission; counsel to the Speaker of the House of Commons; K.C.M.G. 1882.

Marshall has resigned his position at Bristol from severe illness & is in Italy or Sicily.[3]

Believe me,

Yours very faithfully,
W. S. Jevons

Attached to this letter is the following pencilled note:

Monday

My dear Jevons

Best thanks for what you have [done]. Please express my thanks to Mr. Inglis.

Yesterday was my worst for a week: pulse 110. I seem to grow daily weaker.

I fear the thirst and want of sleep worse.

Ever yours
TECL

714.   F. J. MOUAT TO W. S. JEVONS

Local Government Board
Whitehall.
23 Jany. 82

Dear Mr. Jevons

I have not had time until now to go through the paper sufficiently carefully to enable me to answer your note of the 15th..

I am afraid that at present no aid can be expected from the Statistical Society. The Asst Secy[1] is the slowest of all having powers, I am the only one of the Secretaries who has knowledge, however limited, of the subject, and I can barely get through what I have to do officially with any satisfaction to myself.

Some of the Registrar General's people might undertake it, but they might consider themselves disqualified officially — and we have no special committees now to undertake particular inquiries. I am afraid therefore that I can be of no use to you in the matter.

Manchester is undoubtedly a good centre to work from, and I know of

---

[3] Marshall had resigned his position as Principal of University College, Bristol, in 1881 owing to a breakdown in health. He and his wife spent a year in Italy, first in Palermo, then in Florence and Venice. He was able to resume his duties as Professor of Political Economy in Bristol in 1882. See Pigou, *Memorials of Alfred Marshall*, pp. 16–17.

[1] Joseph Whittall, administrative head of the permanent staff of the Society at that time.

no question which more urgently demands solution, or in regard to which the revelations would more surprize and shock the public.

I return your Guardian and am

Yours very truly
F. J. Mouat.

W. S. Jevons Esq.

715.   W. S. JEVONS TO R. H. INGLIS PALGRAVE

2, The Chestnuts,
West Heath,
Hampstead, N. W.
31 January, 82.

Dear Palgrave,

I enclose a note about Cliffe Leslie[1] according to your suggestion.

Yours faithfully,
W. S. Jevons

P.S. Dont be alarmed about this commercial panic. It is not the right time for a collapse, neither the right time of year nor the right time of the cycle. Nor, as many papers remark, are there the elements of bad trading and specn. to make a real crisis here.[2] I object very much to the alarmist tone of the Pall Mall Gazette.[3]

[1] T. E. Cliffe Leslie died on 27 January 1882. *The Economist,* 4 February 1882, p. 133, carried an obituary paragraph which was presumably written by Jevons.

[2] Although the crisis of 1882 was not a severe one in the United Kingdom, available evidence indicates that the peak of the cycle was reached about March 1882, with the downswing continuing until 1885. Cf. Tinbergen, *Business Cycles in the United Kingdom 1870 – 1914* (Amsterdam, 1951); Fels, *American Business Cycles, 1865 – 1897* (Chapel Hill, N.C., 1959).

[3] The *Pall Mall Gazette* during January 1882 carried a series of articles drawing attention to the weakness of French stock markets, growing anxiety about the trend of the London stock exchange, and the likelihood of a move towards higher interest rates and credit restriction. The issue of 31 January 1882 had an article on page 1 entitled 'Insufficiency of a Six per cent Rate' and paragraphs on pages 6 and 12 noting the collapse of L'Union Générale and quoting views of other papers on 'The Financial Crisis'.

716.   G. TOWNEND[1] TO W. S. JEVONS

Peel Bro.^{s} & Co
Thornton Mills
Near Bradford.   Feb^{ry} 1st 1882

Married Women in Factories.

W. Stanley Jevons Esq.

Sir,
    With others I have read with great interest the paper you contribute in the Contemporary Review on the above subject. It is one that deeply interests both emploiers and emploied, and your article is written in such a fair, and kind spirit, I take the liberty of thanking you for the same, and also beg to point out one or two difficulties I fear you have not weighed.—
    The married women, emploied in our Factories are the *greatest* stay, in the general *Line*, and example, if your withdraw them (and child-bearing women means I should say 1/3 more or less of the workers) what class of Hands have you left? boys, girls, and men! I should very much fear the consequences, on the very face of it, it sounds and looks ugly! the married women are the best Hands, having experience and steady habits are conducive to this result. I feel sure to restrict this class of women from liberty to work when they feel competent would have an immoral effect for a steady young man would hesitate to marry if he found the Housekeeping expences would fall upon him when his wife had children, and what should be a joy, might be a sadness, and he might be sick, out of work, or not able to earn wages tho' ever so willing, and yet his wife is debard from earning 15^s/- to 20^s/- per week. The alteration in the last Factory act from 8 years of age to 10 years before admiting children to work has fallen very heavy on a man who had a large family to keep, further restriction I feel sure would be disastrous. —
    I do not write in any antagonistic or mercenary spirit, with the philanthrophy shown in such a princly way by so many large Factorie owners, there is no occasions but here you name, the question of *Labour* is also a most serious one, what with Hostile tarrifes, cheap and longer hours

---

[1] George Townend, since 1851 a director of a firm of worsted manufacturers, founded in 1845 by his father Simeon Townend. In 1866 Theophilus Peel and George F. Peel became fellow directors and the name of the firm was changed to Peel Brothers. The Firm's central offices and warehouse were at Peel Place, Bradford, and there were two factories, Thornton Mills and Globe Mills. After the death of Sir Theophilus Peel in 1911 the firm was acquired by John Emsley, a local businessman, and wound up in 1965. The text of this letter has been reproduced as a literal copy of the manuscript.

of labour in other countries, the various and costley government supervisions, emploiers have to contend with, the withdrawing of this class of workers is a most serious one for the country.

There is just one other point I would touch upon, here I know it is a fact, the care of young children is often given into the hands of depending relatives who would have to be supported in some other way, and I have grave doubts in concluding all the dreadful mortality of infant life is to be traced to those *married* women who are emploied in Factories, and this you rather confirm in quoting Dr Lankester page 11.[2] You have studied and compiled your statistics well but there is just that want of practicle knowledge of Factory life, that can only be got by seeing and rubbing against it. Excuse my presumtion in thus addressing you there is much one can say in writing out this question but I always find business men have a dislike to write upon these social questions, even in defence of themselves and acts of parliament are passed that might have been better had they brought more practical knowledge to bear upon them.

Your Ob Ser
Geo Townend.

717.　J. L. CLIFFORD SMITH[1] TO W. S. JEVONS

National Association for the Promotion of Social Science,
with which is united the
Society for Promoting the Amendment of the Law.
1, Adam Street,
Adelphi, W. C.
Feb. 14. 1882.

Dear Sir,

Since you were here yesterday I have seen M^r. Hastings & also read your article in the *Contemporary*. From the latter I see that the rate of infant mortality is almost as high at *Nottingham* as anywhere else; & as our

---

[2] Edwin Lankester (1814–74), coroner for Middlesex; author of numerous works on public and private health and hygiene.

Townend appears to have been referring here to *The Sixth Annual Report of the Coroner for the Central District of Middlesex from August 1st, 1867, to July 31st, 1868* (1869) pp. 11–12, where Lankester drew attention to the fact that over half the inquests held on children under one year old related to illegitimate children, although only one child in eighteen in England at that time was illegitimate. Jevons did not quote Lankester directly in his article, but referred to the fact that 'according to the late Dr. Lankester . . . illegitimate children are "killed off" before they are one year old'. See *Methods*, p. 162.

[1] J. L. Clifford Smith was the last secretary of the Social Science Association. He edited the commemorative volume published in 1882 to mark the twenty-fifth anniversary of the Society, also *Hospital Management* (1883), the report of a conference held that year under the Society's auspices.

Congress is to be held in the Autumn in that Town, it occurred to us both that that occasion would be a most opportune one for bringing the question forward. Our programme has not however been yet even thought of, & so I can now only throw out the hint as to the mode in which we could perhaps get the subject started.[2]

Yours faithfully,

J. L. Clifford Smith.

W^m. Stanley Jevons Esq.

718. W. PEARCE[1] TO W. S. JEVONS

12, Connaught Terrace,
Plymouth.
February 14/ 82.

Dear Sir

Many years since I was managing partner in a woollen mill in the north and of necessity saw a good deal of the manners & customs the vices & virtues of the factory operatives of both sexes.

Consequently your able article in the Contemporary on the evil results of the employment of childbearing women interested much —

Your statistics as to Infant Mortality cannot be wrongly stated and the injurious effects of opiates on young children are apparent in every manufacturing town.

While residing in the north I came to the conclusion that there was larger amount of Immorality among *married* women than among the *un*married. I found also that many of the older residents had come to the same conclusion. If this supposition be correct and being scarcely capable of proof it can be spoken of only as a supposition, would not this be a powerfully helping evil influence on the health & life of the children borne to such women.

The causes leading to immorality specially in married women are not I think far to seek and would be stronger in factory life than in other work were the sexes are more seperate.

Forgive my troubling you with this letter & as I have had very little to

---

[2] 'During the last few weeks of his life my husband was much occupied with the question of infant mortality, as he had undertaken to prepare a paper on the subject for the meeting of the Social Science Association, held at Nottingham last September. That paper was never to be written, and the results of his many hours of labour were therefore lost . . .Note added by Mrs H. A. Jevons to the reprint of W. S. Jevons's 'Married Women in Factories' *Methods*, p. 179.

[1] It has not proved possible to trace any biographical information about W. Pearce. The text of this letter has been reproduced as a literal copy of the manuscript.

do with factory operatives for several years past I have the more need to apologise.

I am Sir
Yours respectfully
W. Pearce.

W. S. Jevons Esq.

719. W. S. JEVONS TO A. MACMILLAN
[MA]

2, The Chestnuts,
Branch Hill,
Hampstead, N.W.

15 Feb. 1882.

Dear Mr. Macmillan,

It is of course a matter of guess work but I think it would be better to print 1250 copies of "Investigations". Some parts of the book upon the course of prices will I hope possess permanent interest and I should hope for a slow continued sale.

I have relinquished the idea that it is possible to get the book out by April, although Giffen tells me it ought to be out by the time of the Monetary Conference. But apart from the printers' capacity, I find it quite impossible to get my part of the work done rapidly enough. Such a book ought not to be published without a good index which will add a week or two after all else is done.

What I now propose is therefore to make the book rather more perfect and bring it out in November.

Believe me,
Yours faithfully,
W.S. Jevons.

P.S. The printers appear to be very careful and accurate about the work.

719A. W. S. JEVONS TO H. S. FOXWELL
[RDF] (postcard)

Hampstead
22 Feb. 82

Can you give me the exact present address of Professor A Marshall? Some time ago I left at Allens the copy of Josiah Child due to you. Also a dup. of Corbet on Commercial matters,¹ a book of [   ]² which please accept until you get a more perfect copy.

W. S. Jevons.

Written before your card came.

23 Feb. 82

720.   W. S. JEVONS TO J. TAYLOR KAY¹

2 The Chestnuts,
West Heath,
2nd March 82²   Hampstead, N.W.

Dear Mr. Kay,

I forward proofs and copy of your article for MacMillans· Magazine³ which the printer has sent to me by mistake. Probably you had better return the proof to Mr. George Grove the Editor at MacMillans,⁴ 29 Bedford Street Covent Garden.

I have read the proof with much pleasure. It is a very interesting carefully argued paper. I have marked a few corrections and points needing attention.

The only thing I doubt about is your proposal of the *hundred* as an area of gov't. It is an antiquated division very unequal in extent in different counties.

Yours faithfully,
W. S. Jevons

¹ Presumably Thomas Corbet's *An Inquiry into the causes and modes of the wealth of individuals* . . . (1841). No other work by an author of this name was included in Foxwell's first collection (cf. above, Letter 656, p. 107. However, it seems unlikely that the copy referred to in this letter is the same as the one now to be found in the Goldsmiths' Library. The latter does not contain any note indicating a connection with Jevons, and it was Foxwell's usual practice to add such notes when he obtained a book from a fellow economist.

² Two words are illegible here.

¹ James Taylor Kay (1840–1903), Librarian of Owens College, Manchester, from 1871 to 1894; author of *The Owens College. A Descriptive Sketch* (1891) and *The Owens College. Notes on the Library* (1891), as well as a number of papers, mostly on bibliographical subjects.

² The original manuscript of this letter is in the Stanley Withers Collection, Manchester Reference Library.

³ J. Taylor Kay, 'County Government', *Macmillan's Magazine*, 46 (1882) 147–54.

⁴ See Vol. IV, Letter 562, n. 3.

721. W. S. JEVONS TO J. N. KEYNES

2, The Chestnuts,
West Heath,
Hampstead, N.W.

17 March 1882.[1]

My dear Keynes

The enclosed explains itself. I ought to add that I have given a somewhat similar statement to Mr W. H. Brewer who has just been appointed examiner at Victoria University, & who was formerly my substitute lecturer at Owens College. I have been a little puzzled what to do under the circumstances but came to the conclusion that it was best to state what I knew of each.

Believe me

Yours very faithfully
W. S. Jevons.

721A. W. S. JEVONS TO THE SENATE OF THE LONDON UNIVERSITY

2, The Chestnuts,
West Heath,
Hampstead, N.W.

17 March 1882.

It is well known that Mr John Neville Keynes has taken a very distinguished position in Philosophy and Political Economy. He received the Medal at the London M.A. examination in 1876, & took the first place at the Tripos examination in the same subjects in a year when I happened to be an external examiner at Cambridge. He has lately, that is in last November, been my colleague in a Scholarship examination in Political Economy at University College, London.

I can therefore testify with much confidence to his extensive and accurate knowledge of economics, to his soundness of judgment, and his general efficiency as an examiner.

I cannot entertain the least doubt that he would be a very able and efficient examiner if appointed to the vacant examinership in Political Economy.

W. Stanley Jevons.

[1] The original manuscript of this letter is now in the Marshall Library, Cambridge.

722.   W. S. JEVONS TO T. E. JEVONS
        [LJP, 440–1]

2, The Chestnuts,
Branch Hill,
Hampstead, N.W.

19 March 1882

My dear Tom

I ought to write you a few lines if only to thank you for the £20 duly transmitted by Rathbone Bro⁵. I suppose I must hold the £10 for contingencies or for payment to Mrs F. J. R.[1] next Xmas.

I must also say that I have now received the two little clocks which I found a few days ago at the Athenaeum Club. They keep their rooms so hot in the winter that it does not suit my weakened health & I have been seldom going there of late. I will give Josephine[2] her clock the next time we go to Epsom probably in a week or 10 days.

Almost worse than the clocks, was the fact that I found a letter from the Prince of Wales signed *propria manu*, inviting me to the meeting at St James Palace about the Royal Coll. of Music. Not having known of the letter I had neither gone nor returned the card nor sent any answer. However I have now sent a polite explanation to the Secretary & a subscription of five guineas.

I am just finishing the proofs of my book on Labour for the English Citizen Series, but have had a little difference with the Editor of the series[3] who, never having written a book as yet seemed to think he knew more about the work than I. The reprint of my papers on money is also proceeding satisfactorily but a good deal of work is yet needed to complete the book & introduction. I hope you will find it interesting when done.

I think the bimetallists have received a final blow in the sudden flood of gold from America. In fact almost all the commercial writers have their theories shattered by the sudden return of ease to the Money Market.[4] I have never had any fear of a real pressure for the present. In England at least there is really no bad business worth speaking of, and where prices of

---

[1] The widow of Francis James Roscoe, who had died in 1878. Cf. Vol. III, Letter 207, n.. 2.

[2] Jevons's niece, Mary Josephine Hutton. See Vol. III, Letter 280, n. 2.

[3] Henry Craik. See above, Letter 685, p. 137.

[4] Bank Rate had been reduced to 4 per cent on 9 March. *The Economist*, which the previous week had forecast that the rate would not be lowered immediately, commented 'With rates at the chief continental centres lower than here, and the Bank reserve standing at about 13½ millions, with the prospect of being further reinforced by the arrival of the supplies of gold now on their way here, there was really no reason why a downward movement should have been delayed' (*The Economist*, 11 March 1882, p. 277). Although there was certainly no pressure in the money market at this period this was mainly due to lack of demand; a crisis on the Paris Bourse in January had weakened confidence and presaged the onset of a downswing which was to last until 1886.

stocks are high it is from excess of caution, people not knowing what to invest in & therefore buying any safe railways stocks at whatever price they have to pay. The coal trade is rather disappointing at present but it must mend by waiting, & I am getting 5 p c on most of my investments. The iron trade promises well.

I am almost in despair about Ireland, & fear that coercion is a mistake. I told a member of the Government last September that the Gov¹ ought to grant an amnesty to the suspects on the day the Land Act came into operation (Oct 1?)⁵ I believe that if they had taken some such course things would have gone very differently. Although the passing of the Land Act was a great feat of power, the management of such affairs has otherwise been unfortunate and with all his good intentions I fear that Forster⁶ is hardly the kind of man to govern Ireland. Lord Dufferin⁷ or some man of that kind with tact and geniality is needed to influence the Irish.

    With best love to Isabel

Ever yours

W. S. Jevons

722A.   W. S. JEVONS TO H. S. FOXWELL
      [RDF] (postcard)

Hampstead.

22 March 82

Best thanks for "Cantilloniana", both notes being interesting. Could you come & see us here next week at any time most convenient to yourself? If possible stay a night here.

⁵ The Land Law (Ireland) Act 1881 had received the Royal Assent on 22 August 1881. Cf. above, Letter 699, p. 150, where Jevons expressed a different view on the Irish situation.

⁶ William Edward Forster (1819–86), Chief Secretary for Ireland in the Ministry formed by Gladstone in 1880. In April 1882, when the Cabinet decided to release Parnell and those of his supporters detained with him. Forster and Cowper, the Lord Lieutenant of Ireland, resigned. Forster was succeeded as Chief Secretary by Lord Frederick Cavendish. See above, Letter 699, p. 150 and below, Letter 729, p. 189.

⁷ Frederick Hamilton-Temple-Blackwood (1826–1902), first Marquess of Dufferin and Ava, a major Irish landowner and Liberal who had been Chancellor of the Duchy of Lancaster in Gladstone's administration of 1868–72; Governor-General of Canada, 1872–8; Ambassador to the Court of St Petersburg, 1879–81, and to Constantinople, 1881–4.

723.   W. S. JEVONS TO T. E. JEVONS
        [LJP, 442]

2, The Chestnuts,
Branch Hill,
Hampstead, N.W.

30 March 1882.

My dear Tom

. . . .

I am feeling a little more free from work having finished the proofs of my book on the "State in Relation to Labour" & also sent to the printer the main part of the copy of "Investigations in Currency & Finance".[1] I am now going to make a new start with the large book on Pol. Econ. I find that gentle work agrees with me better than anything else, especially such interesting work as that of the large book.

I have just had an offer of an Examinership under the Civil Service Comm[rs] worth £130 a year. I was also asked to examine at Oxford but declined that & one or two other examinerships making nearly £200 for the year. My health will not stand the wear & worry of such work & it does not even pay in the long run.

Your affec. Brother
W. S. Jevons.

724.   W. S. JEVONS TO C. W. FREMANTLE
        [LSE]

2 The Chestnuts,
Hampstead Heath.
1 April, 1882[1]

My dear Sir,

I have been thinking over the subject of the approaching recoinage and will just jot down what occurs to me.

There cannot be any doubt about the necessity of such recoinage whether we consider the facts stated by yourself to the City Lands

---

[1] This is consistent with Foxwell's statement that pp. 1 – 320 of *Investigations* had been printed off before the volume came into his hands.

[1] The text of this letter is taken from a copy, now in the Welby Papers, British Library of Political and Economic Science, written in a clerk's hand on notepaper embossed 'Royal Mint' and headed 'copy 5'.

Committee, the statistics now being prepared by Mr. Martin, or the similar ones formerly drawn up by myself.[2]

Nor can there be any doubt I think as to the mode of withdrawal which must be adopted. Any idea of proclaiming the illegality of the light coins and attempting to place the cost upon the holders must be abandoned when it is understood that the coinage affected would amount to something less than half the whole gold circulation. It is impossible to say what would be the precise effect of any such attempt. Considering that the greater part of the metallic reserves of ordinary Bankers consists of such light coin, the refusal of their customers to take light coin would render them practically, and perhaps even legally, incapable of meeting their liabilities. As the Mint could not possibly replace the light coin in less time than several years, the Banks could not possibly be supplied with legal tender sovereigns in sufficient number, and though notes might always be had by remitting the deficient sovereigns to the Bank of England, yet there are in England no £1 notes. If any apprehensions were excited among the people of a want of gold currency, the result might be a tendency to hold full weight sovereigns which would seriously aggravate the position of bankers and the state of the money market.

In fact I believe the neglect of this subject has brought us to such a dead lock that it is requisite to proceed with some circumspection lest any "scramble for gold" should be created which would result in considerable financial disturbance and give grounds of argument to those who wish to subvert the admirable arrangement of our currency.

I believe that the only way of withdrawing the light coin safely is much what you suggested the other night, namely to do it as quietly and smoothly as possible through the Bank of England. A circular from the Bank to the principal bankers to say that all coins not evidently defaced or

[2] 'On the Condition of the Metallic Currency of the United Kingdom . . .'. Cf. Vol. III, Letter 281.

John Biddulph Martin (1841–97), Honorary Secretary of the Statistical Society, read his paper 'Our Gold Coinage: An Inquiry into its present Defective Condition, with a view to its Reform', before the Institute of Bankers on 19 April 1882; it was published in the *Journal of the Institute of Bankers*, 3 (1882) 297–358.

In his Introduction to *Investigations*, pp. xxxvi–vii, Foxwell quoted extracts from notes made by Jevons at this time on the question of re-coinage and Martin's paper: 'The attention of Mr. J. B. Martin . . . having been drawn to the matter, he very recently undertook to repeat upon a more extensive scale the census which I carried out. . . . His basis of facts indeed is not very much more extensive than mine, the sovereigns examined being [105, 364] against [90, 474], and half sovereigns [145, 743] against [75,036]. . . . Although I could never have any doubts as to the substantial accuracy of my figures, it is evidently desirable that an inquiry of the kind should [receive independent verification]. . . . It may indeed seem somewhat strange that inquiries of this sort, touching matters of direct practical interest to the population, should be left to be carried out by private inquirers like Mr. Martin and myself. . . . It must, of course, be highly satisfactory to find that Mr. Martin confirms, with absolute coincidence, the accuracy of my determination of the average wear of the sovereign. . . .'

fraudulently treated, or of course counterfeit, would be henceforth received at their nominal value would result in the Bank receiving abundance of light gold for you to set the new Mint busily at work. The whole loss ought in my opinion to be borne by the Treasury. For this course sufficient precedent will be found in the case of the great recoinage of 1774, which is alluded to in Lord Liverpool's Treatise[3] (p. 191 ; Bank of England reprint p. 213). "When the deficient gold coins were called in, in the year 1774 to be recoined, their deficiency was compensated to the holders, according to a plan then settled, which will be found in the books of your Majesty's Treasury. This plan was successfully carried into execution without complaint or murmur etc." As you can readily refer to the sources of information mentioned by Lord Liverpool, and possibly have in the Mint Records more authentic accounts than are elsewhere to be found I need not refer to other book-statements which might be discovered.

The only alternative which I can conceive would be to raise the price now given for old gold coins to a point which would just induce persons to send them into the Bank rather than keep them in reserve. If I understand rightly the result of the correspondence given at pp. 64–70 of your First Report, the Treasury then enabled you to raise the price usually given for old gold coin from £3. 17. 6½ to the full £3. 17. 10½ or by 4d. per ounce or by rather more than 1d. in £1.[4] As to the justice and expediency of the change so far as it went there cannot be a shadow of a doubt; but it has been found insufficient to bring the light coin in to an adequate extent. In 1868 I calculated that the recoinage then required would be £26,000,000, the deficiency in value being about £300,000. The quantity of light gold in circulation would seem to be greater now, and will be accurately shown by Mr. Martin's Inquiry. I think the deficiency might be roughly stated at half a million, or say £100,000 a year assuming the recoinage to take five years, which I think it will.

Returning to the former point it might be worth the while for bankers to accept a part of this loss rather than go on for a series of years incurring the inconvenience of light gold, etc. But the result of any such half measure would probably be to leave large masses of light gold congested in country towns and in banks which can maintain the light gold in circulation. There would be little hope of breaking through the present bad habit of picking the new sovereigns for remittance, which seems now to be an established part of bank-routine. What you want is to get light and heavy sovereigns sent in indifferently, so as to remedy the congestion of the gold circulation.

[3] Charles Jenkinson, first Earl of Liverpool, *A Treatise on the Coins of the Realm; in a letter to the King . . .* (1805).

[4] *First Annual Report of the Deputy Master of the Mint*, 1871 [C. 303] XVI, 179.

I cannot understand upon what ground the Government could refuse to undertake the whole cost of recoinage, remembering especially that in regard to silver currency the Mint has for some years past been paying to the Treasury a sum for seignorage not much inferior to the annual cost of withdrawing the light gold. It may be said, indeed, that you incur the liability of withdrawing the worn silver coin. But the cost of that withdrawal as shown in your Annual Reports has by no means absorbed the profit, nor will it probably do so as long as silver remains low in price. In fact if silver is to remain at 52d. per ounce, and you can maintain in circulation a silver currency of say £20,000,000, it follows, if I have calculated rightly, that the metallic value of such currency will be only about £16,500,000. There must therefore be a standing balance of seignorage of £3,500,000 on which the Government will gain interest at $3\frac{1}{4}$ per cent, making £113,750 per annum, in addition to the gain which accrues from the accidental loss and destruction of silver coins, a considerable addition.

On every ground therefore I venture to think that the Government ought to and must withdraw the light gold with the balance of profit on the silver coin.

One word more – any attempt to prevent the circulation of light gold by Proclamation as in 1842, must now be practically impossible. After creating disturbance it would probably be (in fact must be) disregarded, and tend to bring discredit upon the Government resorting to that method.

> I am, My dear Sir,
> Yours faithfully,
> (sd.) W. S. Jevons

The Hon. C. W. Fremantle,
Royal Mint.

725.   W. S. JEVONS TO W. SPOTTISWOODE[1]

4 April 1882

Dear Mr. Spottiswoode,

I take the liberty of drawing your attention to the claims of one of the candidates now proposed for election to the Royal Society, namely Mr. R. H. Inglis Palgrave. He is well known to be one of the most eminent economists of the day – one indeed of very few who survive after the

---

[1] William Spottiswoode (1825–83), President of the Royal Society. Succeeded his father in 1846 as head of the printing and publishing house of Eyre & Spottiswoode, but found time for much original work in pure mathematics and experimental physics.

This letter is reproduced from a copy made in a clerk's handwriting.

recent deaths of Bagehot, W. B. Hodgson, Cliffe Leslie & now Newmarch.[2]

The position of an economist in the candidature is peculiar because the Royal Society has only on rare occasion gone beyond the bounds of physical science. Yet I venture to express the feeling that considering its unique and central position the Royal Society should recognise all branches of Knowledge which partake of scientific character and method. Now this is certainly the character of economic and statistical enquiry as exhibited in recent times and in some of the principal publications of Mr. Palgrave. His "Notes on Banking" is one of the able and scientific publications which is to be found upon the subject, and his Analysis of the Accounts of the Bank of England, and the Bank Rate in England, France and Germany is of the same character.[3] If the list of his works seems not very considerable, the cause is that in matters relating to trade and industry it is the custom to publish much anonymously. A large part of the economic writings of Bagehot & Newmarch were in like manner anonymous. In addition to other acknowledged books such as the Tayler Prize Essay on Local Taxation printed in 1871 by the London Statistical Society or the Analysis of Evidence on Banks of Issue printed in 1876[3] Mr. Palgrave has written a long series of anonymous articles in the "Bankers Magazine" and elsewhere, which have powerfully contributed to the improved comprehension of concrete economic questions. I can perceive that the daily discussions of the Press upon commercial matters are now distinctly more precise, well grounded and scientific than they were fifteen years ago, a change due in great part to Newmarch, Palgrave, and one or two other writers. I must add that the late Mr. Newmarch who was intimately acquainted with Palgrave and his writings, not only signed the certificate of proposal, but intended to address you in support of his election as shown by the post card in his handwriting enclosed. His lamented death has deprived us of his authoritative opinion. It has also diminished the already very small number of representatives of the economic or moral sciences now within the Royal Society. I venture to advocate an addition to the number in the person of Mr. Palgrave.

I am,

Yours faithfully,

W. Stanley Jevons.

(Copy of letter addressed to Mr. W. Spottiswoode, President of the Royal Society in 1882)

[2] William Newmarch died on 23 March 1882, Cliffe Leslie on 27 January 1882; but W. B. Hodgson had died in 1880, Walter Bagehot in 1877.

[3] For details of these papers, see Vol. IV, Letters 359 and 368.

725A.   W. S. JEVONS TO H. S. FOXWELL
[RDF]

2, The Chestnuts,
Branch Hill,
Hampstead, N.W.

8 April 1882

My dear Foxwell

I ought to write & say that as the weather seems so fine & the children want a little change of air, we have decided to go to the seaside next Tuesday for probably three weeks. As you will hardly wish to be in London on Bank Holyday*, it will perhaps be better if you can manage to visit us a few weeks hence when we are back home again, when I should hope you will be less busy.

I fear that lecturing & examining must absorb about all your time. I find that I must give up even examinerships if I am to make much progress in writing. I have however just got to the end of the proofs of the State in Relation to Labour. I hope it may interest you.

Ever yours faithfully
W. S. Jevons.

P.S. Possibly you could come & dine with me at the Political Economy Club on an early occasion & come home here afterwards.

726.   H. S. FOXWELL TO W. S. JEVONS

St. John's Coll: Cambr.
Apr. 10. 1882

My dear Jevons,

Many thanks for your kind note. I hope you will enjoy your seaside trip – which I envy you. I am grinding at College Essays – not the most entertaining of occupations.[1]

I shall hope to see you soon after you return. If the P.E. Club evenings are not either Mondays or Fridays I should be glad to dine there with you. In fact, it does not much matter whether they fall on those days or not – as my lectures will be over soon after 6 this term.

I have been expecting and recommending your "State in Relation to Labour" ever since Xmas. I have not the least doubt it will be very

---

[1] For comment on Foxwell's duties as an examiner, and their effect on his other work, see Keynes, 'Herbert Somerton Foxwell', *Economic Journal*, 46 (1936) 598–9.

interesting. I hope to find that you have taken up – well I wont say a Socialistic position, because some dislike the word: but at all events a position from which you recognize the obligation of the individual to society, and the necessity for some control, in the public interest, of his endeavours to secure his private gain. The more I read about the condition of labour, the more convinced I am of the necessity and advantage of organisation and control. It vexes me to hear the authority of P.E. always appealed to by the selfish rich on the other side. I dont think it will be so much longer, from what I see of the younger generation of economists.

Ever yours very truly,
H. S. Foxwell

727.   W. S. JEVONS TO G. GORE[1]
        [LJN, 440]

Hampstead, 11th April 1882

. . . I thank you very much for the copy of your new book on the *Scientific Basis of National Progress*,[2] which you have been so good as to send me. I have read it with much interest. It develops, very conclusively, the view which you had previously put forth more briefly, and it is impossible not to agree with you for the most part.

I have, however, never quite made up my mind how far it would be practicable to extend *direct* endowment of research. That it is desirable and successful, with certain persons and in certain cases, there can be no doubt. But it is a question how far it could be provided for, incidentally as it were. However, it is too large a subject to discuss by letter, and I certainly agree with you on the whole. . . .

---

[1] George Gore (1826–1908), F.R.S.; Lecturer on Chemical and Physical Science at King Edward School, Birmingham. In addition to the work referred to in this letter his publications included *The Art of Scientific Discovery* (1878) and *The Scientific Basis of Morality* (1899).

[2] *The Scientific Basis of National Progress, including that of Morality* (1882). For Gore's discussion of endowments and state aid to scientific research, see chapter IV, especially pp. 186–7.

727A.   W. S. JEVONS TO H. S. FOXWELL
        [RDF] (postcard)

Cliff House
Bulverhythe
Hastings.
12 April 82.

The Pol. Econ club does meet on Fridays but I hope you will soon be able to attend. Judging from what you say I fancy the new book will almost exactly meet your views. It seems impossible to reconcile the needs of modern society with the ideas of the Individual Rights[1] people.

Yours—
W. S. Jevons.

727B.   W. S. JEVONS TO THE EDITOR OF *THE ECONOMIST*[1]

Sir,

Seeing it stated by Mr. Westgarth in your last week's issue, that I have virtually ceased my opposition to bi-metallism,[2] I beg leave to state that so far as this may be the case, it is not due to any alteration in my opinions. Those opinions were pretty fully stated in my book on "Money and the Mechanism of Exchange", in a paper on the "Silver Question" communicated to the American Social Science Association in 1877, and reprinted in the (London) *Banker's Magazine* for December of that year;[3] also in an article on "Bi-metallism" printed in the *Contemporary Review* of last May.[4]

---

[1] Presumably a reference to the Personal Rights Association, founded in Manchester in 1871, which not only sought to defend the rights of individuals in general, and women in particular, but adopted a strong anti-socialist position. Cf. *Annual Report of the Personal Rights Association for 1910*, which contains an account by the Secretary, J. H. Levy, of the history of the Association in its first forty years.

[1] Published in the issue of 15 April 1882, vol. 40, p. 444.

[2] Jevons was replying to a letter from W. Westgarth, dated 28 March 1882 and published in *The Economist*, 8 April 1882, vol. 40, pp. 415–16, in which it was stated that at a meeting of the International Monetary Association held at the Mansion House on 8 March, 'we were told that one of our highest and most candid economic authorities, Professor Jevons, had virtually ceased his opposition . . .'.

[3] See Vol. IV, Letter 503, n. 1.

[4] See above, Letter 683, n. 1, p. 136. Some further evidence of Jevons's continuing opposition to bimetallism emerges from correspondence between C. W. Fremantle and Louis Mallet in October and November 1885, now preserved in Volume IV of the Welby Papers in the British Library of Political and Economic Science. Replying to a suggestion by Mallet that he had declared 'Bimetallism to be Protection', Fremantle denied this but quoted a passage from his Report to Lord Granville on the Paris Conference of 1881 in which he had written: 'It has been the policy of this

The arguments contained in those publications, especially the last-named article, have not, in the best of my judgment, received any real answer in subsequent controversies. If I find anything more to say I will take the liberty of saying it at my own time. There is not the least reason to fear that the foundations of our excellent system of currency will be subverted for a long time to come, especially considering that the "scramble for gold" has resulted in the Bank of England obtaining quite as much gold as it wants for the present.

I am, Sir, yours obediently,

W. Stanley Jevons.

728.   W. S. JEVONS TO R. H. INGLIS PALGRAVE
[KCP]

St. Leonards.
29th April, 1882.

My dear Palgrave,

I was much pleased to see last night in the *Times* that you were among the select fifteen, and congratulate you upon election.[1] Of course the formal election is not yet completed but it is an understood thing that the Council list is always accepted.

As the meetings are now at 4.30 on Thursday afternoons I fear the time will not be convenient to you, but I shall like to meet you at Burlington House when possible.

We have been here nearly three weeks at our usual lodgings but the weather which was delightful for the first few days has of late been a kind of intermittent storm and the children have caught colds more or less.

I have noted what has appeared in Economist on Bimetallism and thank you for what you have said.[2] I have felt that it would be a hopeless

country to emancipate commercial transactions as far as possible from legal control . . . To fix the relative value of gold and silver by law would be to enter upon a course directly at variance with this principle . . .' *(Parl. Papers*, 1882 (221) liii).

Fremantle then added: 'I find I had a very strong expression of opinion at the time from poor Jevons, who says: "I venture to think that Bi-metallism not only tries to establish an artificial ratio of values, in itself an arbitary thing, but the action of that fixed ratio would be practically to force silver currency upon those who prefer gold. This is undoubtedly an extreme infraction of the freedom of trade and laissez-faire policy to which you refer in your Report" ' (Fremantle to Mallet, 7 November 1885). To this Mallet replied on 9 November – 'Jevons's remark is very curious – and you are entitled to make the most of it – for he was really a great economist – but to my mind it is an astonishing opinion and I cannot but think that further reflection would have opened his eyes.'

[1] Palgrave was among the fifteen candidates selected to stand for election as Fellows of the Royal Society on 4 June 1882 *The Times*, 28 April 1882, p. 10(c).

[2] *The Economist* had at this time been publishing a series of 'Questions for Bimetallists', attacking their arguments; the issue of 22 April 1882 contained an item in this series which included an approving quotation from Jevons's 1877 paper, 'The Silver Question' (loc. cit., p. 472).

if not a useless task to attempt to answer the whole tribe of bimetallists in correspondence and I prefer to say what I have to say in a more deliberate form in my new book on money[3] which is slowly and laboriously progressing.

We return home in a few days,

I am,
Yours very faithfully,
W. S. Jevons.

729. W. S. JEVONS TO T. E. JEVONS
[LJP, 442-3]

2, The Chestnuts,
Branch Hill,

7 May 1882

Hampstead, N.W.

My dear Tom
I have just heard today (Sunday) by rumour of the dreadful murder of Lord F. Cavendish[1] & another in Dublin. I fear it will immensely complicate a situation already nearly hopeless. I confess I doubt the wisdom of the course of the Govt for some time back. I believe that conciliation should have been tried on the passing of the Land Act. Forster's speech of explanation on his resignation is generally blamed.[2] I am very glad of one thing however, namely that my old school friend Chamberlain[3] did not go to Ireland as Secretary, or we should have lost the ablest man in the government, & one whom we shall need in the

[3] *Investigations*, Paper XIV, pp. 330-60.
[1] Lord Frederick Cavendish (1836-82), Liberal M.P. for the West Riding of Yorkshire from 1865, succeeded W. E. Forster as Chief Secretary for Ireland in the spring of 1882. He arrived in Dublin on 6 May and that same evening he and the Under Secretary for Ireland, Burke, were stabbed to death in Phoenix Park. The murders were the work of a secret group, the 'Invincibles', five of whom were later hanged for their part in the crime.
[2] Forster had resigned as Chief Secretary for Ireland on 2 May 1882 over the decision to release from prison the three Irish Members of Parliament, Parnell, Dillon and O'Kelly. In a secret agreement with the government Parnell had undertaken to use his influence to restore order in Ireland, in return for the introduction of an Arrears Bill to wipe out the arrears of rent owed by thousands of Irish tenants. Forster believed Gladstone's conciliatory policy to be premature, and in his speech of resignation in the House of Commons on 4 May he made clear his opinion that the situation in Ireland had not improved sufficiently to end the policy of coercion. See T. Wemyss Reid, *Life of . . . William Edward Forster* (1888) II, 451-6.
[3] Joseph Chamberlain (1836-1914), at this time President of the Board of Trade in Gladstone's Ministry of 1880-5; President of the Local Government Board, 1886; Secretary of State for the Colonies, 1895-1903. Chamberlain belonged to a Unitarian family and spent a year at University College School at the same time as Jevons, 1850-1, before entering his father's business at the age of sixteen. It had been widely expected that Chamberlain, who was opposed to coercion in Ireland, would succeed Forster.

future. I cannot say however that I remember noticing in him at school the qualities of a future Prime Minister.

We have been for three weeks at our seaside retreat "Galley Hill", where however we had unsettled weather & two severe storms. On the second occasion the sea was nothing but wild surf as far as you could see. The children had colds there from which they are now recovered. Harriet is quite well & I think I am gradually getting a little stronger & better, an improvement which I hope to carry on.

I have completed the proofs of my small book on "Labour" which is now left entirely in the hands of the printer & publisher. I am nearly half through the proofs of my reprint of papers on Money but the amount of new work required will take six months to accomplish.

Will Jevons has now got back to Primrose Hill. I am told he speaks warmly of your kindness, but is not so pleased with some of the Americans he met. He is said to be much better than he was in health, having slept very well on the voyage home. The fact is that we considered his health to be anything but satisfactory. London & Literature evidently do not suit him, but I do not know how he can be persuaded to abandon them.[4]

My new piano seems to me a great success. The tone is sweet & clear like that of a bell almost, & the action is exceedingly easy & pleasant—The touch is light & quick, & the third or tone sustaining pedal is a great advantage. It holds up the dampers on any notes just played and may be almost constantly used after a little practice. Altogether Brinsmead is a great success.[5]

There is a considerable relapse in Coal & Iron shares, & I regret not selling some when they were 25 per cent above their present mark simply because I have lost that profit. But everything points to a prosperous future. The Company in which I have most largely invested – John Brown & Co of Sheffield has had a run of orders for armour plates[   ].[6] Yet the price of the shares remains low – simply because the public cannot judge. I am getting about 5 p.c.

[1] The only published work definitely attributable to William Edgar Jevons is a poem entitled 'A Birthday Ode – April 23rd. Written for a Shakespere [sic] Celebration', which is included in a volume of poems by his wife, Mary Ann Jevons, *The Syrens: and other Poems* (1880). The Jevons Family Papers also contain an unpublished poem, 'Stabat Mater', about the mother of a Norwegian shepherd mourning her son. It was written in 1881, the year in which W.E. Jevons had accompanied Jevons on a tour of Norway. See above, Letter 691, p. 143.

[5] Jevons had evidently bought a piano manufactured by John Brinsmead (1814–1908). The reference to a third pedal indicates that it was a grand piano, for which he would probably have paid about £120. The firm established by Brinsmead in 1836 was expanding rapidly at this time and by 1900 he had become the leader of the trade in Britain. However, despite spectacular commercial success both at home and in export markets in the face of stiff German competition, Brinsmead was never really accepted as a first-class maker by international standards. For an account of the firm during the nineteenth century, see *Fortunes Made in Business: life struggles of successful people* (1901).

[6] The rest of this sentence is illegible.

interest all round with every prospect of something much better in a year or two.

   Your affec. brother
     W. S. Jevons.

730. W. S. JEVONS TO H. R. GRENFELL[1]
  [LJN, 443]

           Hampstead, 7th May 1882

. . . I should like to say how sorry I was not to be able to attend the meeting of the Political Economy Club,[2] when you brought the subject of Bimetallism forward. I have been far from well of late, and not able to go about to debates. For the same reason I should not feel able to avail myself of an invitation, even if you were to act upon the suggestion you threw out on Friday evening.

I have been following the controversies on the subject with much interest, and am in fact busily engaged upon a volume, partly consisting of reprints of former papers, with a good deal of new matter, more or less bearing upon Bimetallism. So much labour is, however, required in completing the volume in the way I wish, and in seeing it through the press, that I cannot undertake to answer the numerous arguments put forward in the *Bullionist*[3] and other publications. My own impression is that this question cannot be wholly 'laid', and that it will recur from time to time in the future as it has in the past. But it seems to me requisite to draw a clear distinction between the speculative aspects of Bimetallism and the practical conclusion applying to us here and now in England. . . .

[1] Henry Riversdale Grenfell (1824–1902), M.P. for Stoke from 1862; Governor of the Bank of England, 1881. An advocate of bimetallism, he spoke and wrote mainly on currency questions. Joint author with H. H. Gibbs (Lord Aldenham) of *The Bimetallic Controversy* (1886).

In LJ, p. 443. Mrs Jevons incorrectly referred to him as 'W. R. Grenfell'.

[2] On 3 March 1882, Grenfell had proposed the question 'What ground is there for asserting that the old economical doctrine that the precious metals depend ultimately for their value on the cost of production should be qualified; and, if there be any such ground, to what extent?' *Political Economy Club . . . Questions Discussed, 1821–1920*, 6 (1921) 106.

[3] *The Bullionist*, a weekly financial and commercial journal, published from January 1866 to December 1899; continued as the *Daily Bullionist* from 7 December 1899 to 2 June 1900, then merged in *The Financier*.

731.   H. R. GRENFELL TO W. S. JEVONS
    [LJN, 457–8]

8th May 1882

. . . In reply to your most kind letter of yesterday, I beg to say that I quite concur with you in saying that it is necessary to draw a clear distinction between the speculative and practical aspects of the Silver Question. The worst of all these questions is that those capable of reducing them to theoretical expressions are very often incapable of understanding what happens in business.

I served a sort of apprenticeship to Lord Halifax,[1] as far as the parliamentary and political view of currency was concerned, but I always found it most difficult to explain what really happens in business to him. On the other hand, it is equally impossible for those whose whole minds are occupied with the daily search after a profit, which commerce is, to clear away irrelevant matter from a discussion which ought to be as clearly defined in its terms as a problem in Euclid.

Before you finish your labours now on hand, would it assist you to know what is really going on? I should like very much to impart to you what I know on this point, unless you are already in communication with those better informed than myself.

In order to get to practical work it seems necessary to avoid trailing hares across the paths of those seriously desirous of a solution. You will forgive me for saying that the proposition for the issue of one pound notes partakes of the nature of a hare.

Palgrave's proposition to discuss "Bank Money" is of the same nature. Likewise his assertion that it is a banking rather than a currency question.[2] There seem to me to be three practical solutions:

1. To leave it alone.

2. To make gold the universal standard, leaving silver to be used as an inferior currency at the value settled in each country, and internationally at the price of the day.

3. To resort to bimetallism – that is, not necessarily for England to join in an agreement, but by offering such terms as would induce those interested to make an agreement.

No. 2 does not appear to me to differ in any essential point from No. 1.

Can you enlighten me as to whether it does, and if it does, to what extent? I ask you this because practically No. 2 is what is proposed by

---

[1] Charles Wood (1800–85), created Viscount Halifax, 1866; M.P. for Halifax, 1832–65; Joint secretary to the Treasury, 1832; Chancellor of the Exchequer, 1846; Secretary of State for India, 1859–66.

[2] Cf. *The Economist*, 6 May, 1882, Vol. 40, pp. 531, 534–5.

Lord Grey,[3] C. Daniell,[4] and numbers of "haute finance" people in many countries, whose opinions are of great importance, but who have not taken part in the written discussions. . . .

732.   W. S. JEVONS TO H. R. GRENFELL
       [LJN, 458]

Hampstead 12th May 1882

. . . In answer to your very interesting letter, I may say that it would be a somewhat intricate matter to define exactly how your second proposition, pointing to a universal gold standard, differs from the first – that is, the present state of things. Practically there is so large – in fact, by far the largest part of the population of the world, who only use silver, and are too poor to use much if any gold, that I do not think a gold standard could be introduced in the next ten or fifteen years much beyond the present limits. I do not think that it is practicable or at present desirable to introduce a gold standard into India, so that I should be perfectly satisfied about making any concession in that respect for the next ten, fifteen, or even twenty years, but that seems to me to be all we have to offer if a one pound note currency be out of the question.

It comes to this, then, that as we have really nothing to give but what we should give without a conference, I do not see that we have any place there. We cannot prevent the other nations coining what money they like, and our currency is too well established to admit of alteration. In a short time I should like very much to know what is going on, and perhaps I may hope to have the pleasure a few weeks hence of calling on you at the bank,[1] at some time convenient to yourself. . . .

733.   W. S. JEVONS TO R. H. INGLIS PALGRAVE

2, The Chestnuts,
Branch Hill,
Hampstead, N.W.
13 June 82.

My dear Palgrave,
   I was pleased to see your name among the final list of F.S.S's in the *Times*,[1] and trust you will enjoy your new name – handle for many years.

³ Henry George Grey (1802–94), third Earl Grey, styled Viscount Howick, 1807–45, Whig statesman; Secretary for War, 1835–9; Secretary of State for War and the Colonies, 1846–52.
⁴ Claremont John Daniell, of the Bengal Civil Service, author of *The Gold Treasure of India* (1884) and *Discarded Silver, a plan for its use as money* (1886).
¹ The Bank of England. Grenfell was Governor at this time.
¹ *The Times*, 13 June 1882, p. 5(d): Jevons evidently made a slip here, in referring to 'F.S.S's'.

I regret I cannot meet you on Thursday at Burlington House, as you perhaps know you require to shake the President's hand and go through a formal ceremony before you are really passed thro the Mint, and some "Fellow" has to present you. Sir Jos. Hooker or any other friend will do you that office, or in any case you can be enrolled next session just as well.

I am going through a rather severe course of Wagner's Music,[2] and cannot miss the Mastersingers on Thursday night, and at this distance from town and in my weak state of health I cannot manage an afternoon as well as an evening engagement.

Wagner's music is a capital antidote to Bimetallism, commercial crises and other intricate subjects in which I am deeply immersed. I am going again over the question of the relation of crises to solar variations a propos of my book on Currency, and am sufficently convinced of the truth of the theory though it may not be possible at present to meet every difficulty.

I do not understand the U.S. silver certificates but John L. Shadwell who has studied the subject tells me that they cannot drive out the gold in the manner of the double standard because there is not *free coinage*. You cannot buy silver and have it coined and turned into certificates, but you must buy certificates with gold. If this be so which I do not guarantee there is no more a double standard in the U.S. than there would be in England if the Bank exercised the power of holding $\frac{1}{5}$ reserve in silver.

I cannot see that Hartington's answer to Briggs as fully reported commits us to anything new.[3]

It would in my opinion be fatal to any govt. to suggest the idea of a silver standard in this country.

Yours faithfully,

W. S. Jevons.

[2] See below, Letter 739, p. 198.

[3] There had been an International Monetary Conference at Paris in 1881, which was to be reconvened on 12 April 1882 and was expected to take important decisions on the coinage of silver; but when the date arrived the Conference was postponed (*The Economist*, 15 April 1882, p. 444)

Hartington, in reply to a question in the Commons on 12 June 1882 from W. E. Briggs, M.P. for Blackburn, as to whether the government intended to urge the re-assembling of the Paris Conference, stated:

'. . . on the 12th of April last I was informed . . . that the Governments of France and the United States had proposed an adjournment of the Monetary Conference . . . until further progress had been made in arriving at a definite basis of future discussion, subject to an understanding as to the date of its re-assembling during the present year. On the part of the Government of India I concurred in the propriety of this proposal, and stated my readiness to give the necessary instructions to its representatives to attend the Conference, whenever it was found practicable, to fix the date of its meeting. As the Governments of France and the United States have throughout taken the initiative in this matter, it would appear to be rather for them than for Her Majesty's Government to take the necessary steps to promote the early re-assembling of the Conference. I cannot state when it is likely to re-assemble.' (*Hansard*, third series, CCLXX, 829, 12 June 1882.)

734. W. S. JEVONS TO W. E. A. AXON [1]

2 The Chestnuts,
Branch Hill,
Hampstead, N.W.

17 June 1882.

My dear Axon

I shall be happy to lend you my copy of Visserings book. [2] As it is bound I will send it by parcel company in the course of the next day or two.

I was certainly interested in your article [3] (not knowing it however to be yours) and was rather taken aback to find you mention several books on paper money unknown to me. But I am more & more convinced of the impossibility of exhausting the world of books.

I think Visserings publication is a very remarkable feat & deserves to be well known to English students. The particulars given in the book are very curious but I have never properly utilised them yet.

I will consider whether I have any brief article for your new periodical. [4]

I have thought of a little note I may perhaps send. In any case please put me down as a subscriber.

I am
Yours faithfully
W. S. Jevons.

735. L. WALRAS TO W. S. JEVONS

Ouchy sous Lausanne,
24 juin 1882 [1]

Léon Walras

très souffrant [2] d'une névrose cérébro cardiaque qui a pris, depuis neuf ou dix mois, un caractère plus accentué, ne peut que remercier M. Jevons de l'envoi de son dernier volume [3] en l'assurant de son bon souvenir.

---

[1] Willam Edward Armitage Axon (1846–1913), Manchester journalist and bibliographer; assistant in the Manchester Public Free Libraries, 1861–6; deputy chief librarian, 1866–74; a member of the editorial staff of the *Manchester Guardian*, 1874–1905.

[2] Willem Vissering, *On Chinese Currency. Coin and paper money . . . With facsimile of a Banknote* (Leiden, 1877).

[3] No article meeting this description, attributable to Axon, has been traced.

[4] *The Field Naturalist and Scientific Student,* edited by W. E. A. Axon, 9 nos (Manchester, 1882–3). Cf. below, Letter 736, p. 196.

[1] The original of this note is not now among the Jevons Papers. It is here reproduced from the draft (written on a visiting card) in Fonds Walras, FW 1, 278/16. Cf. Jaffé, *Walras Correspondence*, 1, 724.

[2] Walras had here written 'depuis plusieurs mois', but deleted the phrase.

[3] *The State in Relation to Labour.*

736.   W. S. JEVONS TO W. E. A. AXON

2, The Chestnuts,
West Heath,
Hampstead, N.W.

30 June 1882

My dear Axon

I have now sent off the book on Chinese Currency by parcel carriage paid. Excuse dilatoriness. Please keep it at your entire convenience & in returning it address to me care of Mr Allen

Bookseller
432 Euston Road
Near Portland Road

Delivery by the companies is uncertain up here.

I have thought of a subject on which to write you a brief article namely "A reflected rainbow", [1] but I cannot do it until I get into the quiet of the country a week or two hence.

Yours faithfully
W. S. Jevons

737.   W. S. JEVONS TO H. RYLETT
[LJN, 444–5]

Hampstead, N.W., 2d July 1882.

. . . Not having read Davitt's speech in detail I cannot speak of it, but I do not believe in nationalisation of the land. [1] I am strongly in favour of any scheme tending towards peasant proprietorship, and would like to see the State risk a good deal of money on the enterprise. But the Government must not be the landlords. The people must be their own landlords as soon and in proportion as they can be made to be so; but of course I am aware of the great difficulties in the way. Anything is better than the present state of things. I do not think you need trouble yourself much about Bastiat's opinions in regard to land. [2] They are not, in my

[1] W. S. Jevons, 'Reflected Rainbows', *The Field Naturalist and Scientific Student*, edited by W. E. A. Axon (Manchester, 1883) pp. 64–5.

[1] In a speech at Liverpool on 6 June 1882 Michael Davitt elaborated on the details of his programme for 'the land for the people' and declared himself 'in favour of the land becoming the national property of Ireland' as against Parnell's advocacy of peasant proprietorship. Cf. *The Times*, 7 June 1882, p. 10.

[2] F. Bastiat, *Harmonies Economiques*, chap. IX, 'Propriété foncière', *Œuvres Completes* (1855) tome VI, pp. 266–313. The general conclusion of Bastiat's argument had certainly little relevance to the case of Ireland in 1882: 'Aussi longtemps que dans un pays il y a abondance de terre à défricher, le propriétaire foncier . . . ne jouit d'aucun privilège, d'aucun monopole, d'aucun avantage exceptionnel . . .' (loc. cit., p. 288).

opinion, well founded. I have not read George's pamphlet nor his book;[3] but from glancing over the latter I am not inclined to take it up while so many better books are available.

The remarks in the *Economist* on your letter were not written by me. Having shown your letter to the Editor in the course of discussion, he wished to print it as a text — and omitting your name I saw no reason to refuse.[4]

Being an economist and not a politician, I hardly like to venture upon the wide and stormy field of the Irish Question. There can, however, be little doubt that the progress of events tends to justify your position more than it was formerly easy to foresee. I never, indeed, believed in Forster's coercion policy, which struck at the wrong parties, and was calculated rather to irritate than to suppress or amend what was wrong.

I may also add, that though I was formerly of the opposite opinion, both the course of events and the course of my studies have tended to suggest grave doubts as to whether the whole tendency of English agrarian law, policy, and practice is not radically wrong.

In England the immense wealth and social power of the landowners has disguised the question, but it has broken out in Ireland, and it will break out sooner or later elsewhere. I have quite satisfied myself that whatever may be the economic results, the social and political results of an opposite agrarian policy are infinitely superior to what we experience. Some day I may perhaps try to write out these opinions and support them, but it is too heavy a subject to venture upon in a hurry. . . .

738.   W. S. JEVONS TO L. BODIO
       [LJN, 445]

Hampstead, N.W., 4th July 1882

. . . I return my warm thanks for the beautiful volumes and atlas of the *Monograph of Rome and the Campagna*,[1] which arrived safely a day or two ago. They will have a place of honour in my library, and are full of

---

[3] See above, Letter 699, nn. 5 and 6, p. 151.

[4] Presumably a reference to Rylett's letter published the previous December (see above, Letter 704, p. 157), as no further correspondence on the Irish question, purporting to come from Rylett, appeared in *The Economist* up to the date of this letter. Jevons's comments here explain the style of Rylett's letter, which was published without signature or date, but clearly addressed to a former teacher, obviously Jevons himself. Rylett had apparently referred to the editorial comments which had preceded the letter, and which included the following remarks: 'The following letter tells a sad story to those who have the interest of Ireland at heart. It is written, as will be seen, by a man who has studied political economy and still remembers its technical language, though hardly its teachings. . . .'

[1] Cf. Vol.IV, Letter 563, n. 5.

interest for me. Since the visit which I had the pleasure of paying to Rome and Italy about ten years ago, I have not ceased to feel a peculiar interest in everything relating to the places visited.

I thank you also for the *Archivio di Statistica*[2] and other publications safely received. I have found them very valuable of late, in connection with a work on Money which I am preparing, and of which I shall hope in a few months to forward you a copy.

I welcome especially the contributions to a history of prices which I find in several places, including the article in the *Monograph*.

I had the honour to forward you, few days ago, a copy of my small book on *The State in relation to Labour,* which, though small, has been the object of much thought to me. . . .

739. W. S. JEVONS TO T. E. JEVONS
      [LJN, 446–8]

Galley Hill, Bulverhythe,
Near Hastings, 19th July 1882

. . . I am very sorry indeed that so long a time has elapsed since I wrote to you. The last two months, however, form the most busy and distracting time of the year to me, and letter-writing is too much like my ordinary occupation to be relaxation.

You will be pleased to hear perhaps that one of the distractions which took up much time this season was a full course of Wagner's music, which both Harriet and I enjoyed in a degree which we could not have anticipated. We subscribed both for the German opera season and the Richter concerts,[1] and went out about three times a week. The concerts were good enough indeed. It was impossible that a hundred of the best German musicians, led by such an incomparably skilful conductor as Richter, could produce anything but the best music.

Wagner's newer operas, however, produced as they were at Drury Lane, produced a wholly new impression, such as one will never forget. Having heard the *Flying Dutchman* much praised, I was a good deal disappointed with it, and even *Lohengrin* became thin and weak compared with what was to follow. *Tännhäuser,* however, which we heard twice, and would willingly hear a few times more, stands out as an altogether striking and perfect composition. It is impossible to forget either the 'Pilgrim's March' or the 'Siren Voices.' The *Meistersinger*[2]

---

[2] *Archivio di Statistica,* fondato da T. Pateras (Rome, 1876–83).

[1] On the Richter concerts, see above, Letter 681, n. 2, p. 134.

[2] In 1882 *Die Meistersinger* and *Tristan und Isolde* were presented at Drury Lane by Hans Richter, while *Der Ring des Nibelungen* was first performed at His Majesty's Theatre under the conductorship of Seidl.

proved to be a work of a totally different character, and having never before been performed in London, took the musical world there quite by surprise. On the first time of hearing, I was rather wearied by parts which are certainly long, however beautiful, but on a second and third hearing I became reconciled to the whole. The third act especially, in which the Guilds of Nürnberg assemble for the prize song contest, is a beautiful sight, sustained as it is by a continuous stream of music, such as Wagner only could write.

We also heard *Tristan and Isolde* once, a work of an entirely different character again, being a kind of musical tragedy, more, in fact a kind of musical picture of the Arthurian knight and the unfortunate bride whom he was sent to fetch to the king. There are only some half-dozen characters in the whole, and hardly any chorus; but the manner in which Madame Sucher[3] and Herr Winkelmann[4] riveted your attention throughout a long evening was again a wholly new thing. The music was in the highest degree Wagnerian, and I have not retained a scrap of it in my head; nevertheless it was music which seemed to bind the whole story together into one absorbing and beautiful whole. Harriet says that she shall never forget the picture of the noble and faithful knight, and I shall not forget the picture of the love-torn maiden Isolde, as she sat upon the deck of the ship.

Madame Sucher is in fact an incomparable actress, singer, and musician – all three combined in an almost unique manner. In the concert room she disappointed me, being stiff and almost harsh in the power of her voice. But in the theatre she was all life, and grace, and music such as one will not perhaps hear again.

These performances made a great sensation in London, and I was glad to assist, at least by being present, at what I consider the complete triumph of true music and art over the wretched Italian opera. No doubt the English and Italian opera will die hard; and *Tristan and Isolde* was clearly above the comprehension of the London public as a general rule. But *Tännhäuser* and the Meistersinger charmed every hearer, and I think you may consider that the 'music of the future' has established its hold in England.

. . . We have now got down to our quiet seaside retreat, where we have a beautiful stretch of shore yet almost our own, and pleasant quiet lanes, and fields and bits of wood, where we can do as we like. At Hampstead you are summoned if you touch a wild-flower.

[3] Rosa Sucher (1849–1927), German operatic soprano who became a prima donna at the Berlin Opera. She made her London début in 1882, creating a remarkable impression both as singer and actress by the wide range of parts in which she appeared.

[4] Hermann Winckelmann (1849–1912), German tenor, who also made a great impression on London audiences on his first appearance there in 1882.

Unfortunately Winn caught cold in one eye at Hampstead and has yet to be kept in the house, and the weather is unsettled and windy. But we hope that the children will be all as well as 'Boy', who is in high spirits racing about the sands and constructing all kinds of edifices on the shore.

I hope you got a copy of my *State in Relation to Labour*. I have as usual much on hand, but intend to take things as easily as possible for the future.

We have the *Times* daily, and I am following the tragic events in Egypt[5] with horror combined with interest. The Arab race are evidently preparing the way for their own complete downfall and eventual extermination, and we can only console ourselves that they are opening the way to a better civilisation.

. . . I am going to overthrow my critics on the Employment-of-Married-women question, having pretty surely ascertained, by a comparison of the census and Registrar General's reports, that the mortality of children under five years of age is proportional to the percentage of women over twenty years employed in industrial occupations. . . .

740.   W. S. JEVONS TO W. E. A. AXON

Cliff House
Galley Hill
near Hastings.

19 July 1882

My dear Axon

I now forward copy of the article "Reflected Rainbow" hoping that it is suitable both in matter & length for your periodical.

If you can send a proof to the above address it will be returned by next post.

Thanks for the copy of your son's article. It is highly promising in fact highly remarkable for a boy of his age.[1]

I think your new pub\u207f. is well conceived & well executed, & hope it will succeed as fully as it deserves.

Yours truly
W. S. Jevons.

[5] Since early in 1882 the strength of the nationalist movement in Egypt, led by Arabi Pasha, had threatened the Anglo-French control of the country. The British and French fleets were ordered to Alexandria in May; rioting in the city and the continued defiance of the nationalists caused the British fleet to bombard the forts of Alexandria on 11 July. Nine days later Gladstone sent an army, commanded by Sir Garnet Wolseley, into Egypt to suppress the revolt; the campaign culminated in Wolseley's defeat of Arabi Pasha at Tel-el-Kebir on 13 September 1882.

[1] No evidence has survived concerning this article by Axon's son, one of the three children of his second marriage.

741. W. S. JEVONS TO A. MACMILLAN
   [MA]

Cliff House,
Galley Hill,
Near Hastings.

20 July 1882.

Dear Mr. Macmillan,

I now enclose some of the diagrams for the "Investigations in Currency etc." with a few directions to the lithographer. When I see the effect of colour put on from the stone I shall know better what to do with the remaining diagrams, which are however yet uncompleted. They demand a good deal of labour in calculation, planning, and drawing.

Thanks for the specimen page of bibliography which will do very well. If any change is made it should be as you suggest in compressing the type a little more. I suppose all the lines are at present leaded. But in a few weeks I hope to have the copy completed and then will write again.

At the same time I fear I must make the improvement of my health the first consideration at present. I embarked upon this book rather hastily because it was believed that there was going to be a great bimetallic controversy and a conference. That has entirely collapsed for the present. [1]

By gradually labouring at it I hope to make the book one of permanent interest. But if I shall seem to digress from my original proposal or otherwise cause unreasonable expense, I shall be prepared to hear what you have to say on the subject.

I am,
Yours faithfully
W. Stanley Jevons.

742. F. Y. EDGEWORTH TO HARRIET JEVONS

5 Mt. Vernon,
Hampstead.
Aug. 16th. [1882]

Dear Mrs. Jevons,

I cannot refrain from expressing my deep regret at the loss of my venerated friend. I shall always remember with gratitude the kind encouragement and a peculiar intellectual sympathy which he extended

[1] Cf. above, Letter 733, n. 3, p. 194.

to one whose studies were in the same direction however immeasurably behind his. It is difficult to realize that I shall never more meet Mr. Jevons on the ice or heath be fascinated by his philosophic smile and drink in his words. I shall always regard it as one of the privileges of my life to have come under the influence of his serene and lofty intellect.

Sympathising sincerely with you in your irreparable loss.

I am

Yours faithfully

F. Y. Edgeworth.